The GHOST FLEET™

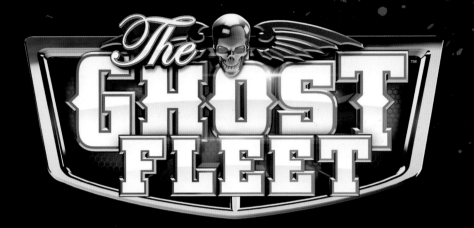

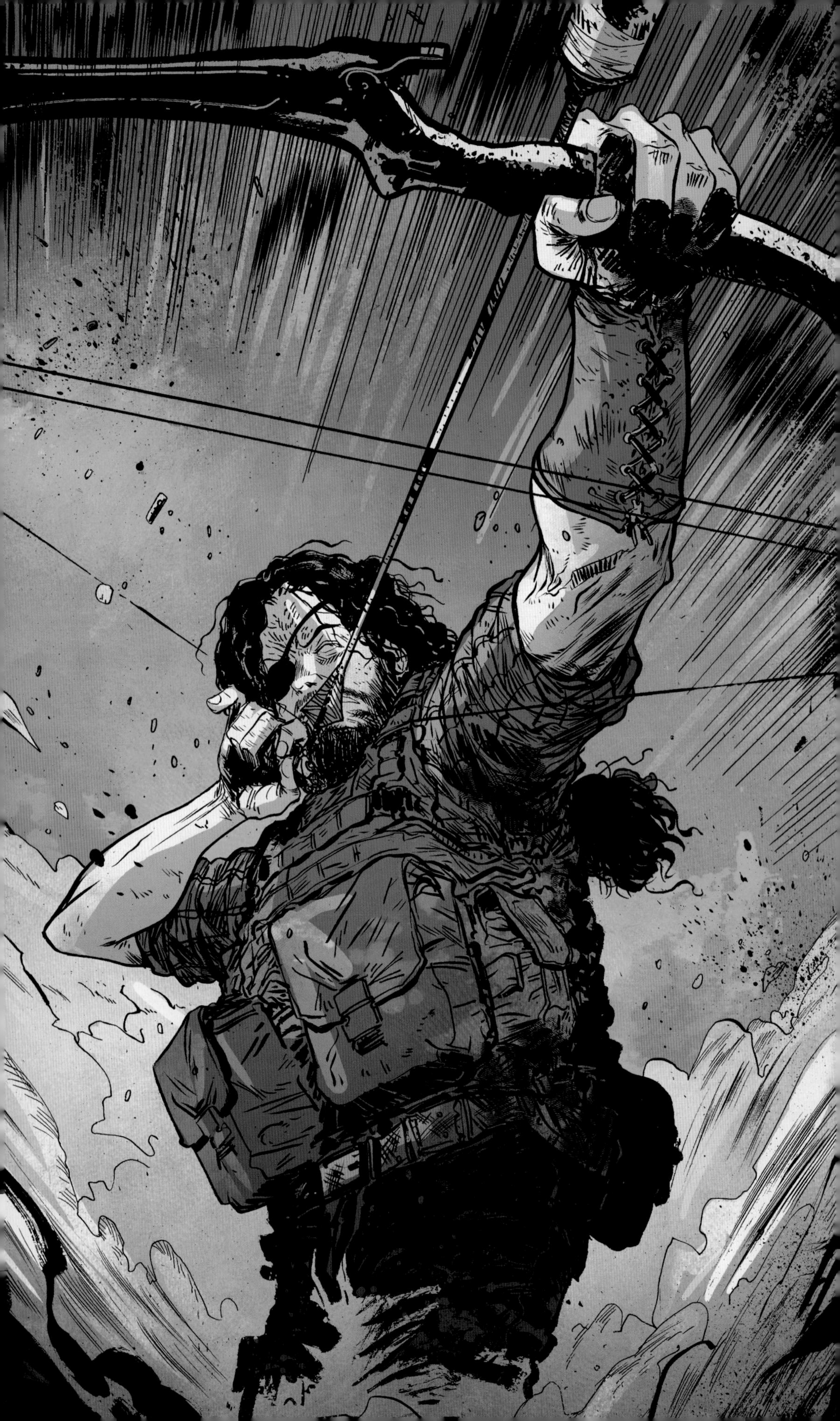

THE GHOST FLEET™

DEADHEAD

Written by
DONNY CATES

Art by
DANIEL WARREN JOHNSON

Colors by
LAUREN AFFE

Letters by
CRANK!

Military Adviser
PHIL KOST

Cover and chapter breaks by
DANIEL WARREN JOHNSON
and LAUREN AFFE

DARK HORSE BOOKS

DONNY
To Lizzy: For believing in me and for being a total badass.

DANIEL
For Mom and Dad. I love you guys.

Publisher **MIKE RICHARDSON**

Designer **RICK DeLUCCO**

Logo Design **DAVID NESTELLE**

Digital Production **RYAN JORGENSEN**

Assistant Editor **EVERETT PATTERSON**

Editor **PATRICK THORPE**

Special thanks to Annie Gullion and Frank Barbiere.

This volume collects issues #1 through #4 of Dark Horse Comics' series *The Ghost Fleet*.

Published by
Dark Horse Books
A division of Dark Horse Comics, Inc.
10956 SE Main Street
Milwaukie, OR 97222

DarkHorse.com
International Licensing: (503) 905-2377
Comic Shop Locator Service: (888) 266-4226

First edition: June 2015
ISBN 978-1-61655-649-5
10 9 8 7 6 5 4 3 2 1

Printed in China

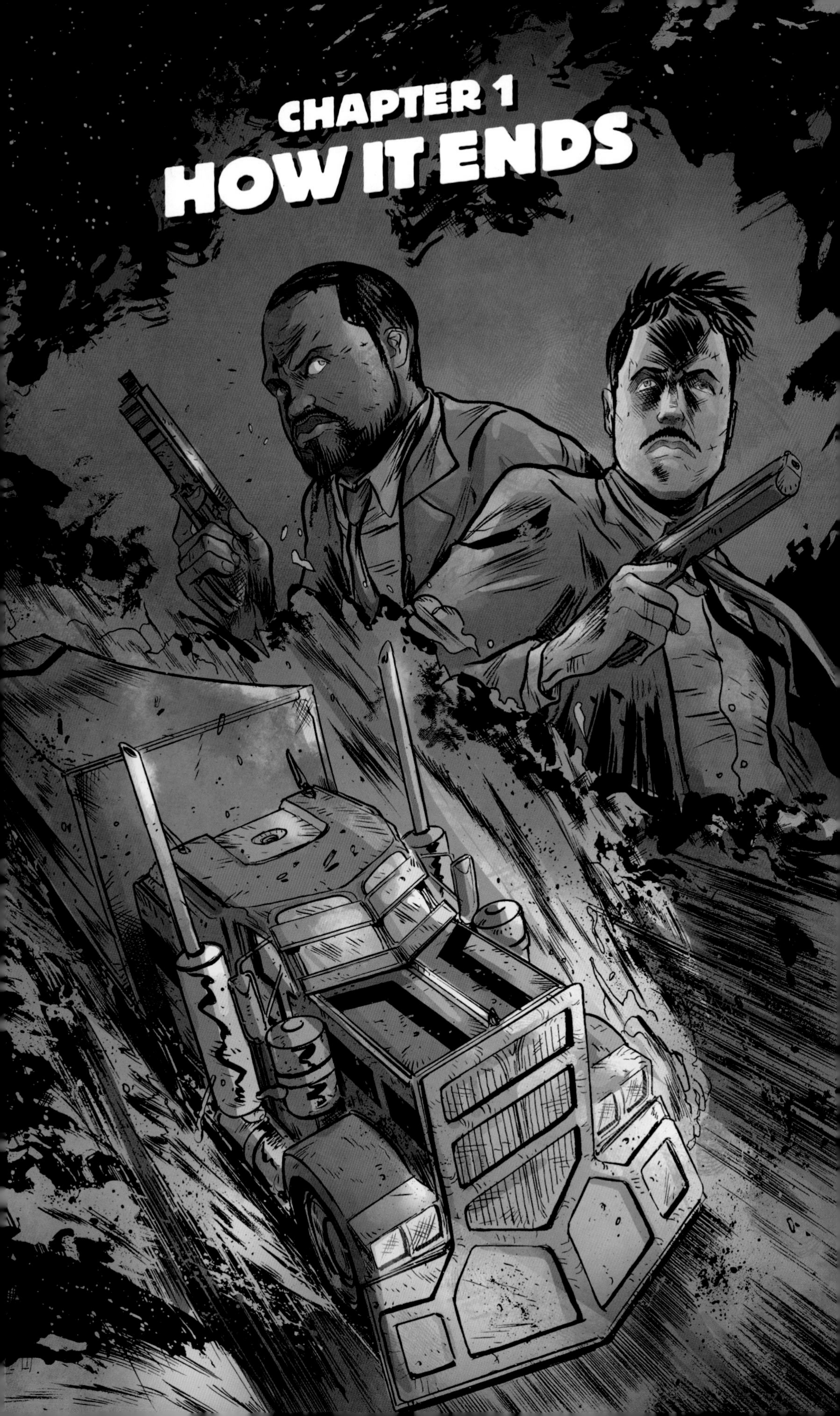
CHAPTER 1
HOW IT ENDS

JANUARY 8, 1815.
THE BATTLE OF NEW ORLEANS.

THIS IS NOT HOW OUR STORY BEGINS.

GENERAL ANDREW JACKSON, FACING DEATH AT THE HANDS OF THE BRITISH, STRIKES A DEAL WITH THE PIRATE JEAN LAFITTE. THE PRIVATEER PROVIDES JACKSON WITH AID IN EXCHANGE FOR A PARDON FOR HIM AND HIS MEN. THIS IS FAIRLY WELL KNOWN...

LAFITTE ALSO SHARED WITH JACKSON WAYS KNOWN ONLY TO MEN OF HIS...PARTICULAR PROFESSION.

SECRET ROADS, HIDDEN PASSAGES... WAYS OF MOVING *SENSITIVE CARGO* AND *CLASSIFIED INFORMATION* THAT WOULD BE IMPOSSIBLE TO TRACK. HE TAUGHT JACKSON HOW TO MOVE IN THE SHADOWS...

HE TAUGHT HIM TO BUILD A *GHOST FLEET*.

BUT THIS IS NOT HOW OUR STORY BEGINS...

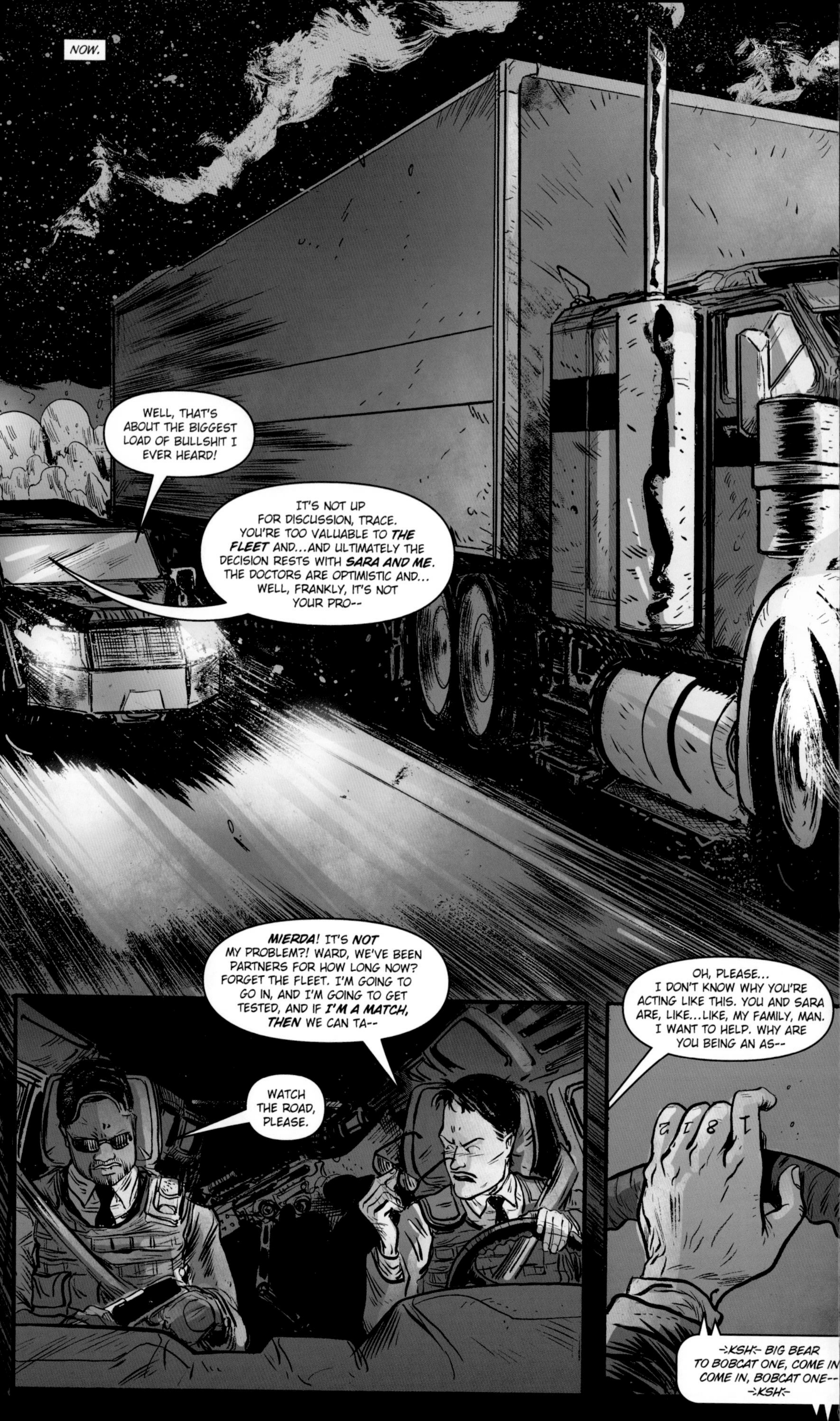
NOW.
WELL, THAT'S ABOUT THE BIGGEST LOAD OF BULLSHIT I EVER HEARD!
IT'S NOT UP FOR DISCUSSION, TRACE. YOU'RE TOO VALUABLE TO THE FLEET AND...AND ULTIMATELY THE DECISION RESTS WITH SARA AND ME. THE DOCTORS ARE OPTIMISTIC AND... WELL, FRANKLY, IT'S NOT YOUR PRO--
MIERDA! IT'S NOT MY PROBLEM?! WARD, WE'VE BEEN PARTNERS FOR HOW LONG NOW? FORGET THE FLEET. I'M GOING TO GO IN, AND I'M GOING TO GET TESTED, AND IF I'M A MATCH, THEN WE CAN TA--
WATCH THE ROAD, PLEASE.
OH, PLEASE... I DON'T KNOW WHY YOU'RE ACTING LIKE THIS. YOU AND SARA ARE, LIKE...LIKE, MY FAMILY, MAN. I WANT TO HELP. WHY ARE YOU BEING AN AS--
1 8 1 2
-KSH- BIG BEAR TO BOBCAT ONE, COME IN. COME IN, BOBCAT ONE-- -KSH-

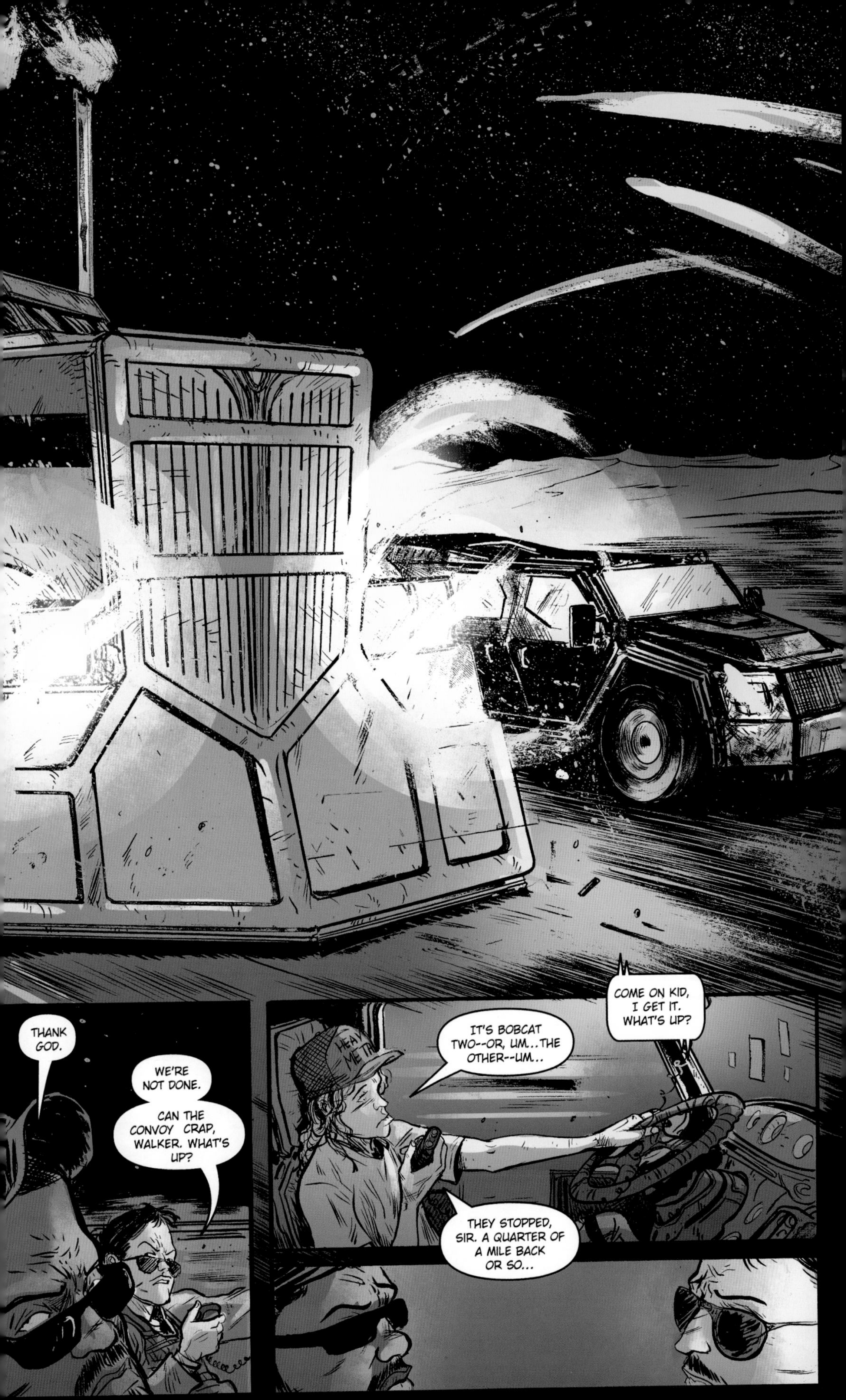
THANK GOD.
WE'RE NOT DONE.
CAN THE CONVOY CRAP, WALKER. WHAT'S UP?
IT'S BOBCAT TWO--OR, UM...THE OTHER--UM...
COME ON KID, I GET IT. WHAT'S UP?
THEY STOPPED, SIR. A QUARTER OF A MILE BACK OR SO...

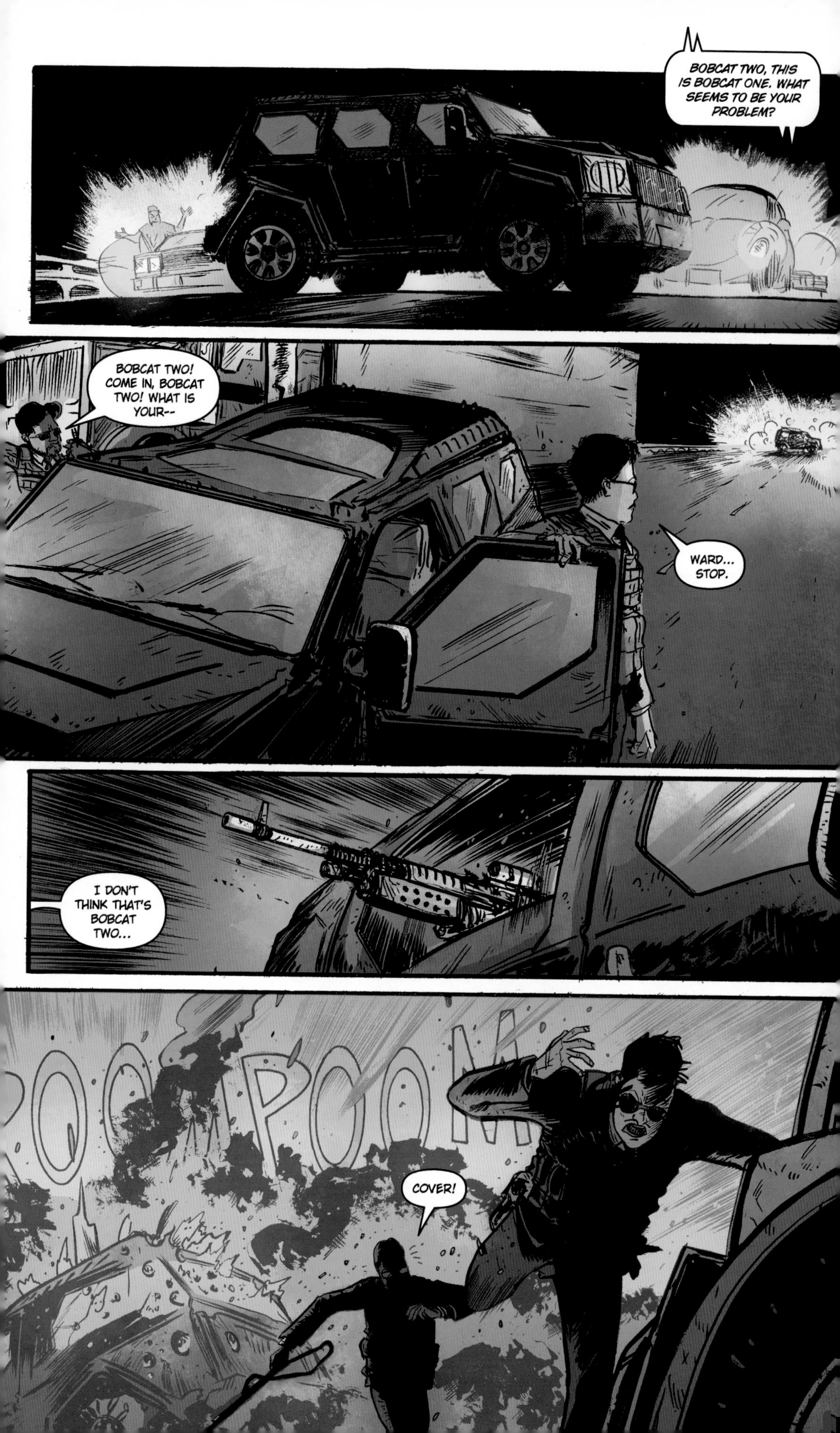
BOBCAT TWO, THIS IS BOBCAT ONE. WHAT SEEMS TO BE YOUR PROBLEM?
BOBCAT TWO! COME IN, BOBCAT TWO! WHAT IS YOUR--
WARD... STOP.
I DON'T THINK THAT'S BOBCAT TWO...
POOM POOM
COVER!

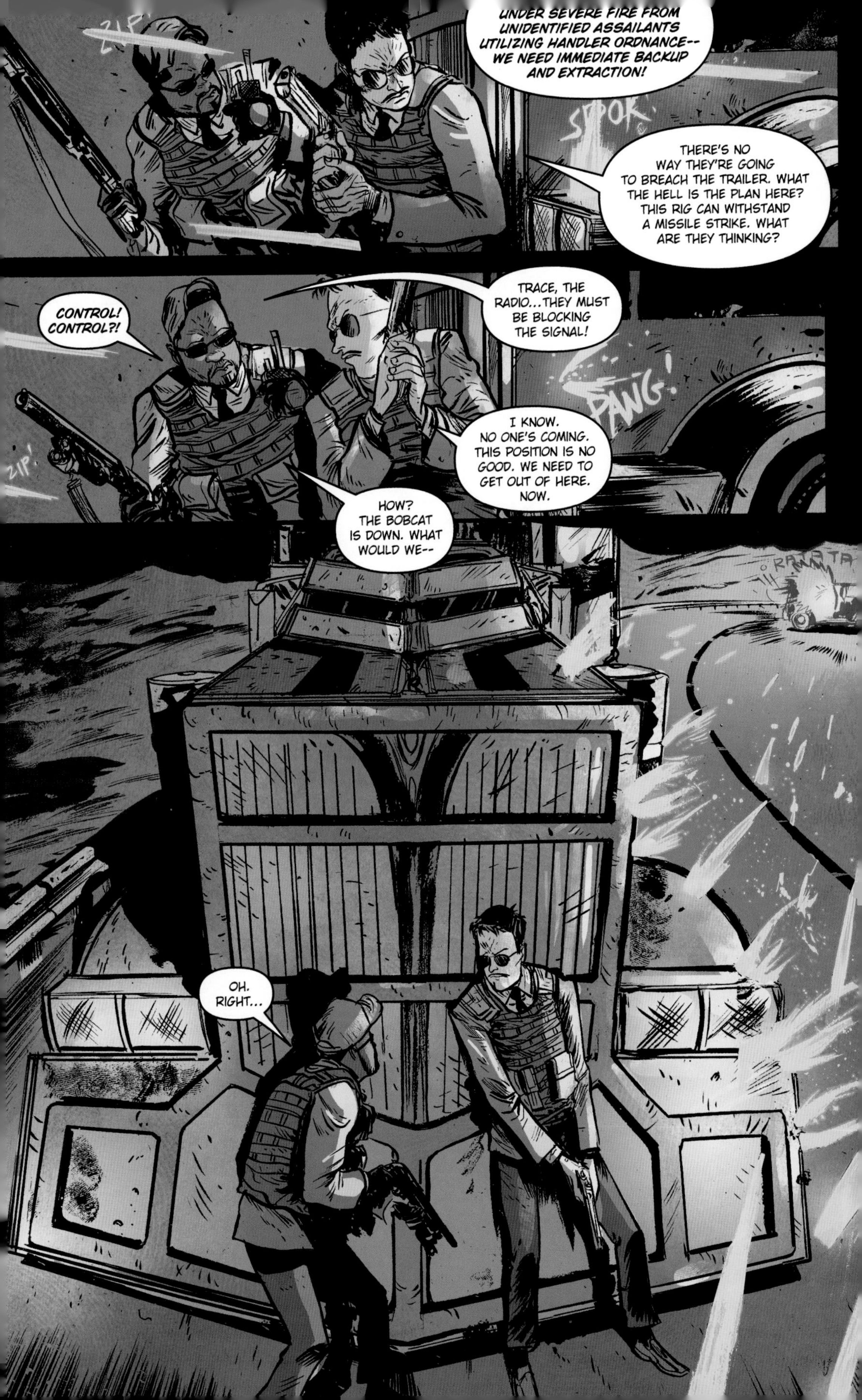
ZIP
UNDER SEVERE FIRE FROM UNIDENTIFIED ASSAILANTS UTILIZING HANDLER ORDNANCE-- WE NEED IMMEDIATE BACKUP AND EXTRACTION!
SPPOK
THERE'S NO WAY THEY'RE GOING TO BREACH THE TRAILER. WHAT THE HELL IS THE PLAN HERE? THIS RIG CAN WITHSTAND A MISSILE STRIKE. WHAT ARE THEY THINKING?
CONTROL! CONTROL?!
TRACE, THE RADIO...THEY MUST BE BLOCKING THE SIGNAL!
PANG!
ZIP!
I KNOW. NO ONE'S COMING. THIS POSITION IS NO GOOD. WE NEED TO GET OUT OF HERE. NOW.
HOW? THE BOBCAT IS DOWN. WHAT WOULD WE--
RATATA
OH. RIGHT...

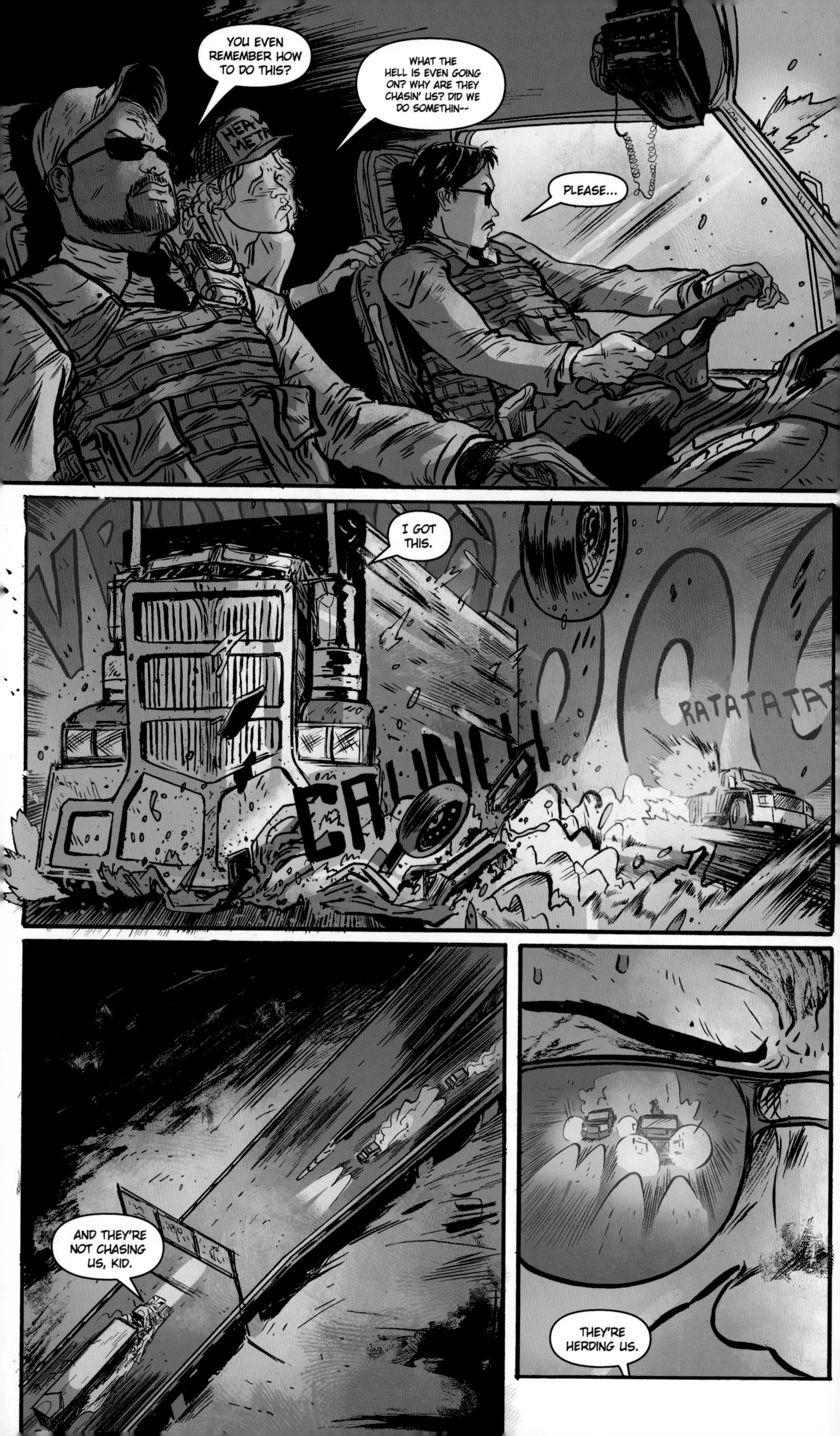
YOU EVEN REMEMBER HOW TO DO THIS?
WHAT THE HELL IS EVEN GOING ON? WHY ARE THEY CHASIN' US? DID WE DO SOMETHIN--
PLEASE...
I GOT THIS.
CRUNCH
RATATATAT
AND THEY'RE NOT CHASING US, KID.
THEY'RE HERDING US.

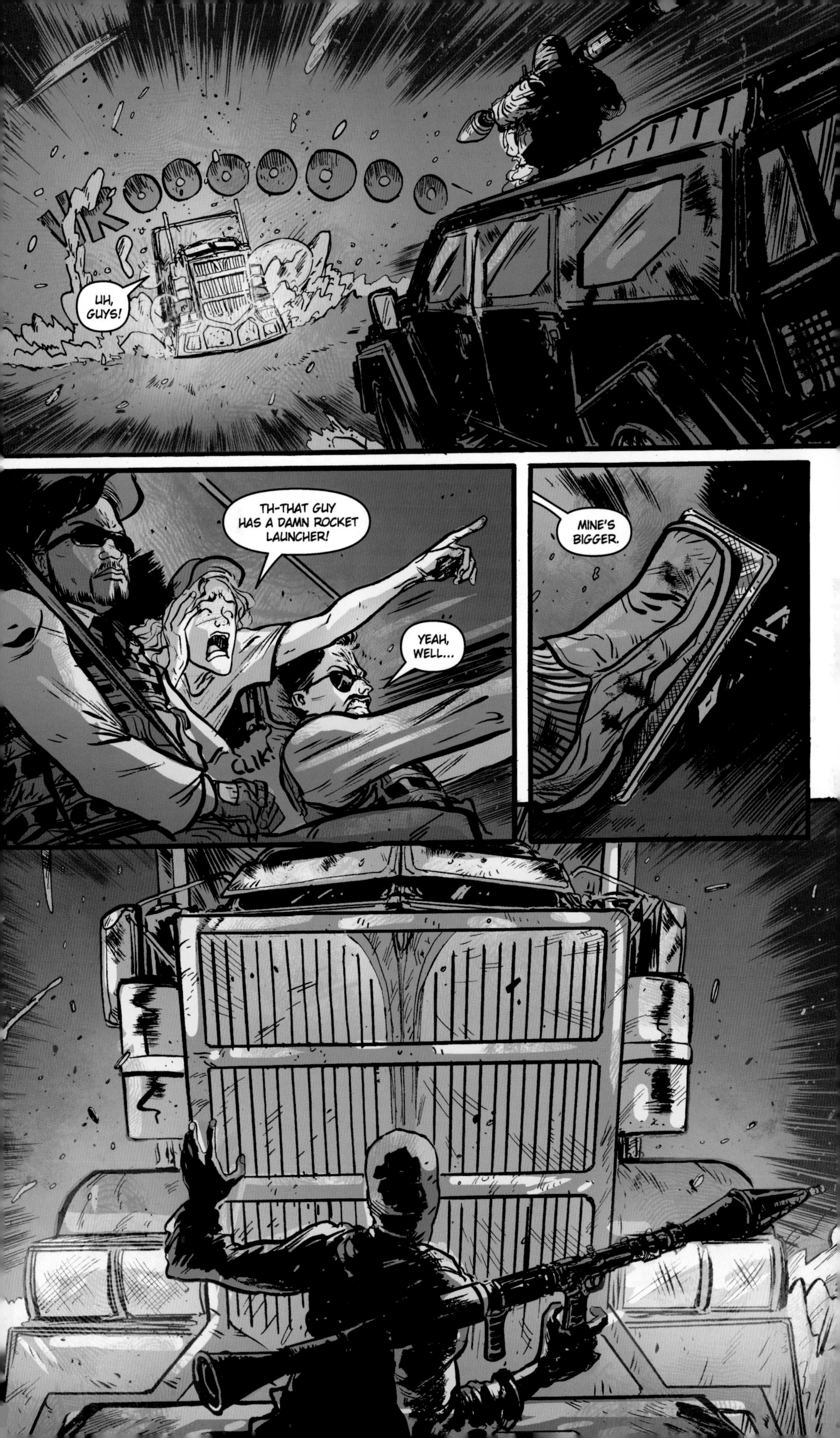
VKOOOOOOOO
UH, GUYS!
TH-THAT GUY HAS A DAMN ROCKET LAUNCHER!
YEAH, WELL...
CLIK!
MINE'S BIGGER.

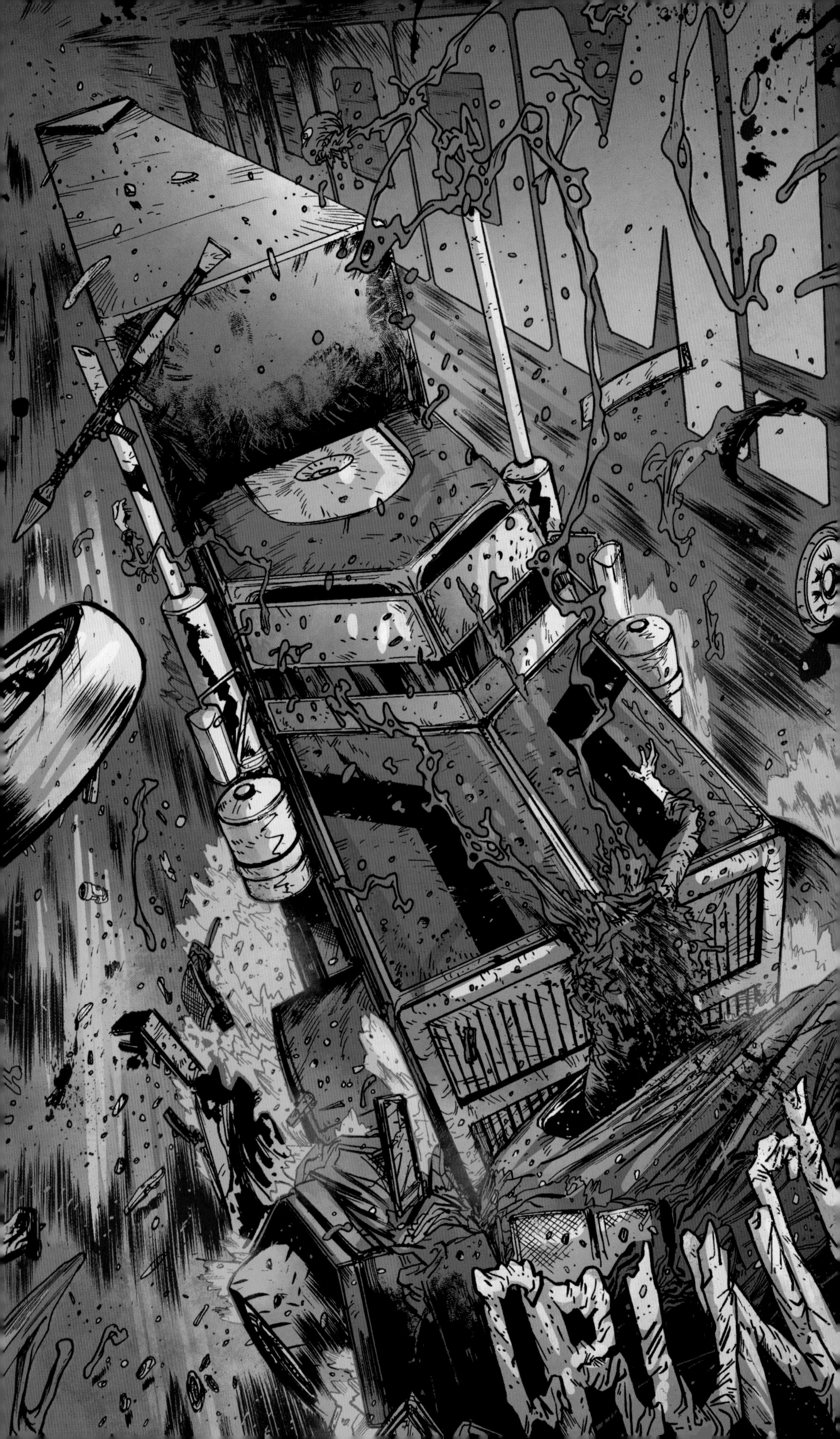

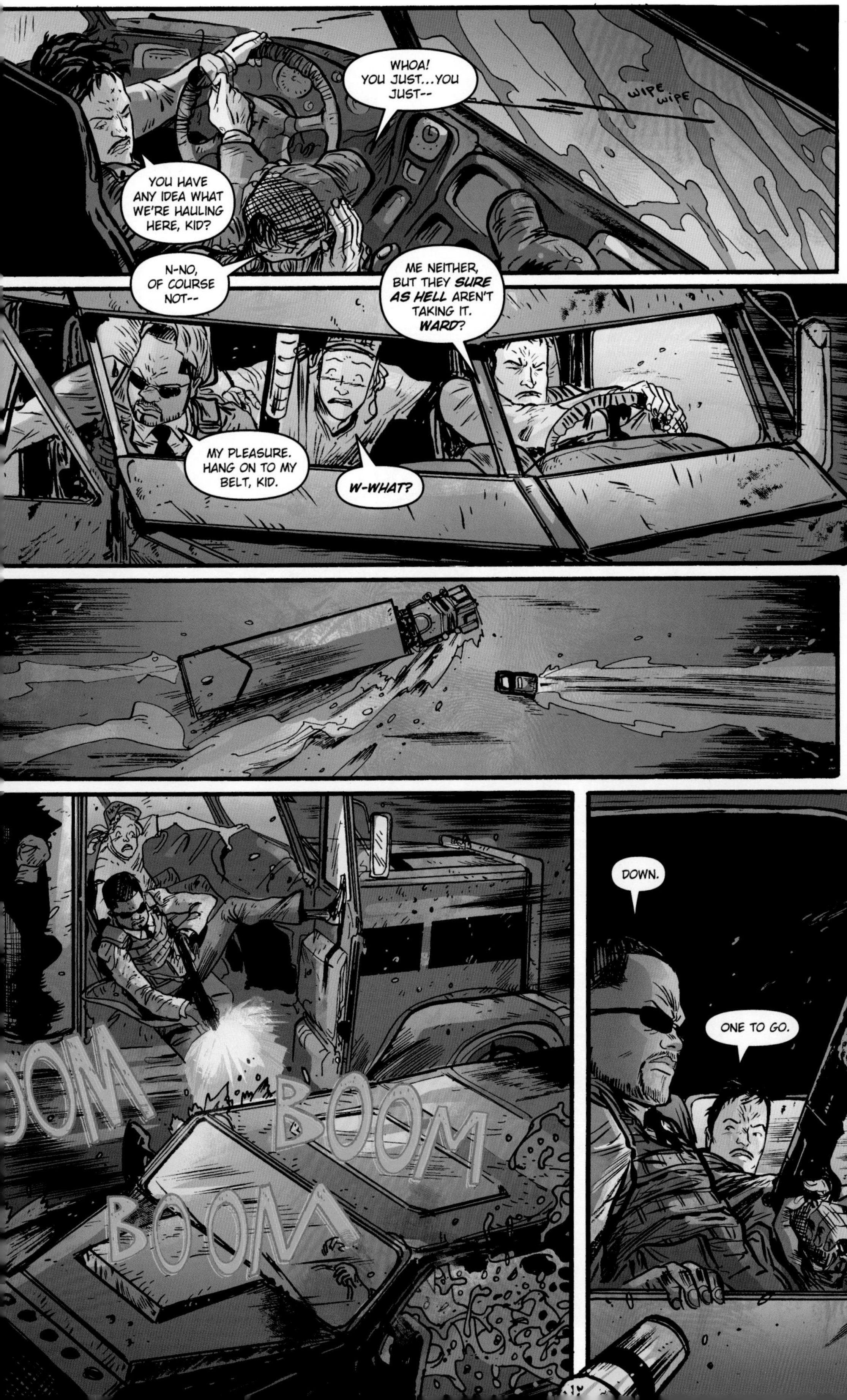
WHOA! YOU JUST...YOU JUST--
WIPE WIPE
YOU HAVE ANY IDEA WHAT WE'RE HAULING HERE, KID?
N-NO, OF COURSE NOT--
ME NEITHER, BUT THEY **SURE AS HELL** AREN'T TAKING IT. **WARD**?
MY PLEASURE. HANG ON TO MY BELT, KID.
W-WHAT?
BOOM
BOOM
DOWN.
ONE TO GO.

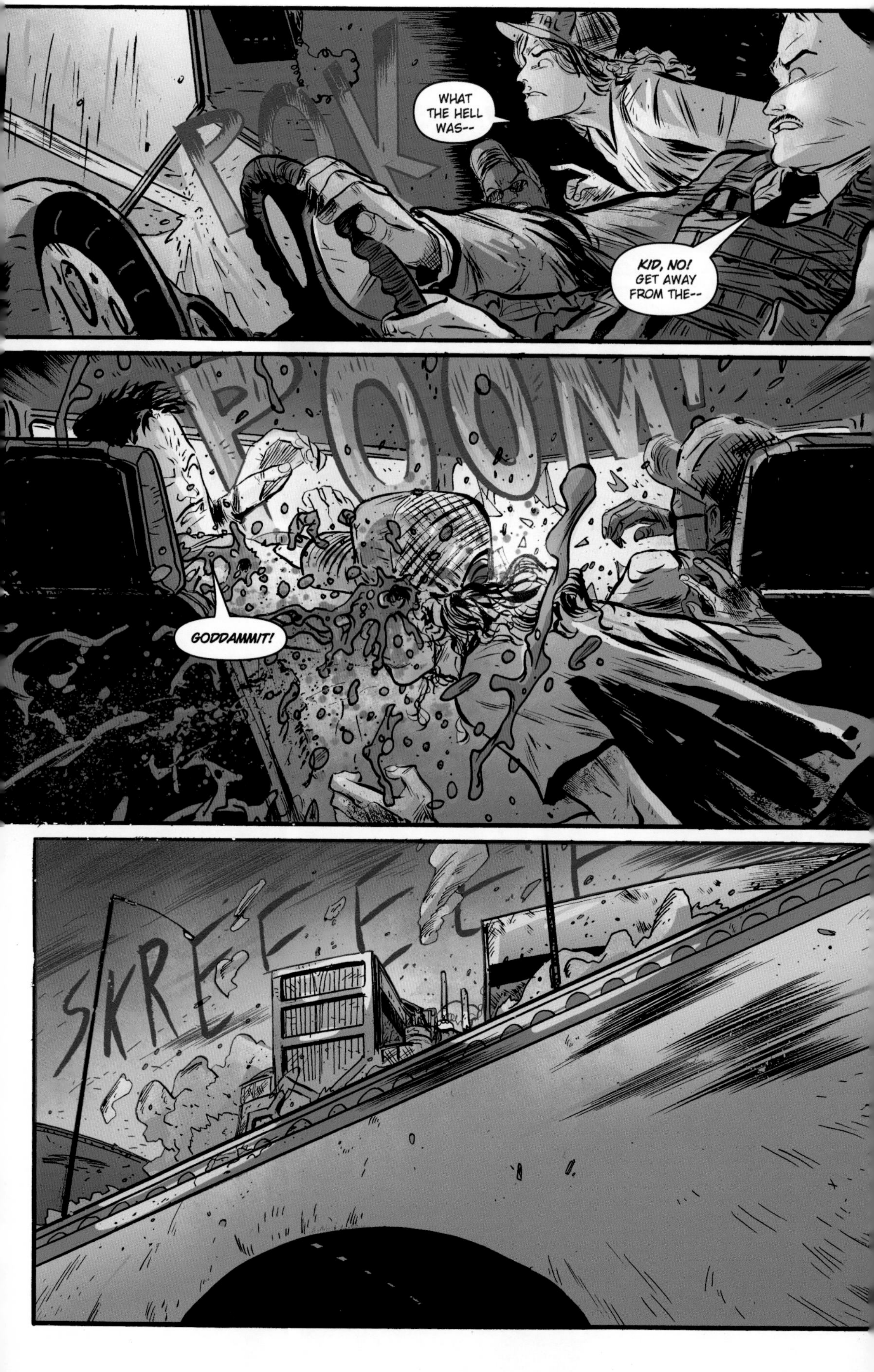
POK
WHAT THE HELL WAS--
KID, NO! GET AWAY FROM THE--
BOOM!
GODDAMMIT!
SKREEEE

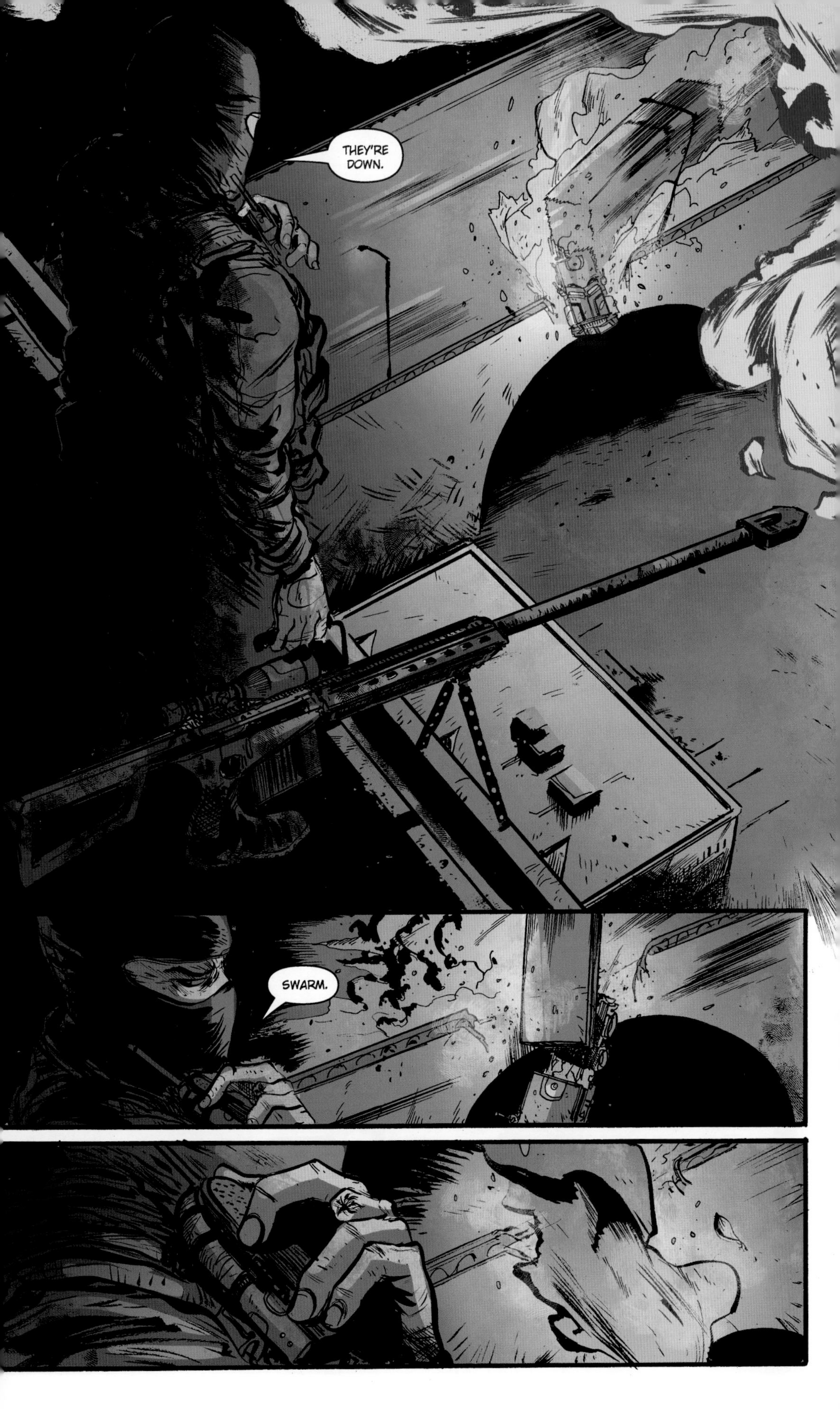
THEY'RE DOWN.
SWARM.

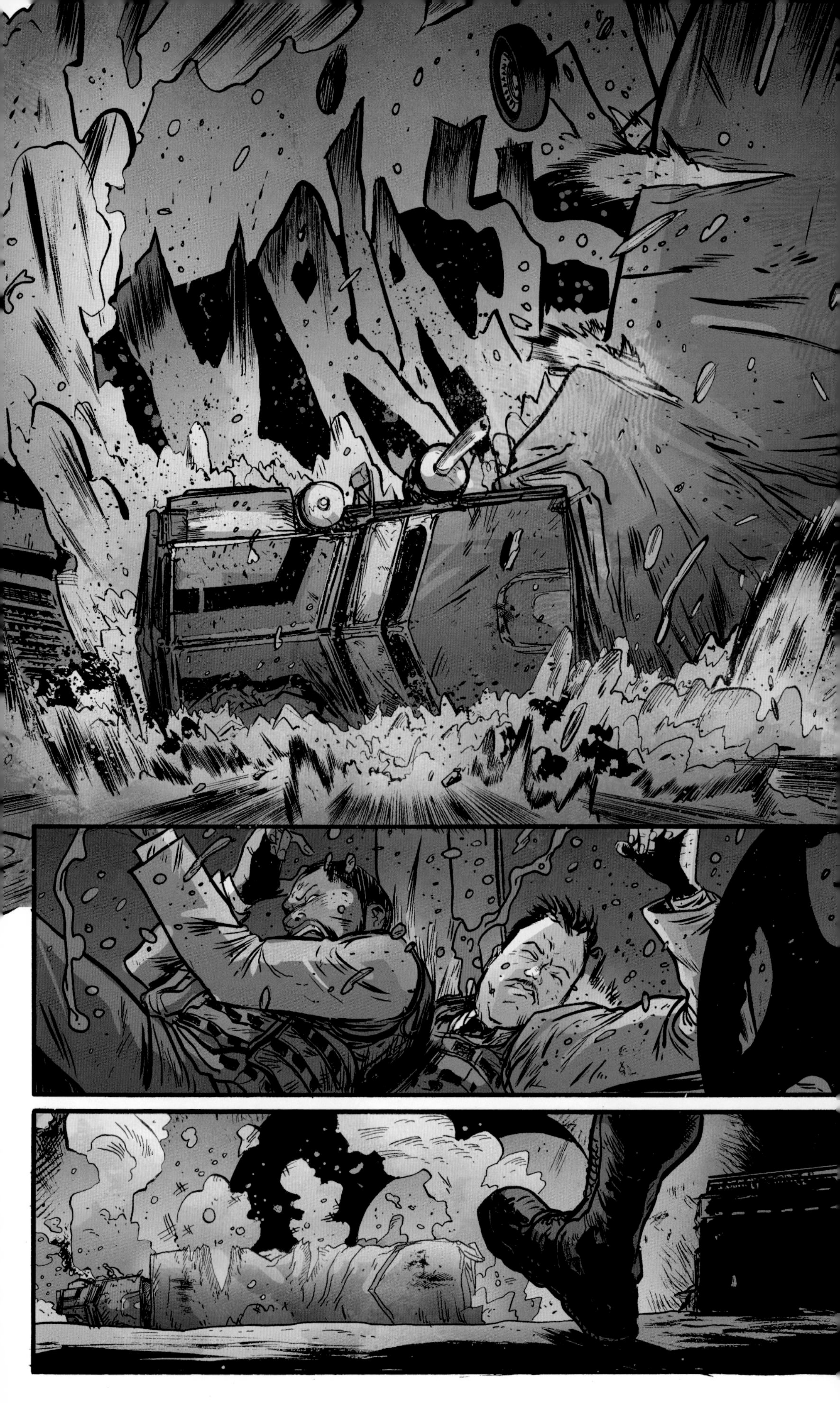

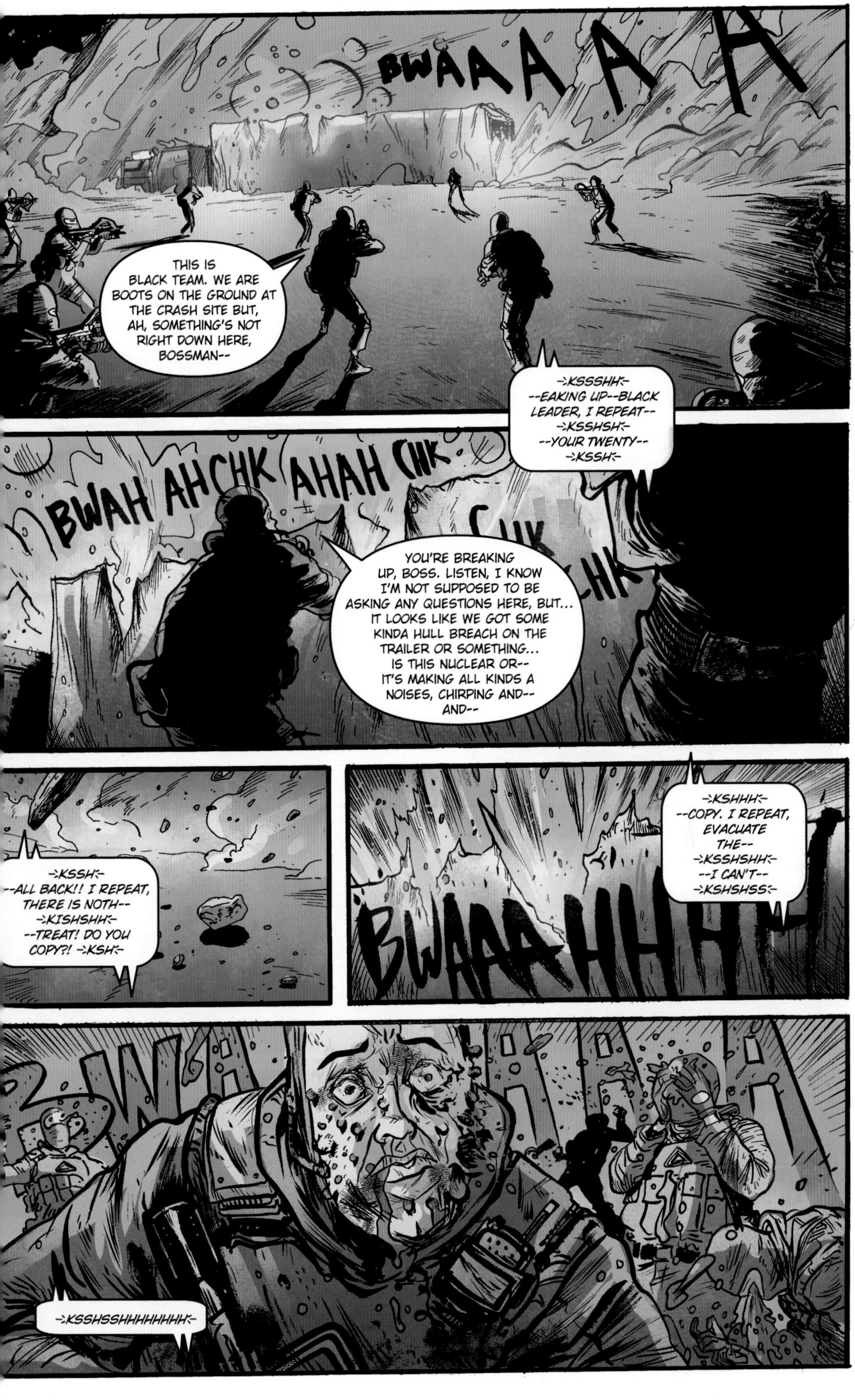
BWAAAAAA
THIS IS BLACK TEAM. WE ARE BOOTS ON THE GROUND AT THE CRASH SITE BUT, AH, SOMETHING'S NOT RIGHT DOWN HERE, BOSSMAN--
-KSSSHH- --EAKING UP--BLACK LEADER, I REPEAT-- -KSSHSH- --YOUR TWENTY-- -KSSH-
BWAH AHCHK AHAH CHK
CHK
CHK
YOU'RE BREAKING UP, BOSS. LISTEN, I KNOW I'M NOT SUPPOSED TO BE ASKING ANY QUESTIONS HERE, BUT... IT LOOKS LIKE WE GOT SOME KINDA HULL BREACH ON THE TRAILER OR SOMETHING... IS THIS NUCLEAR OR-- IT'S MAKING ALL KINDS A NOISES, CHIRPING AND-- AND--
-KSSH- --ALL BACK!! I REPEAT, THERE IS NOTH-- -KISHSHH- --TREAT! DO YOU COPY?! -KSH-
-KSHHH- --COPY. I REPEAT, EVACUATE THE-- -KSSHSHH- --I CAN'T-- -KSHSHSS-
BWAAHHHH
-KSSHSSHHHHHHHH-

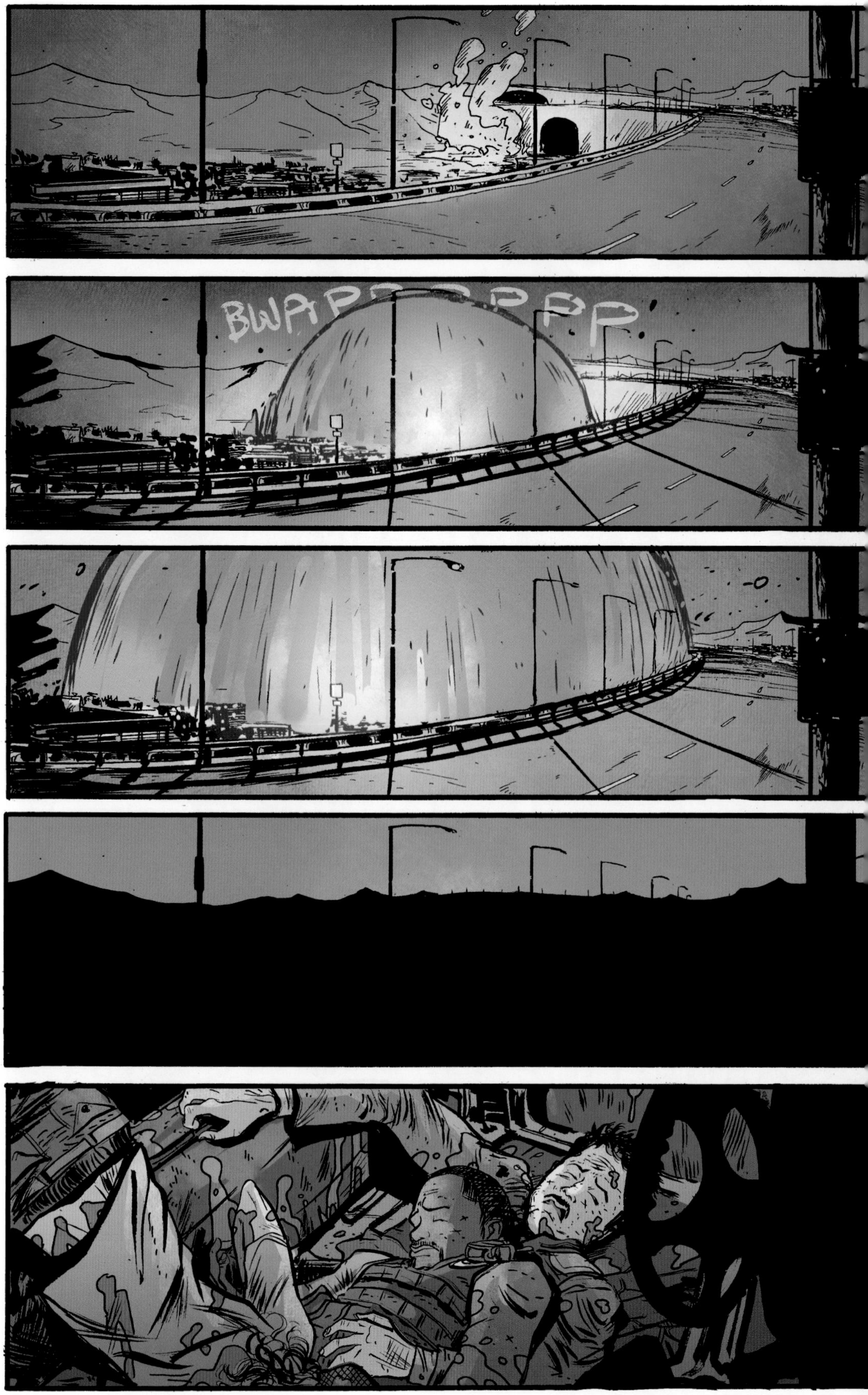
BWAPPPPPPP

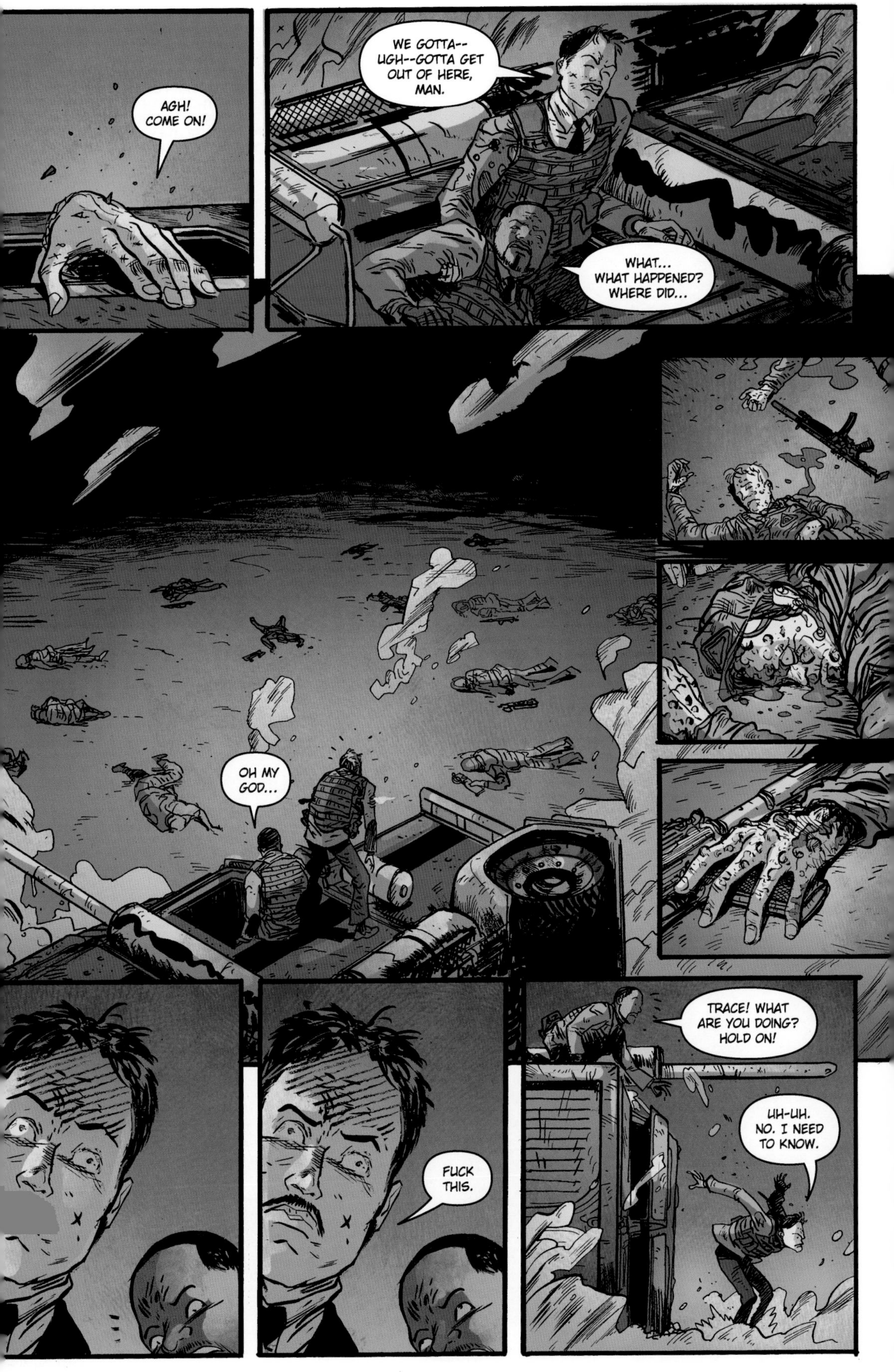
AGH! COME ON!
WE GOTTA-- UGH--GOTTA GET OUT OF HERE, MAN.
WHAT... WHAT HAPPENED? WHERE DID...
OH MY GOD...
FUCK THIS.
TRACE! WHAT ARE YOU DOING? HOLD ON!
UH-UH. NO. I NEED TO KNOW.

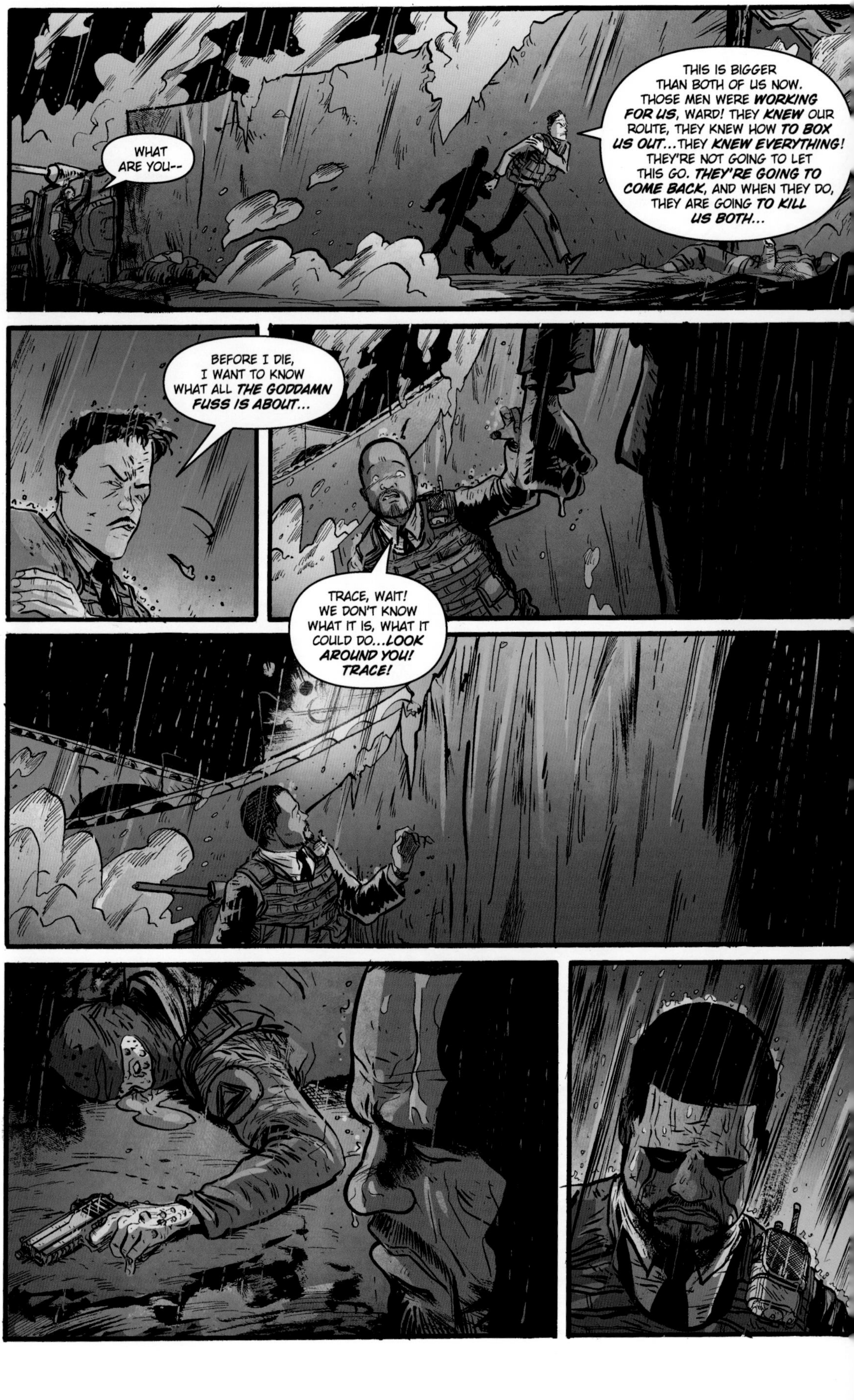
WHAT ARE YOU--
THIS IS BIGGER THAN BOTH OF US NOW. THOSE MEN WERE *WORKING FOR US*, WARD! THEY *KNEW* OUR ROUTE, THEY KNEW HOW *TO BOX US OUT*...THEY *KNEW EVERYTHING*! THEY'RE NOT GOING TO LET THIS GO. *THEY'RE GOING TO COME BACK*, AND WHEN THEY DO, THEY ARE GOING *TO KILL US BOTH*...
BEFORE I DIE, I WANT TO KNOW WHAT ALL *THE GODDAMN FUSS IS ABOUT*...
TRACE, WAIT! WE DON'T KNOW WHAT IT IS, WHAT IT COULD DO...*LOOK AROUND YOU! TRACE!*

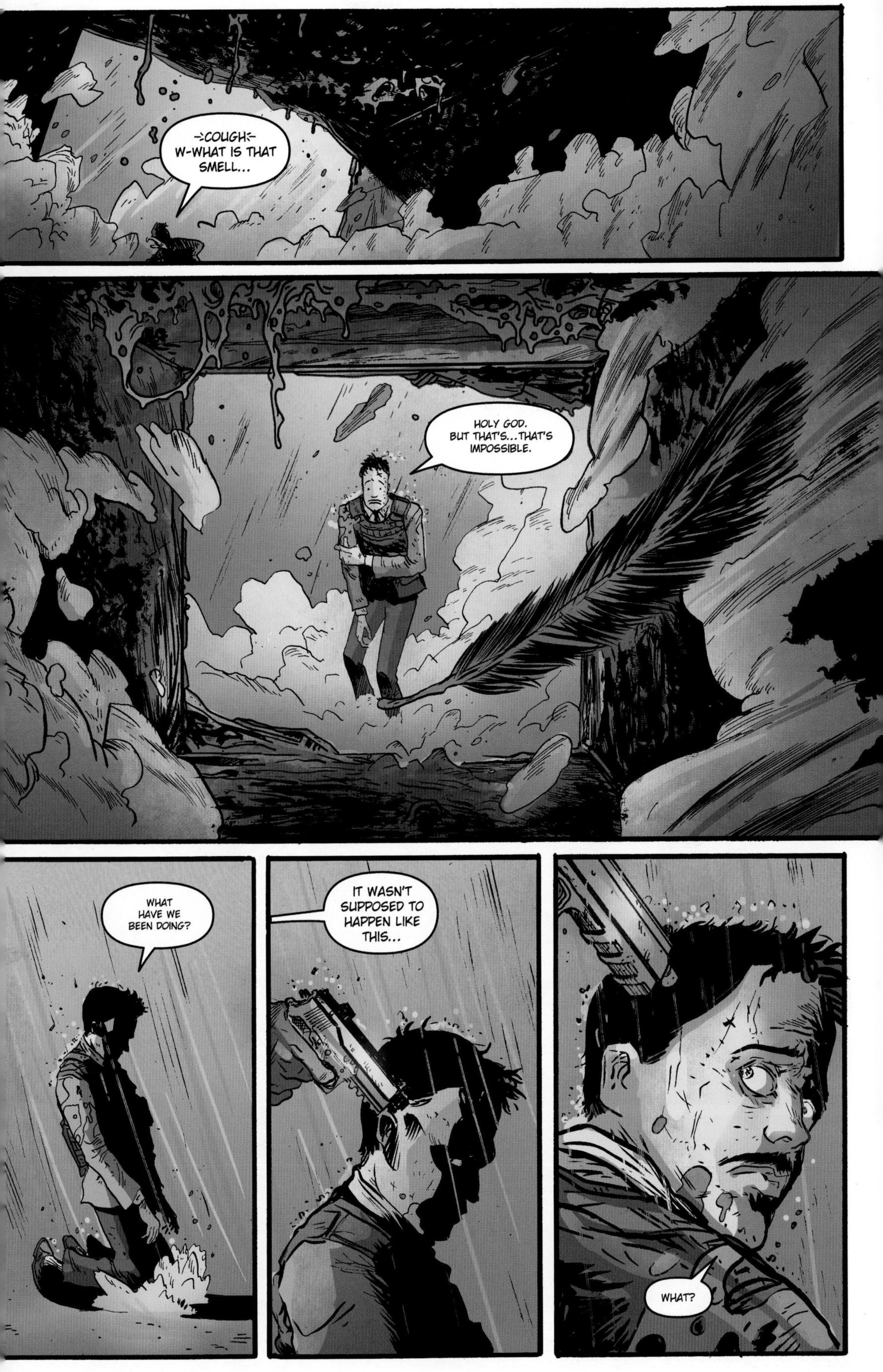

-COUGH-
W-WHAT IS THAT SMELL...
HOLY GOD. BUT THAT'S...THAT'S IMPOSSIBLE.
WHAT HAVE WE BEEN DOING?
IT WASN'T SUPPOSED TO HAPPEN LIKE THIS...
WHAT?

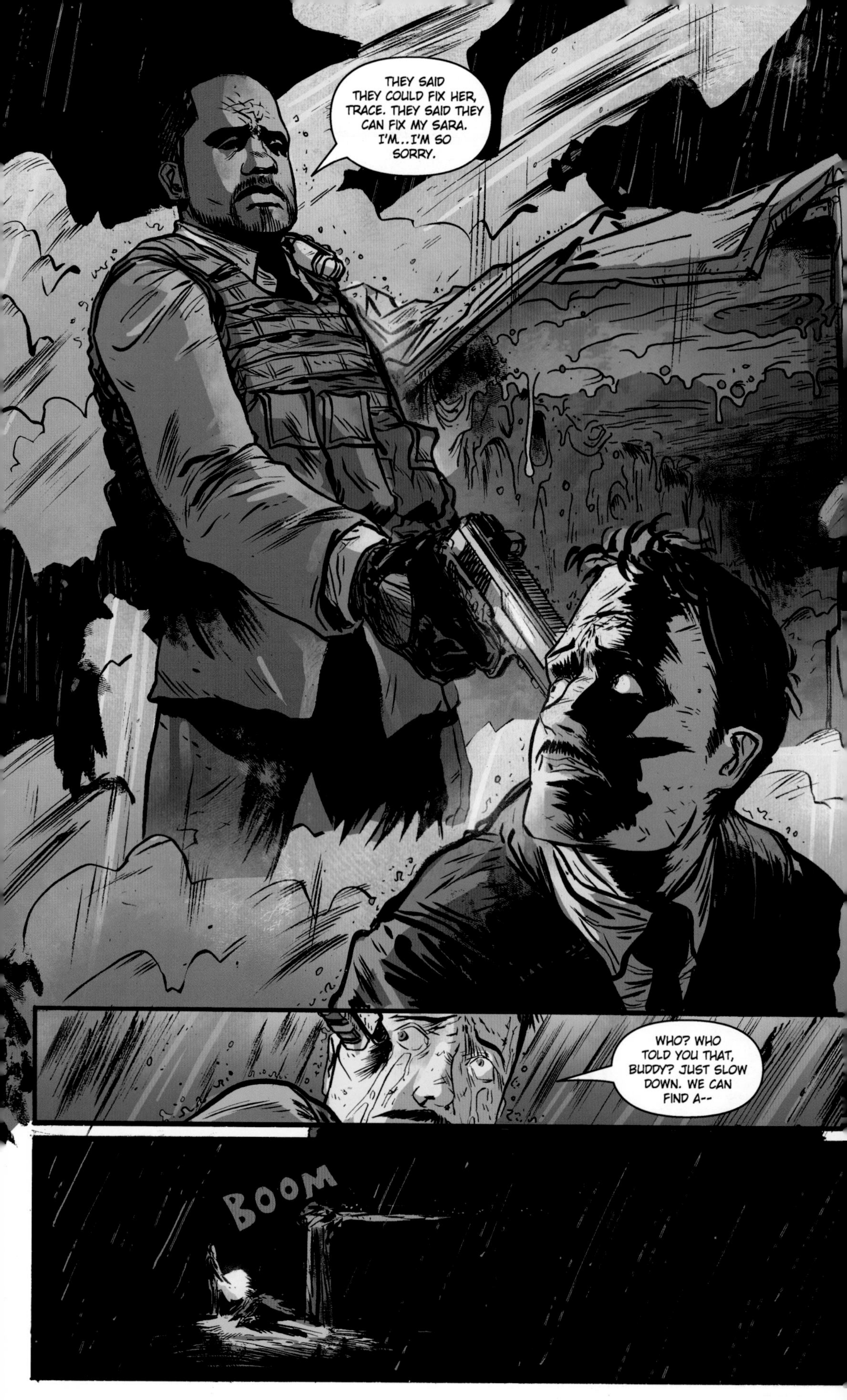
THEY SAID THEY COULD FIX HER, TRACE. THEY SAID THEY CAN FIX MY SARA. I'M..I'M SO SORRY.
WHO? WHO TOLD YOU THAT, BUDDY? JUST SLOW DOWN. WE CAN FIND A--
BOOM

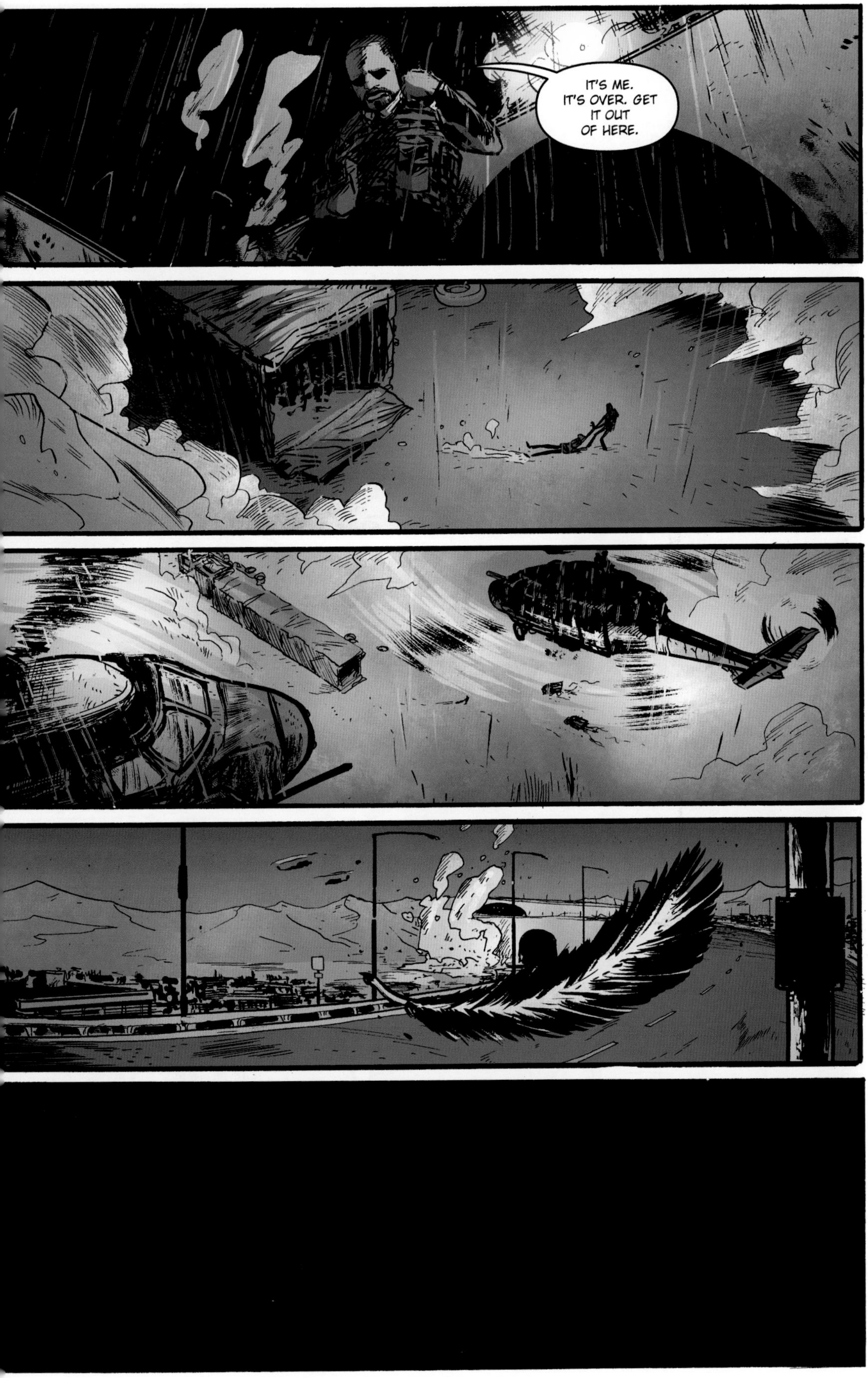
IT'S ME. IT'S OVER. GET IT OUT OF HERE.

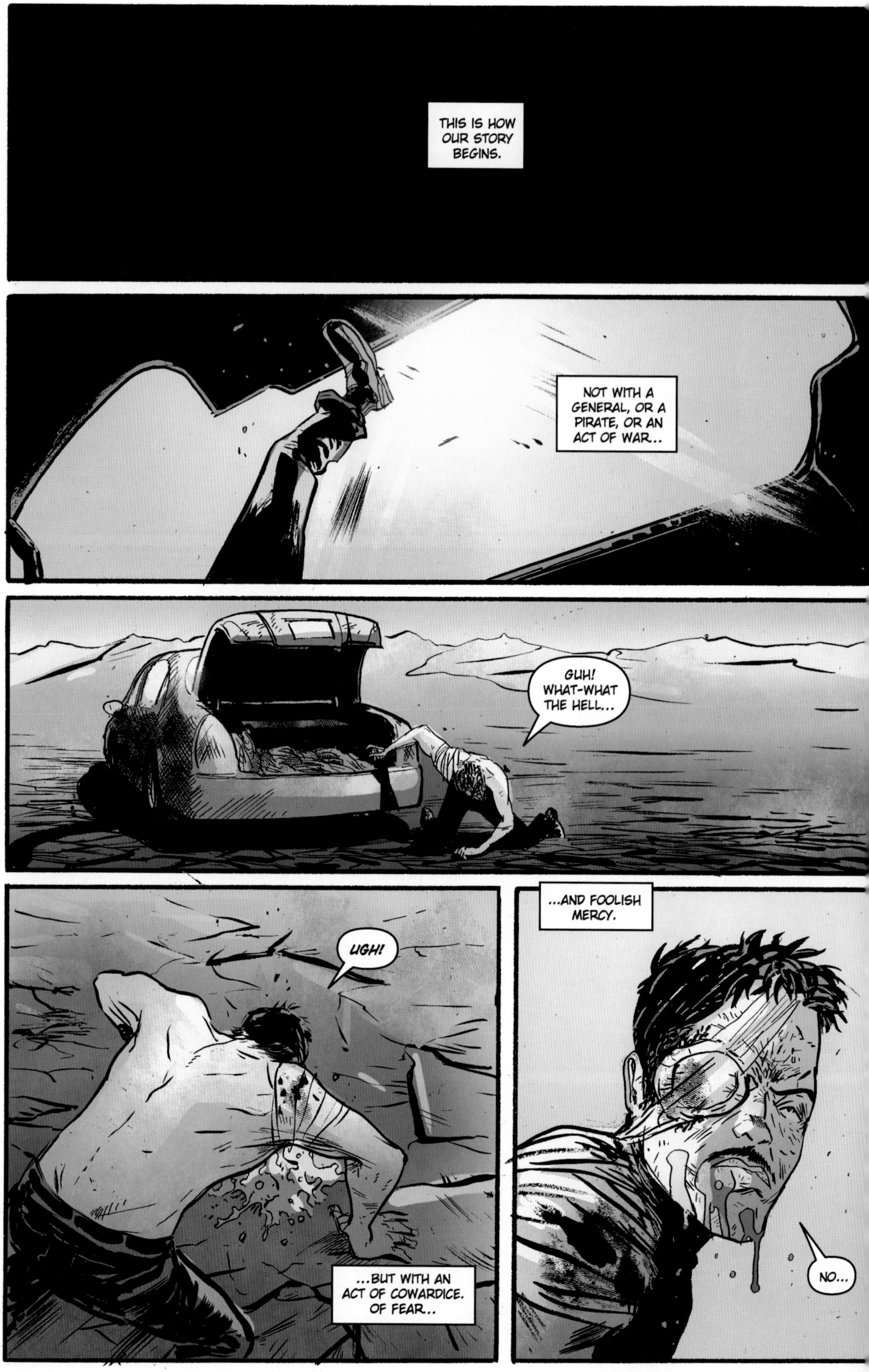
THIS IS HOW OUR STORY BEGINS.
NOT WITH A GENERAL, OR A PIRATE, OR AN ACT OF WAR...
GUH! WHAT-WHAT THE HELL...
UGH!
...BUT WITH AN ACT OF COWARDICE. OF FEAR...
...AND FOOLISH MERCY.
NO...

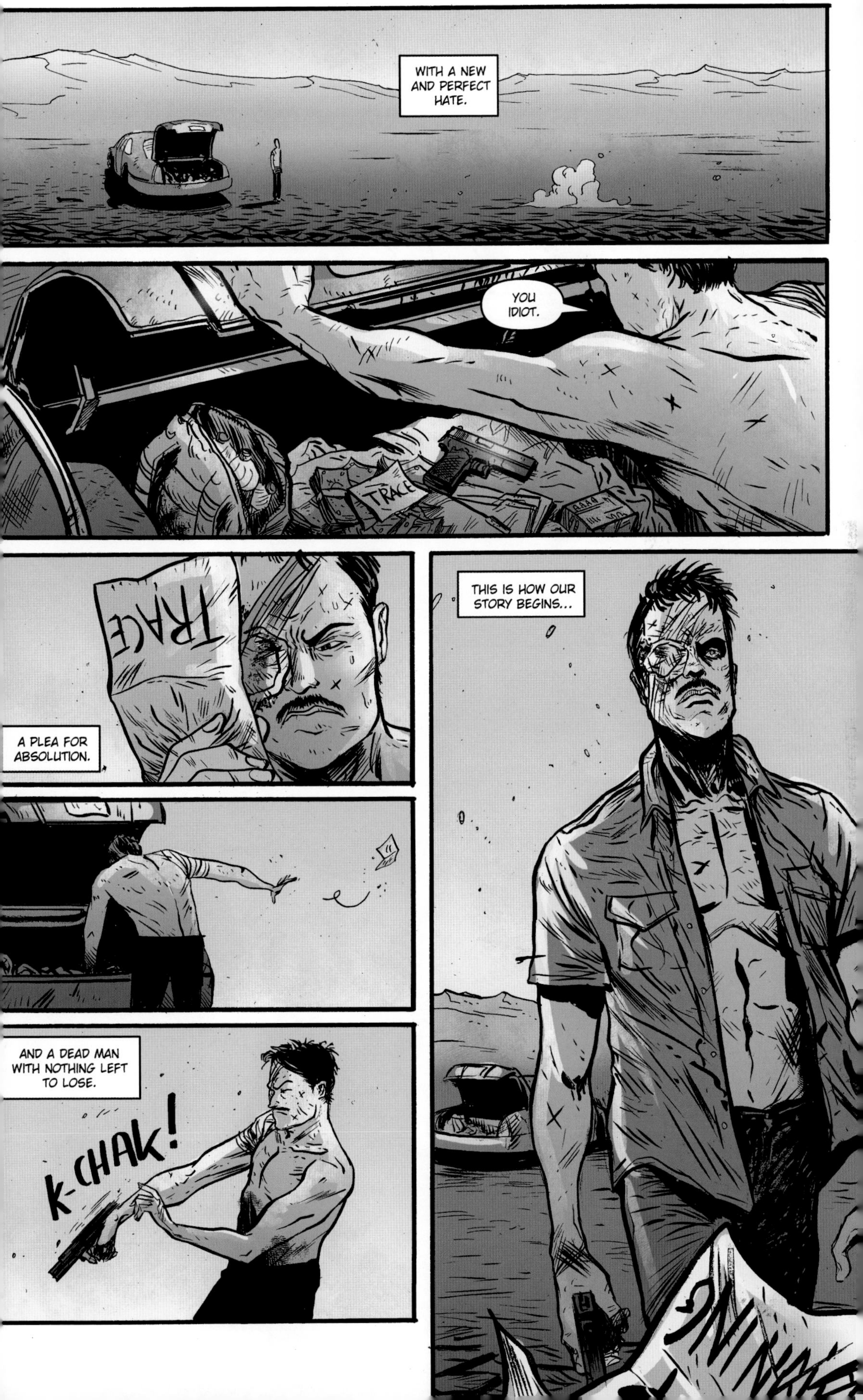
WITH A NEW AND PERFECT HATE.
YOU IDIOT.
TRACE
TRACE
A PLEA FOR ABSOLUTION.
AND A DEAD MAN WITH NOTHING LEFT TO LOSE.
K-CHAK!
THIS IS HOW OUR STORY BEGINS...

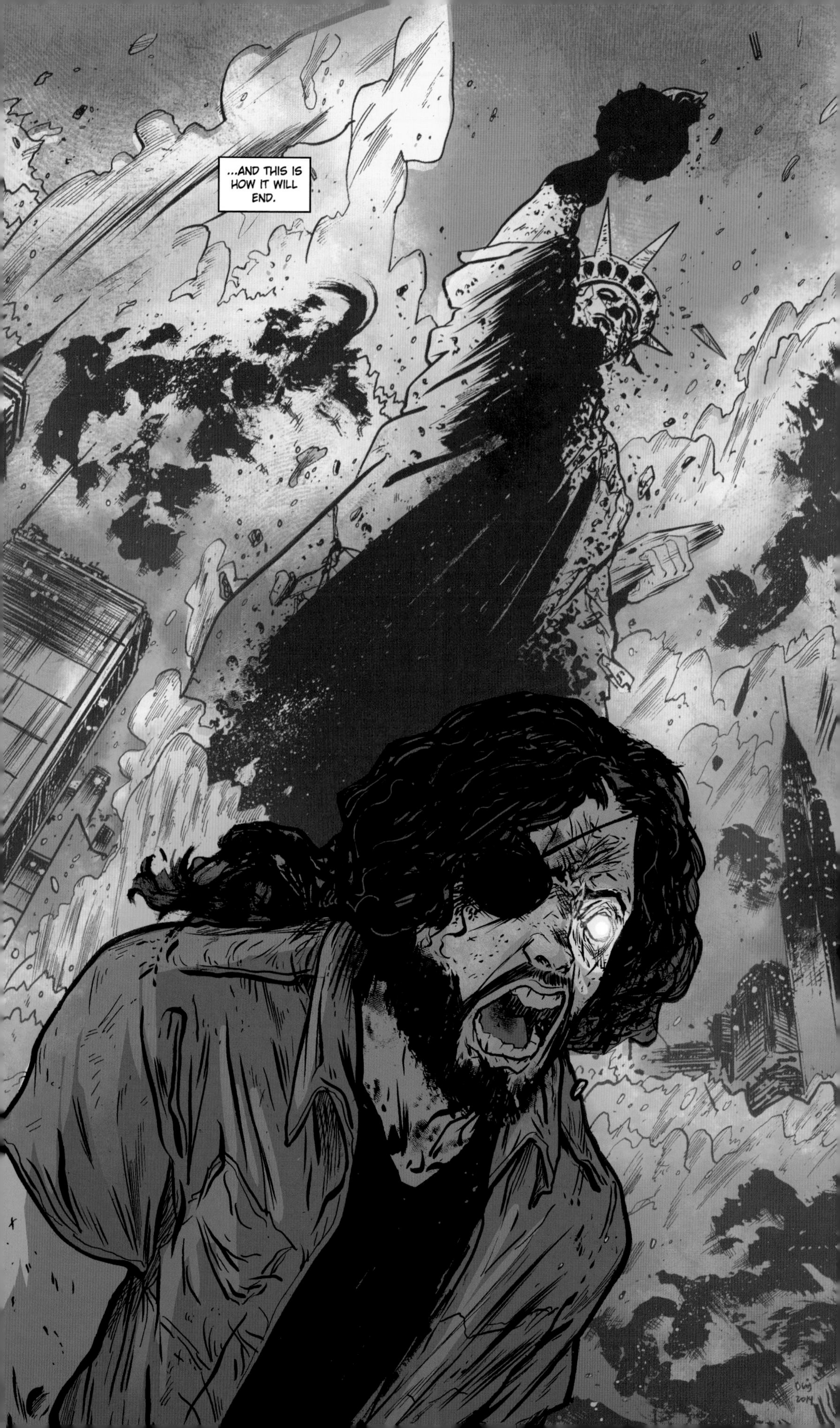
...AND THIS IS HOW IT WILL END.

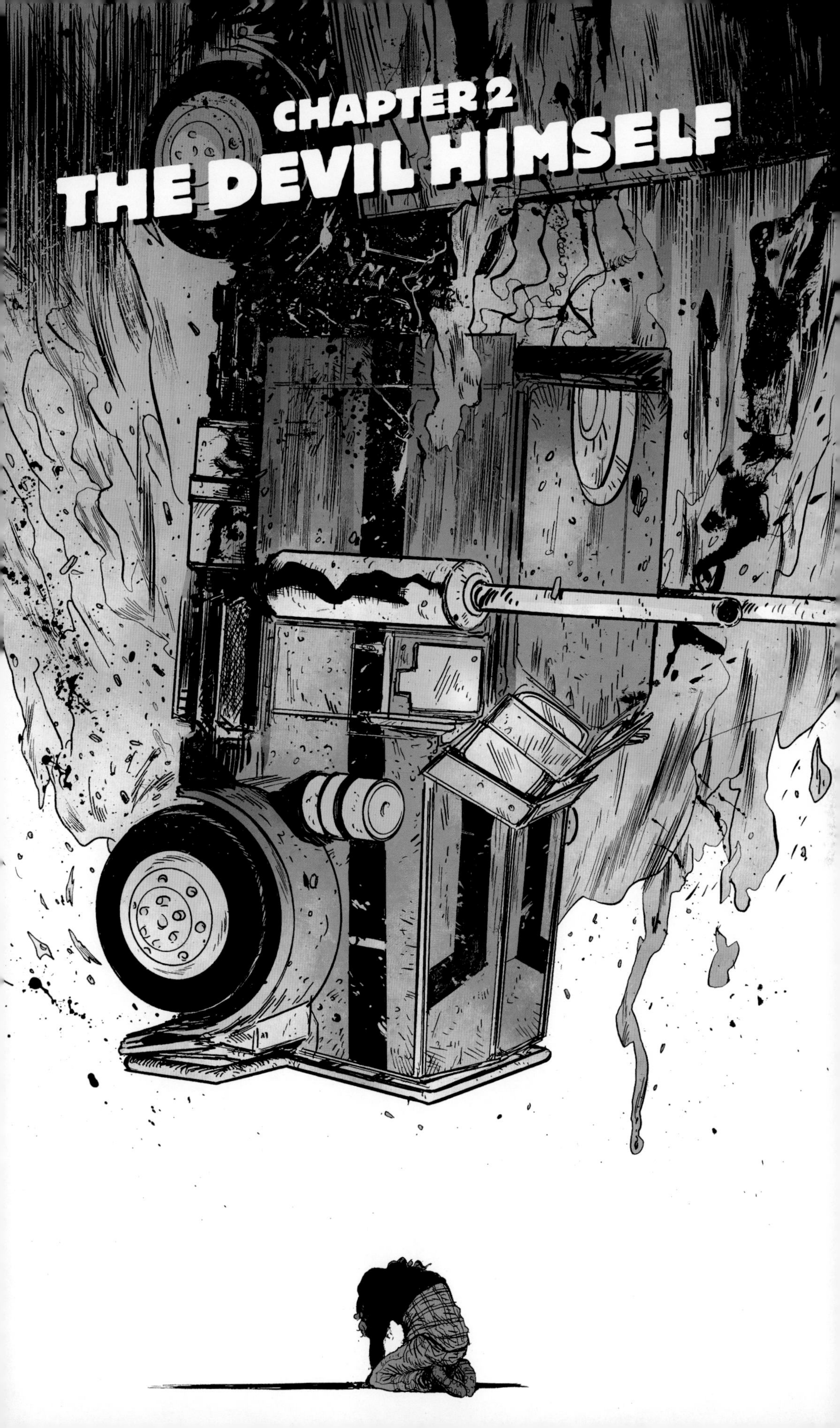
CHAPTER 2
THE DEVIL HIMSELF

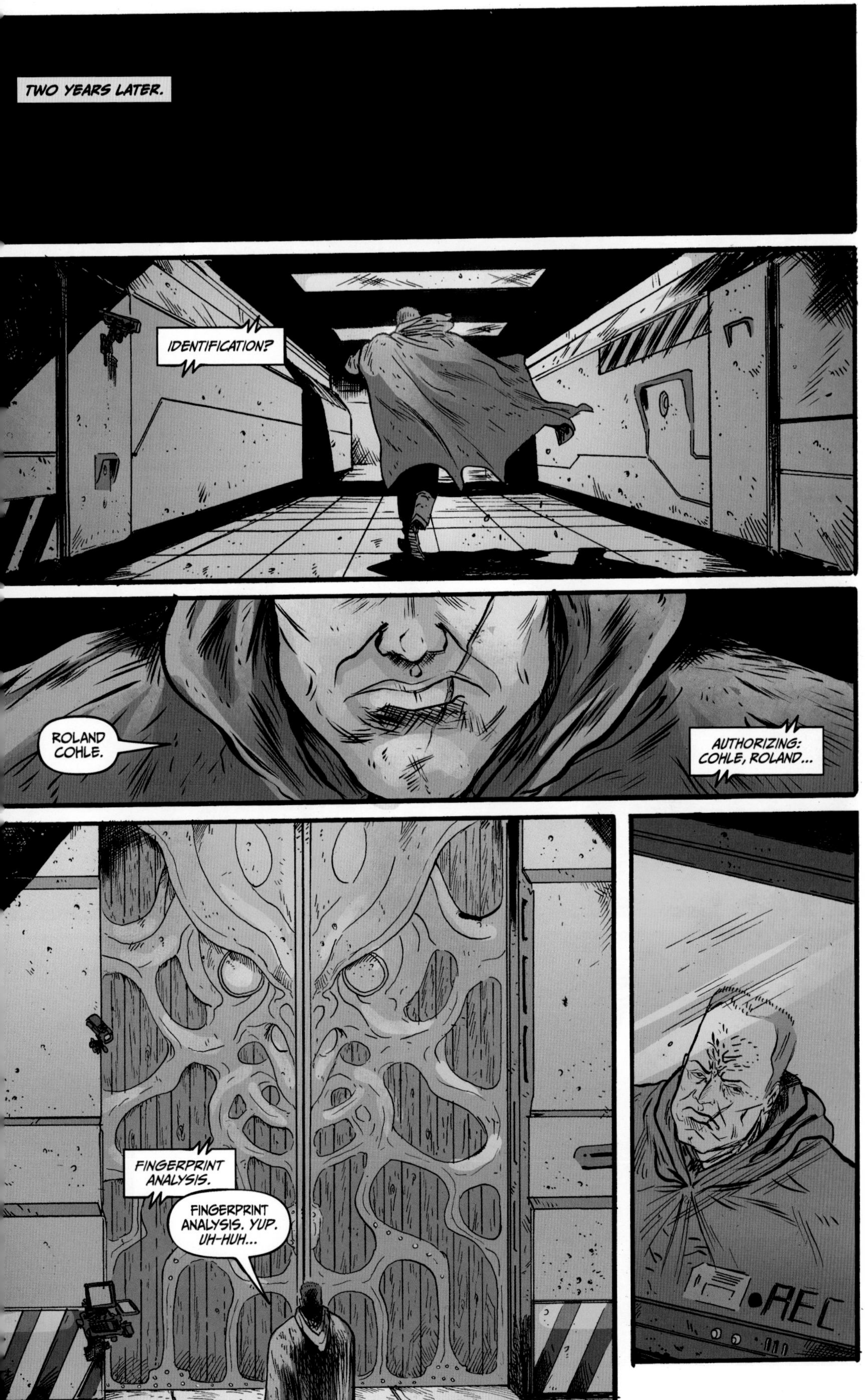
TWO YEARS LATER.
IDENTIFICATION?
ROLAND COHLE.
AUTHORIZING: COHLE, ROLAND...
FINGERPRINT ANALYSIS.
FINGERPRINT ANALYSIS. YUP. UH-HUH...
REC

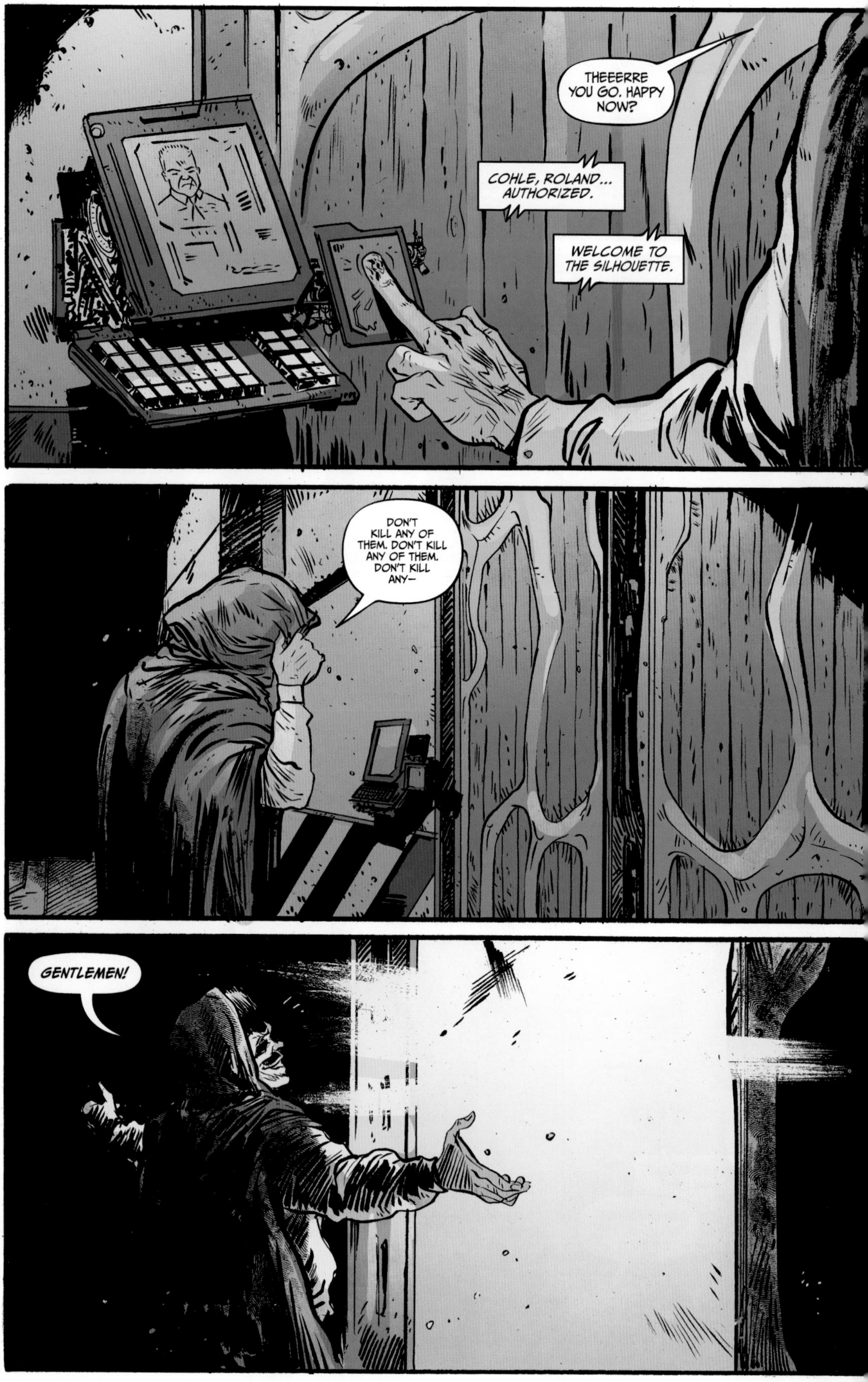
THEEERRE YOU GO. HAPPY NOW?
COHLE, ROLAND... AUTHORIZED.
WELCOME TO THE SILHOUETTE.
DON'T KILL ANY OF THEM. DON'T KILL ANY OF THEM. DON'T KILL ANY—
GENTLEMEN!

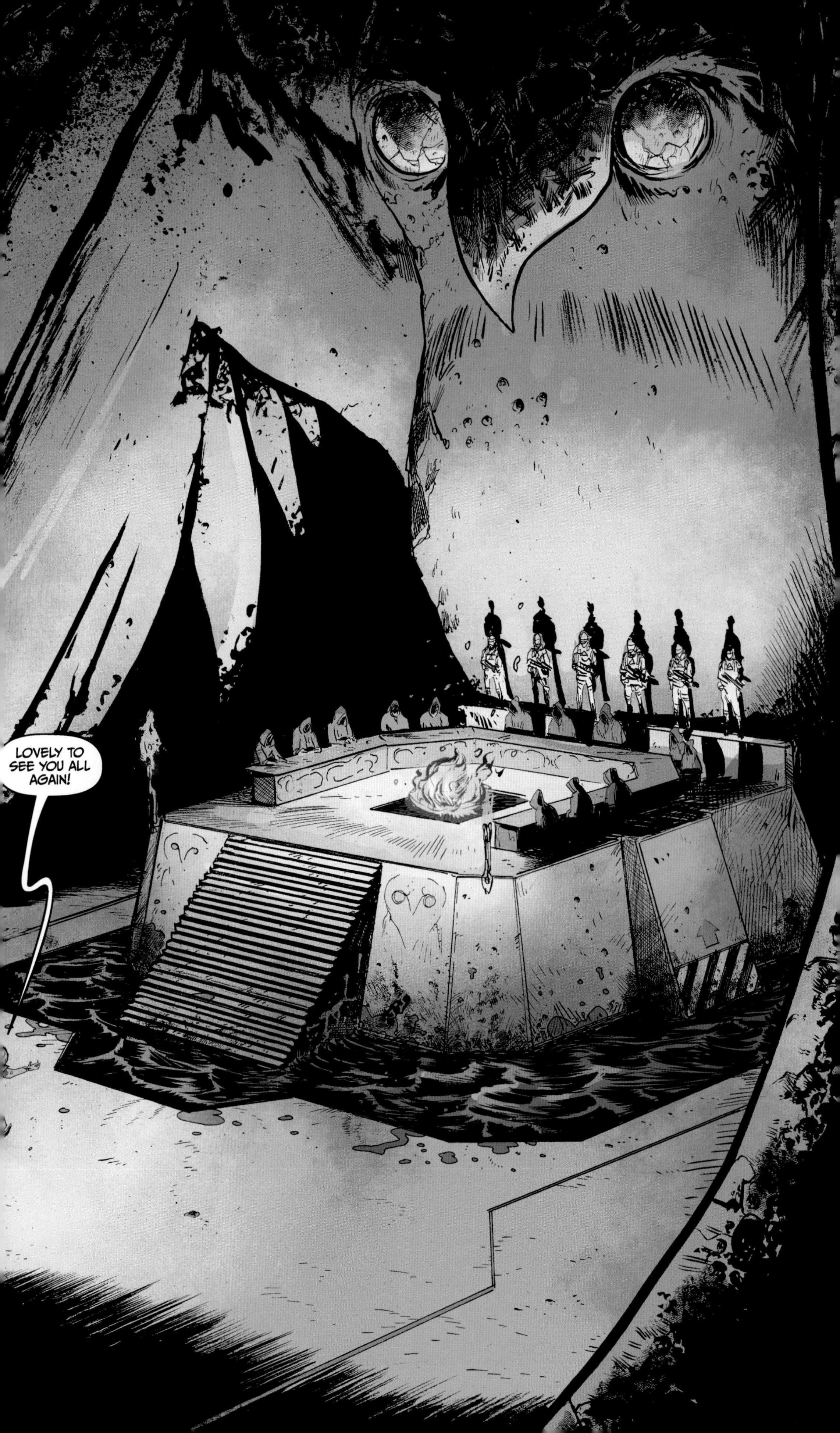
LOVELY TO SEE YOU ALL AGAIN!

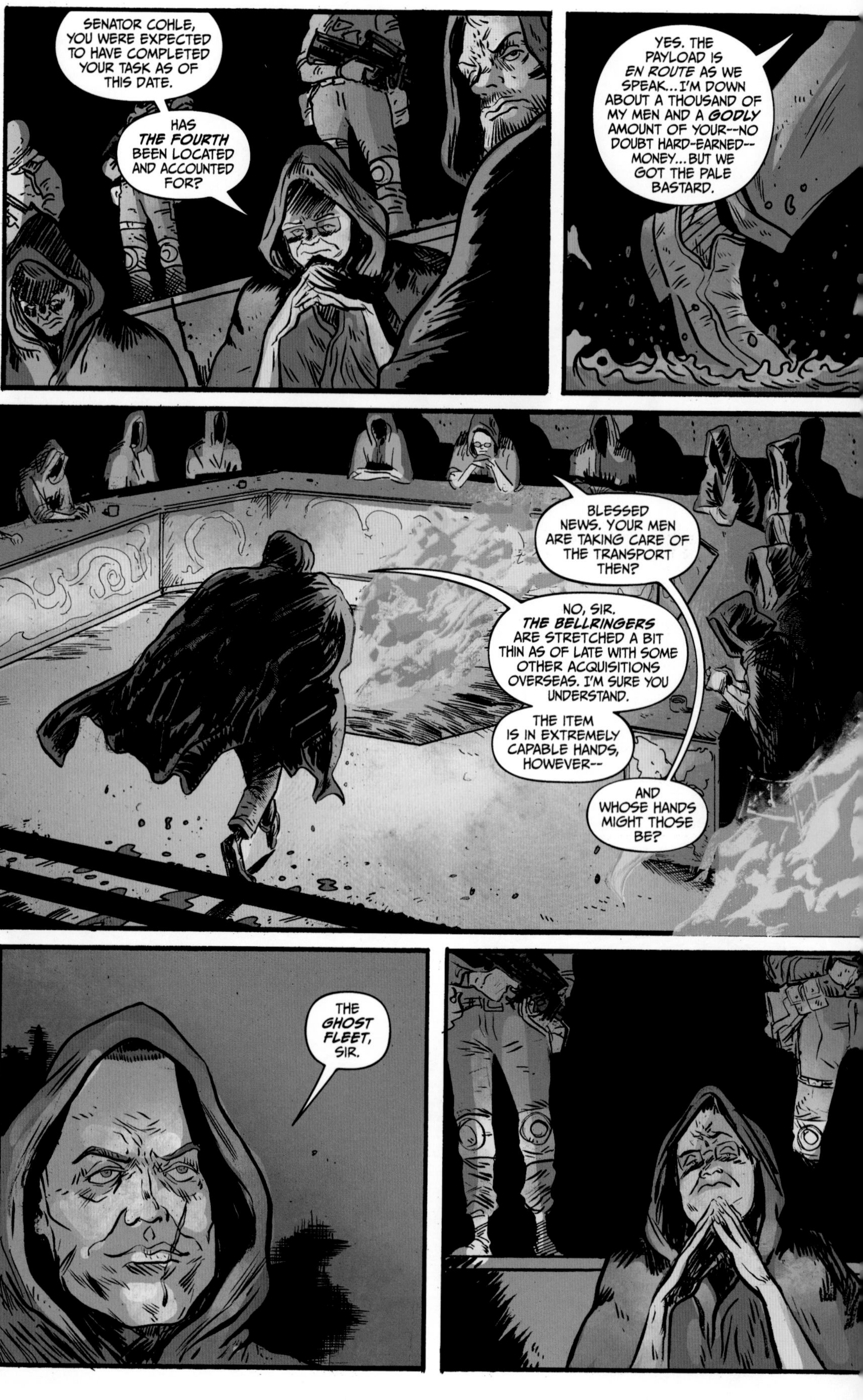
SENATOR COHLE, YOU WERE EXPECTED TO HAVE COMPLETED YOUR TASK AS OF THIS DATE.
HAS *THE FOURTH* BEEN LOCATED AND ACCOUNTED FOR?
YES. THE PAYLOAD IS *EN ROUTE* AS WE SPEAK... I'M DOWN ABOUT A THOUSAND OF MY MEN AND A *GODLY* AMOUNT OF YOUR--NO DOUBT HARD-EARNED--MONEY... BUT WE GOT THE PALE BASTARD.
BLESSED NEWS. YOUR MEN ARE TAKING CARE OF THE TRANSPORT THEN?
NO, SIR. *THE BELLRINGERS* ARE STRETCHED A BIT THIN AS OF LATE WITH SOME OTHER ACQUISITIONS OVERSEAS. I'M SURE YOU UNDERSTAND.
THE ITEM IS IN EXTREMELY CAPABLE HANDS, HOWEVER--
AND WHOSE HANDS MIGHT THOSE BE?
THE *GHOST FLEET*, SIR.

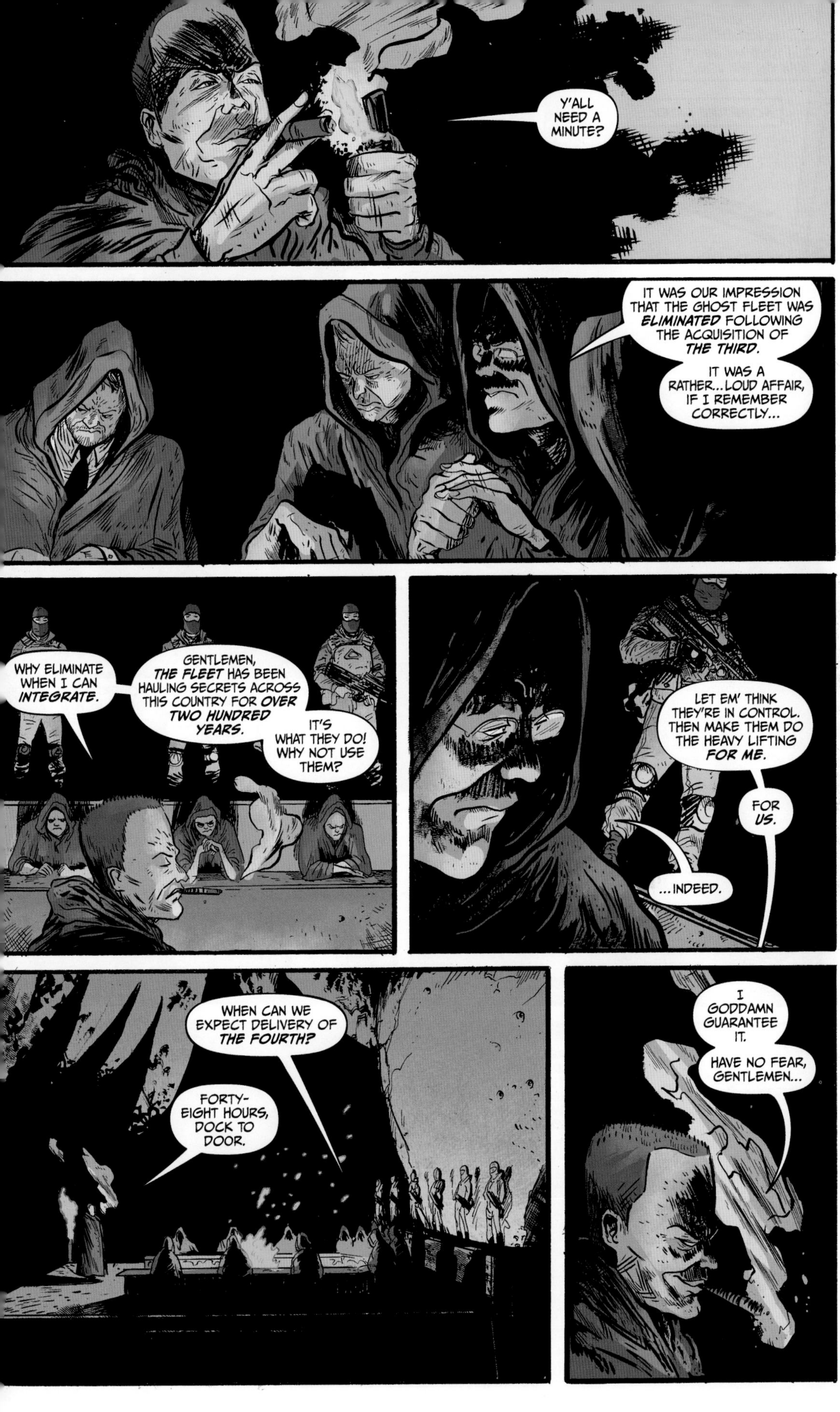
Y'ALL NEED A MINUTE?
IT WAS OUR IMPRESSION THAT THE GHOST FLEET WAS ELIMINATED FOLLOWING THE ACQUISITION OF THE THIRD.
IT WAS A RATHER...LOUD AFFAIR, IF I REMEMBER CORRECTLY...
WHY ELIMINATE WHEN I CAN INTEGRATE.
GENTLEMEN, THE FLEET HAS BEEN HAULING SECRETS ACROSS THIS COUNTRY FOR OVER TWO HUNDRED YEARS.
IT'S WHAT THEY DO! WHY NOT USE THEM?
LET EM' THINK THEY'RE IN CONTROL. THEN MAKE THEM DO THE HEAVY LIFTING FOR ME.
FOR US.
...INDEED.
WHEN CAN WE EXPECT DELIVERY OF THE FOURTH?
FORTY-EIGHT HOURS, DOCK TO DOOR.
I GODDAMN GUARANTEE IT.
HAVE NO FEAR, GENTLEMEN...

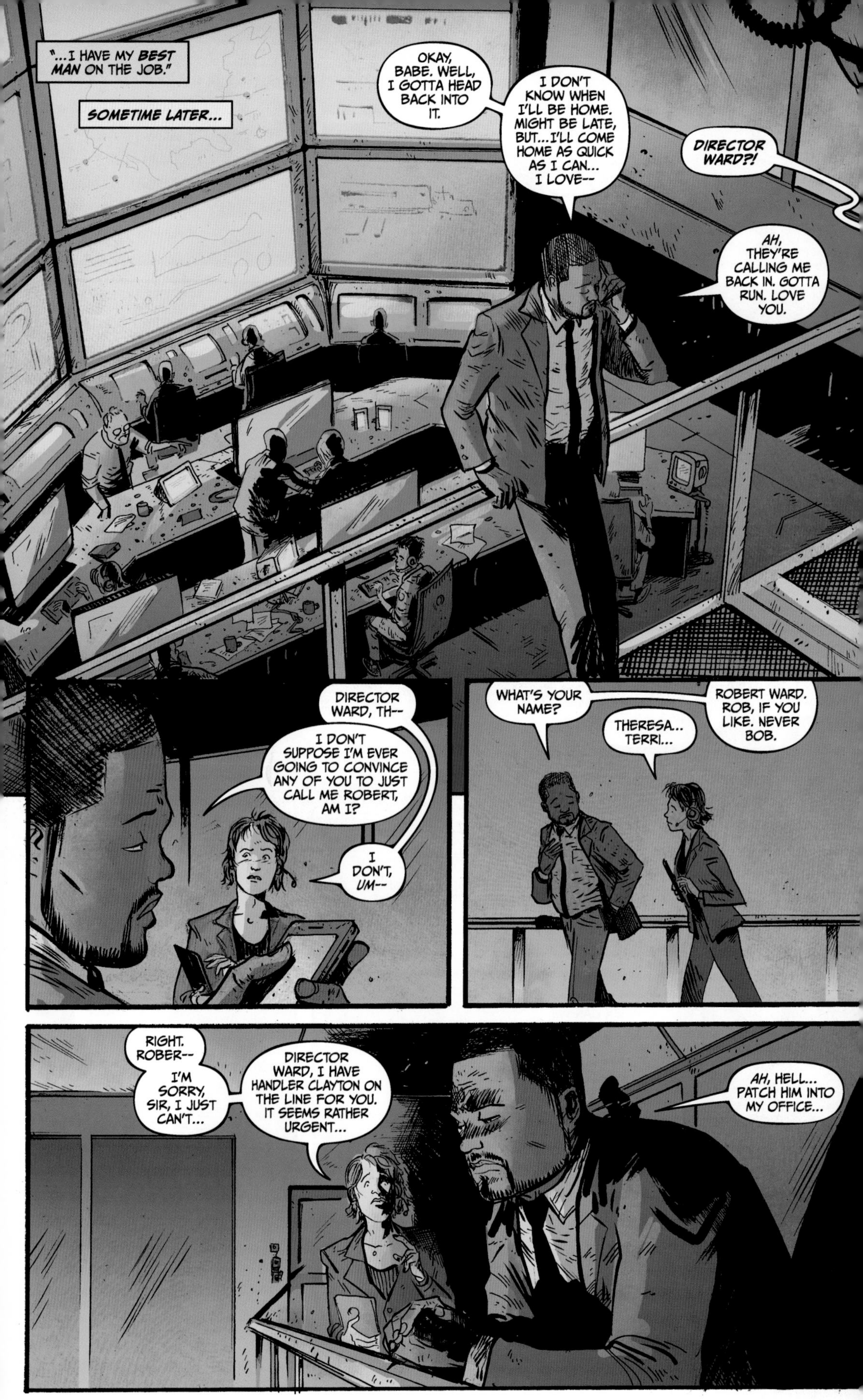
"...I HAVE MY BEST MAN ON THE JOB."
SOMETIME LATER...
OKAY, BABE. WELL, I GOTTA HEAD BACK INTO IT.
I DON'T KNOW WHEN I'LL BE HOME. MIGHT BE LATE, BUT...I'LL COME HOME AS QUICK AS I CAN... I LOVE--
DIRECTOR WARD?!
AH, THEY'RE CALLING ME BACK IN. GOTTA RUN. LOVE YOU.
DIRECTOR WARD, TH--
I DON'T SUPPOSE I'M EVER GOING TO CONVINCE ANY OF YOU TO JUST CALL ME ROBERT, AM I?
I DON'T, UM--
WHAT'S YOUR NAME?
THERESA... TERRI...
ROBERT WARD. ROB, IF YOU LIKE. NEVER BOB.
RIGHT. ROBER--
I'M SORRY, SIR, I JUST CAN'T...
DIRECTOR WARD, I HAVE HANDLER CLAYTON ON THE LINE FOR YOU. IT SEEMS RATHER URGENT...
AH, HELL... PATCH HIM INTO MY OFFICE...

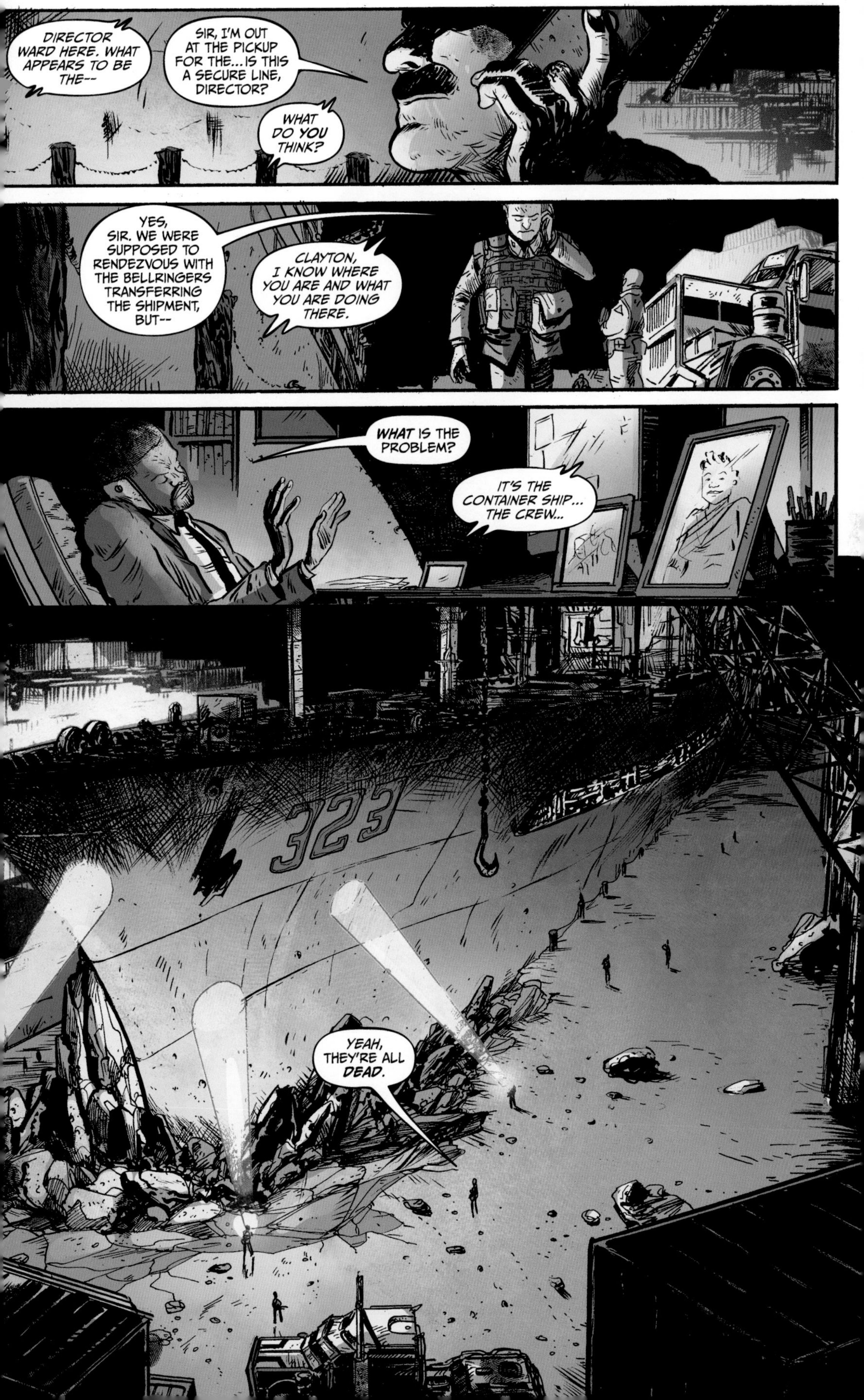
DIRECTOR WARD HERE. WHAT APPEARS TO BE THE--
SIR, I'M OUT AT THE PICKUP FOR THE...IS THIS A SECURE LINE, DIRECTOR?
WHAT DO YOU THINK?
YES, SIR. WE WERE SUPPOSED TO RENDEZVOUS WITH THE BELLRINGERS TRANSFERRING THE SHIPMENT, BUT--
CLAYTON, I KNOW WHERE YOU ARE AND WHAT YOU ARE DOING THERE.
WHAT IS THE PROBLEM?
IT'S THE CONTAINER SHIP... THE CREW...
323
YEAH, THEY'RE ALL DEAD.

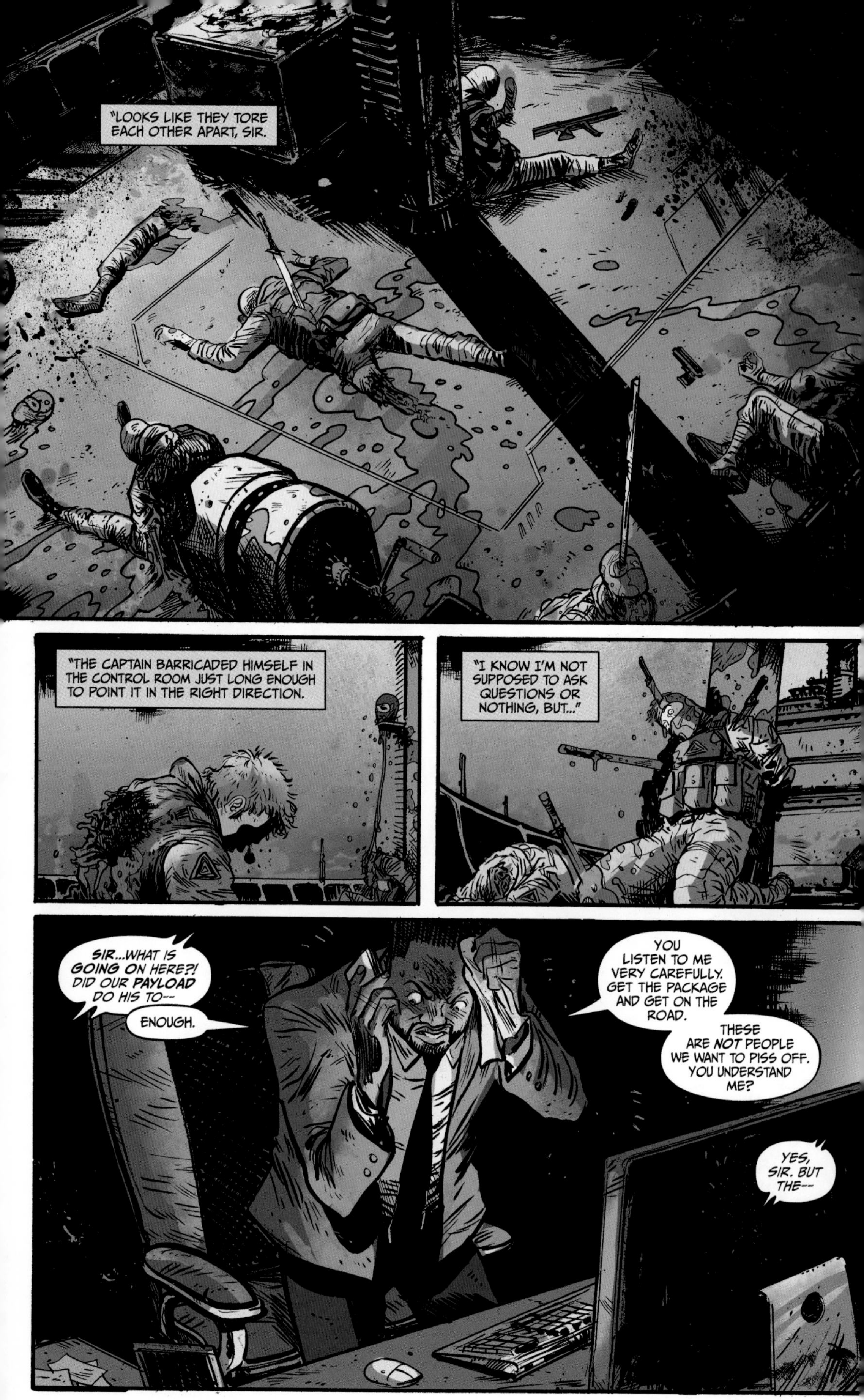
"LOOKS LIKE THEY TORE EACH OTHER APART, SIR.
"THE CAPTAIN BARRICADED HIMSELF IN THE CONTROL ROOM JUST LONG ENOUGH TO POINT IT IN THE RIGHT DIRECTION.
"I KNOW I'M NOT SUPPOSED TO ASK QUESTIONS OR NOTHING, BUT..."
SIR...WHAT IS GOING ON HERE?! DID OUR PAYLOAD DO HIS TO--
ENOUGH.
YOU LISTEN TO ME VERY CAREFULLY. GET THE PACKAGE AND GET ON THE ROAD.
THESE ARE NOT PEOPLE WE WANT TO PISS OFF. YOU UNDERSTAND ME?
YES, SIR. BUT THE--

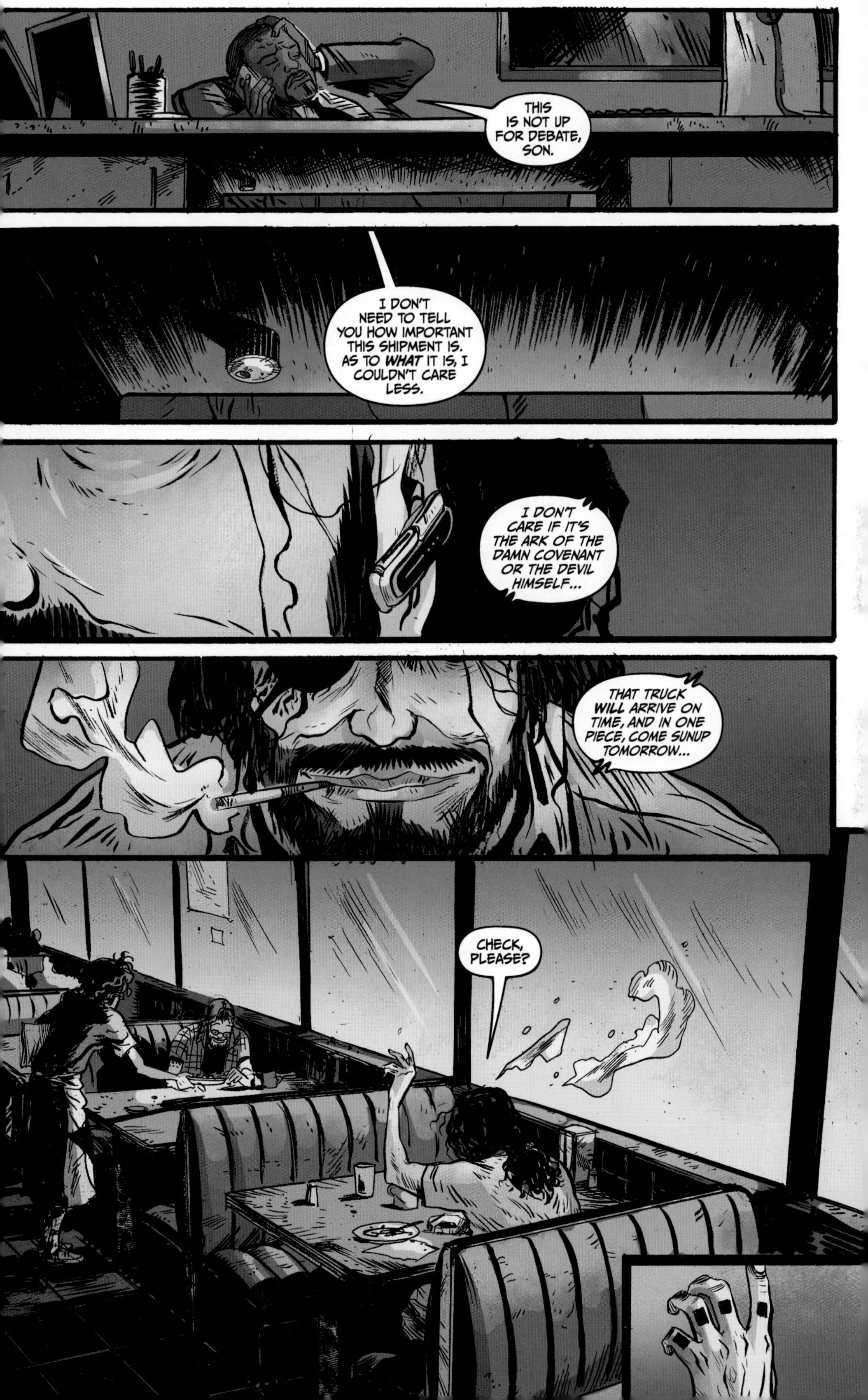
THIS IS NOT UP FOR DEBATE, SON.
I DON'T NEED TO TELL YOU HOW IMPORTANT THIS SHIPMENT IS. AS TO *WHAT* IT IS, I COULDN'T CARE LESS.
I DON'T CARE IF IT'S THE ARK OF THE DAMN COVENANT OR THE DEVIL HIMSELF...
THAT TRUCK *WILL* ARRIVE ON TIME, AND IN ONE PIECE, COME SUNUP TOMORROW...
CHECK, PLEASE?

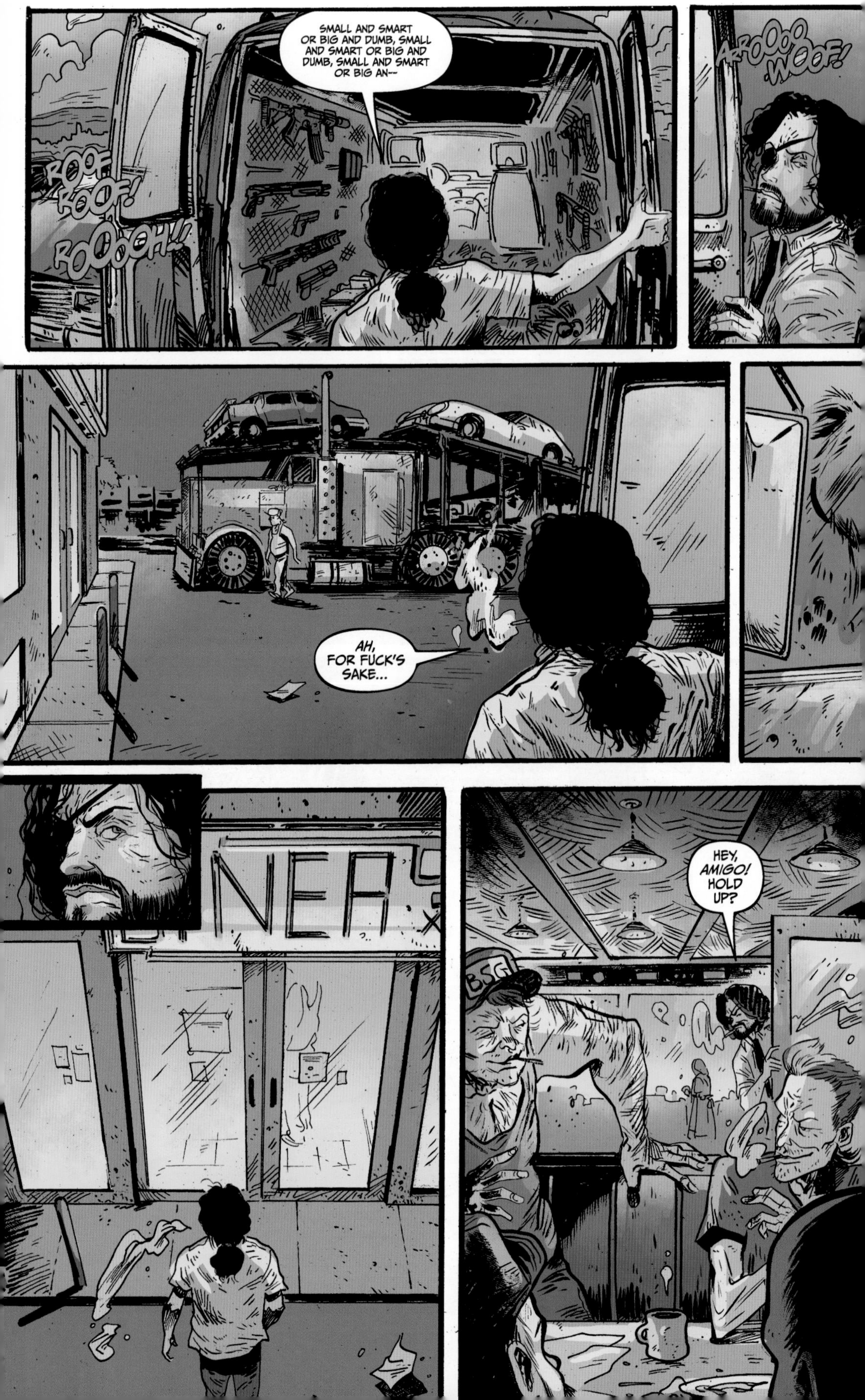
SMALL AND SMART OR BIG AND DUMB, SMALL AND SMART OR BIG AND DUMB, SMALL AND SMART OR BIG AN--
ROOF KOOF!
ROOOOH!!
AROOOO WOOF!
AH, FOR FUCK'S SAKE...
HEY, AMIGO! HOLD UP?

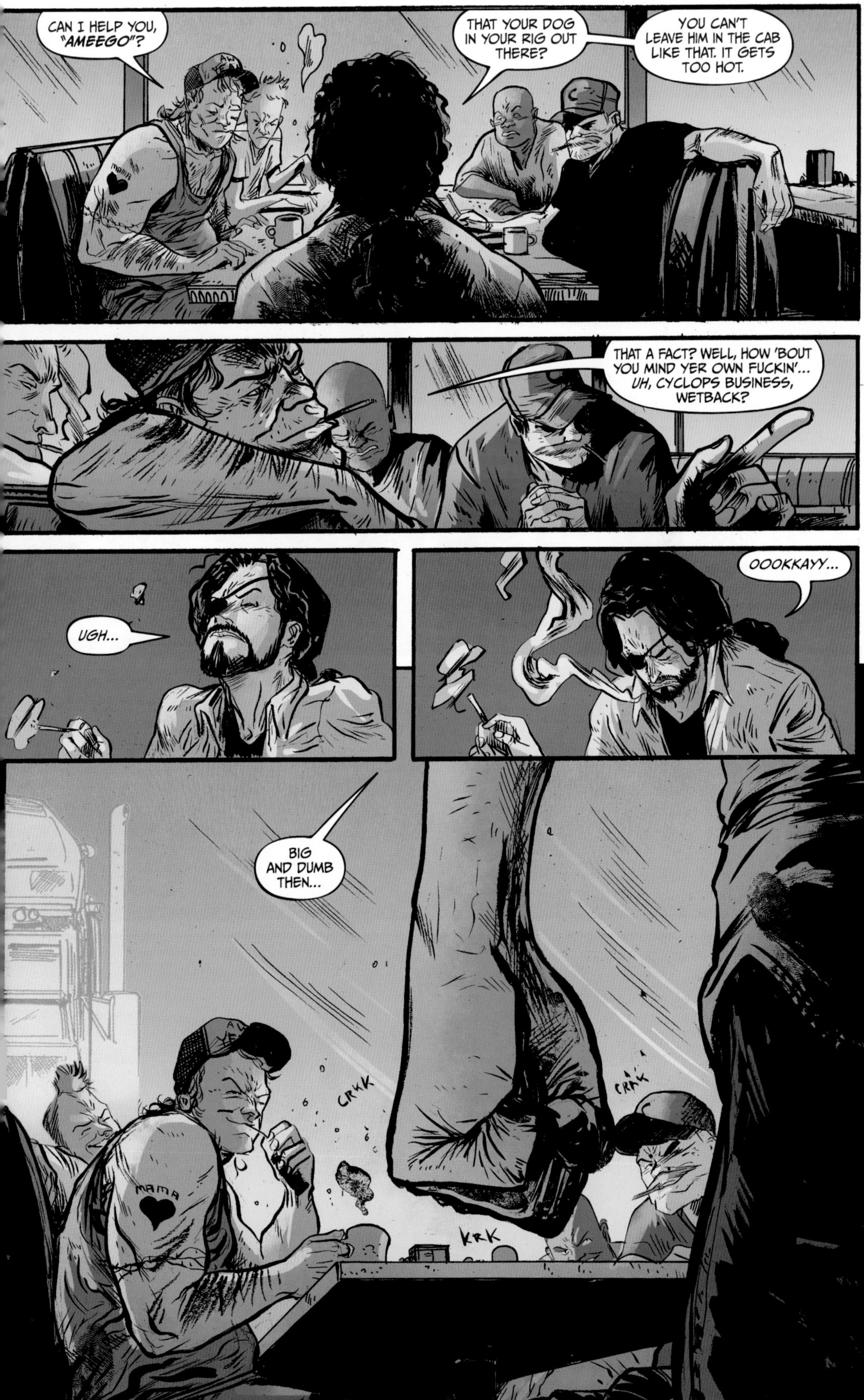
CAN I HELP YOU, "AMEEGO"?
THAT YOUR DOG IN YOUR RIG OUT THERE?
YOU CAN'T LEAVE HIM IN THE CAB LIKE THAT. IT GETS TOO HOT.
THAT A FACT? WELL, HOW 'BOUT YOU MIND YER OWN FUCKIN'... UH, CYCLOPS BUSINESS, WETBACK?
UGH...
OOOKKAYY...
BIG AND DUMB THEN...
CRKK
CRKK
KRK

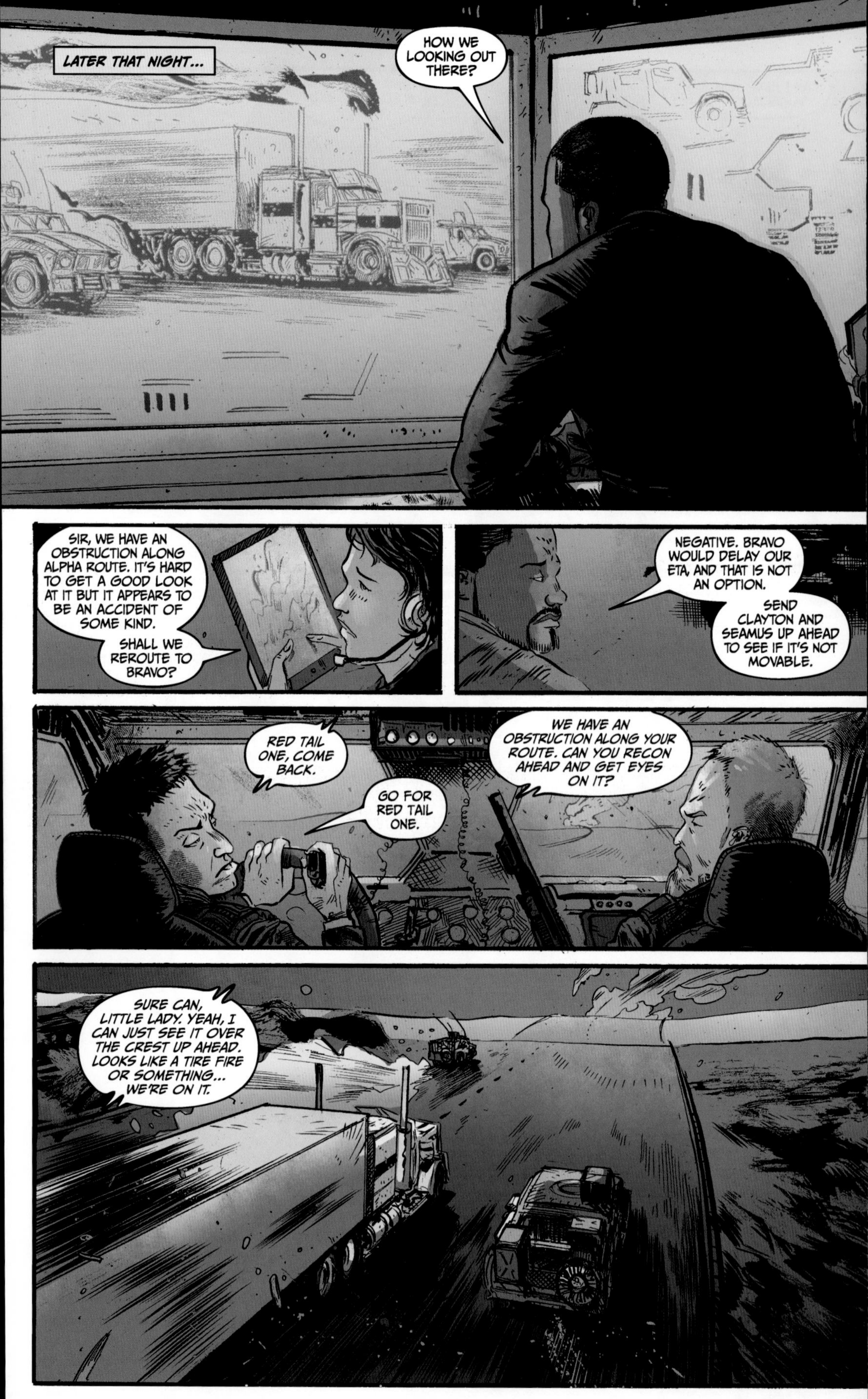
LATER THAT NIGHT...
HOW WE LOOKING OUT THERE?
SIR, WE HAVE AN OBSTRUCTION ALONG ALPHA ROUTE. IT'S HARD TO GET A GOOD LOOK AT IT BUT IT APPEARS TO BE AN ACCIDENT OF SOME KIND.
SHALL WE REROUTE TO BRAVO?
NEGATIVE. BRAVO WOULD DELAY OUR ETA, AND THAT IS NOT AN OPTION.
SEND CLAYTON AND SEAMUS UP AHEAD TO SEE IF IT'S NOT MOVABLE.
RED TAIL ONE, COME BACK.
GO FOR RED TAIL ONE.
WE HAVE AN OBSTRUCTION ALONG YOUR ROUTE. CAN YOU RECON AHEAD AND GET EYES ON IT?
SURE CAN, LITTLE LADY. YEAH, I CAN JUST SEE IT OVER THE CREST UP AHEAD. LOOKS LIKE A TIRE FIRE OR SOMETHING... WE'RE ON IT.

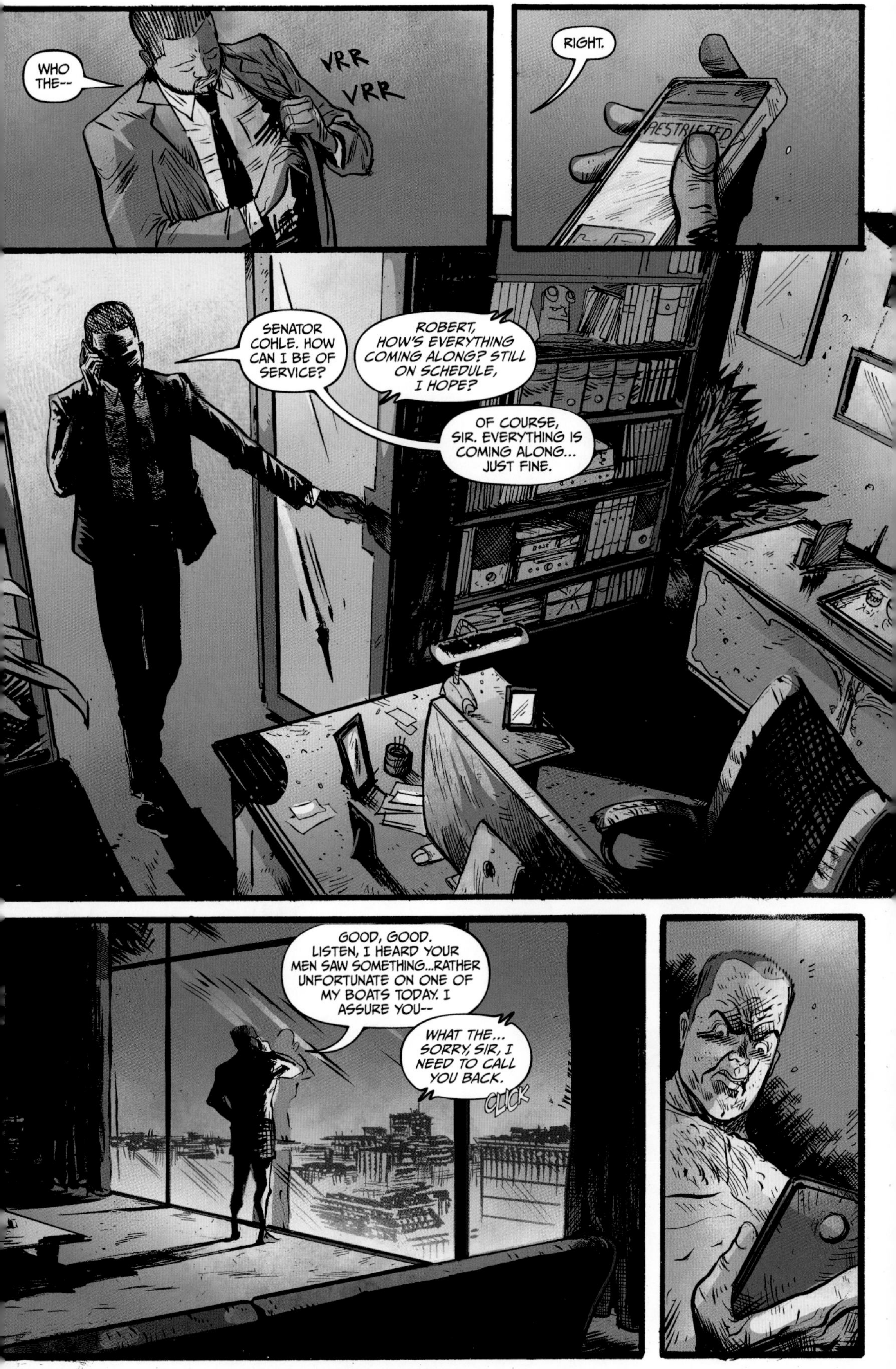
WHO THE--
VRR VRR
RIGHT.
RESTRICTED
SENATOR COHLE. HOW CAN I BE OF SERVICE?
ROBERT, HOW'S EVERYTHING COMING ALONG? STILL ON SCHEDULE, I HOPE?
OF COURSE, SIR. EVERYTHING IS COMING ALONG... JUST FINE.
GOOD, GOOD. LISTEN, I HEARD YOUR MEN SAW SOMETHING...RATHER UNFORTUNATE ON ONE OF MY BOATS TODAY. I ASSURE YOU--
WHAT THE... SORRY, SIR, I NEED TO CALL YOU BACK.
CLICK

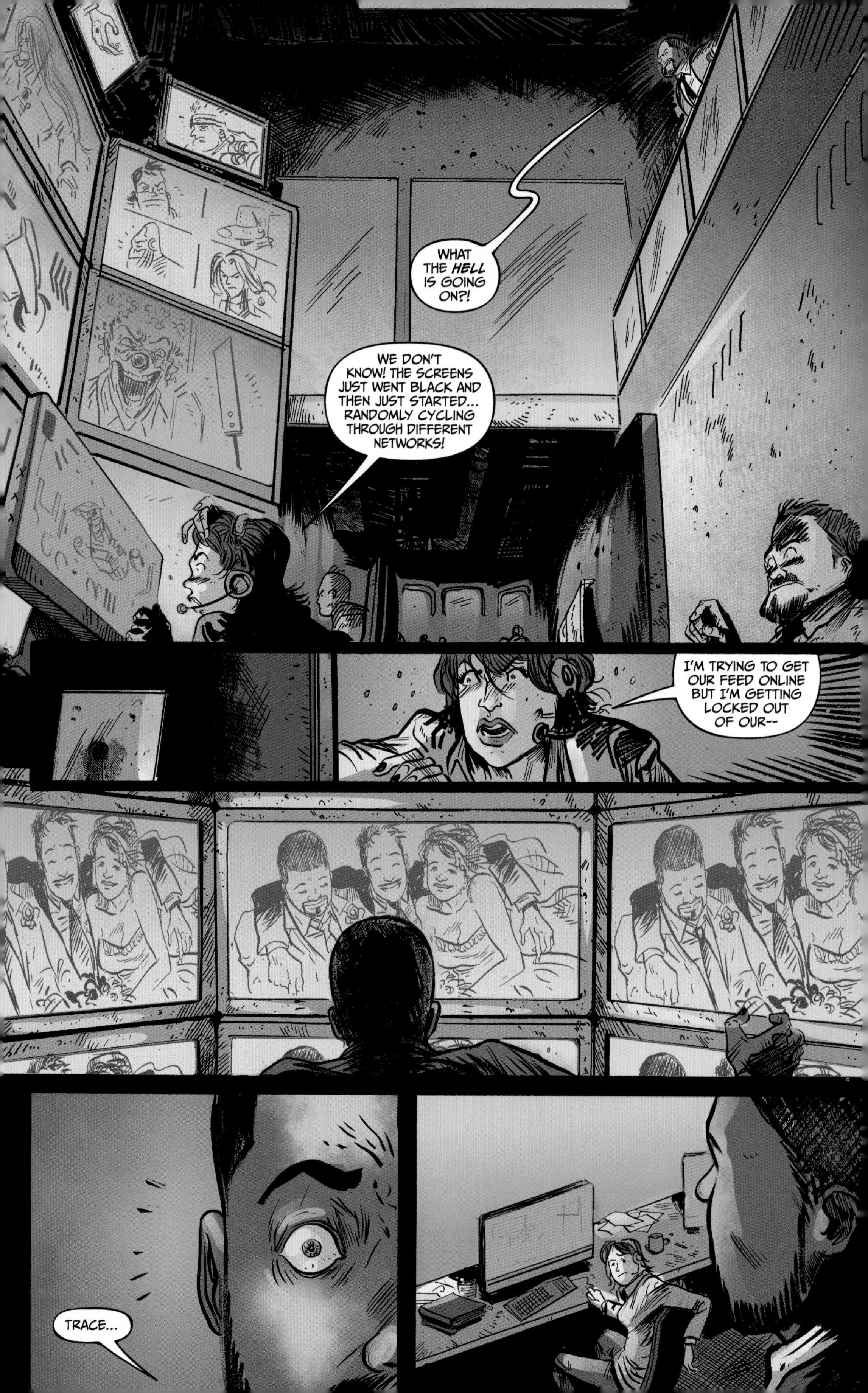
WHAT THE HELL IS GOING ON?!
WE DON'T KNOW! THE SCREENS JUST WENT BLACK AND THEN JUST STARTED... RANDOMLY CYCLING THROUGH DIFFERENT NETWORKS!
I'M TRYING TO GET OUR FEED ONLINE BUT I'M GETTING LOCKED OUT OF OUR--
TRACE...

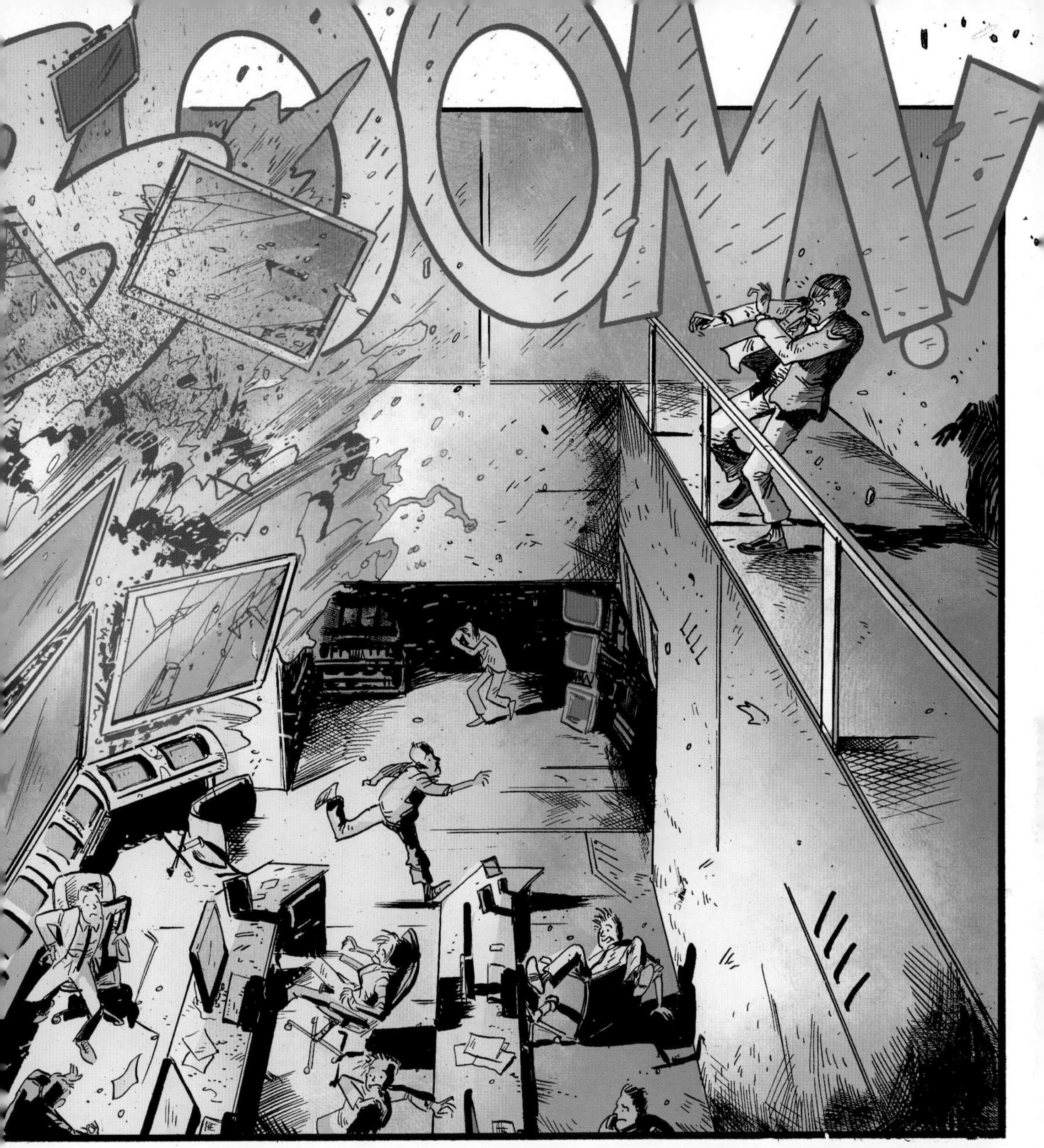
OOM!

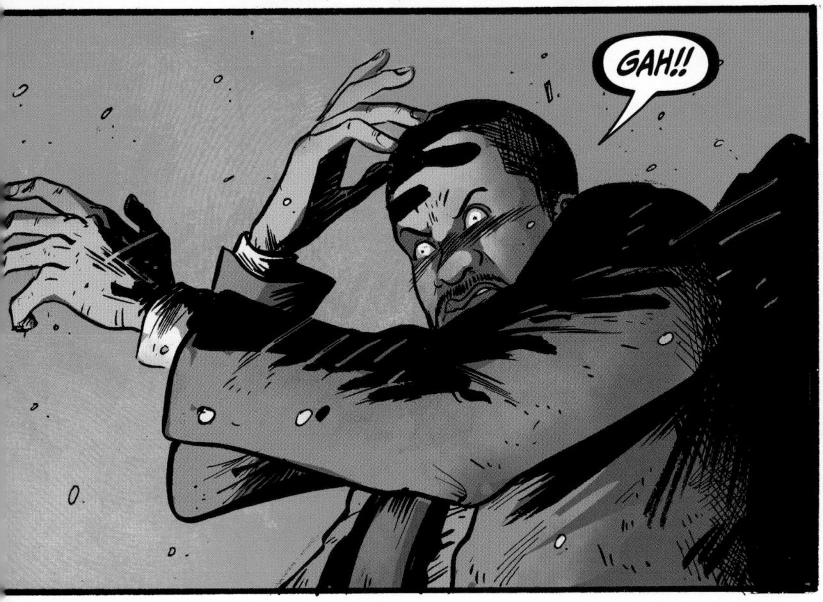
GAH!!

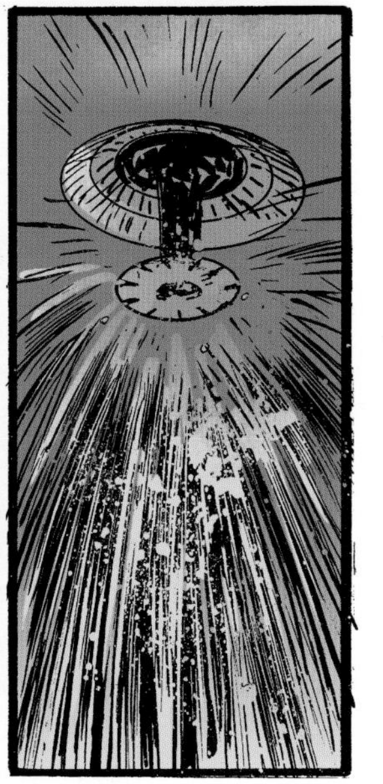

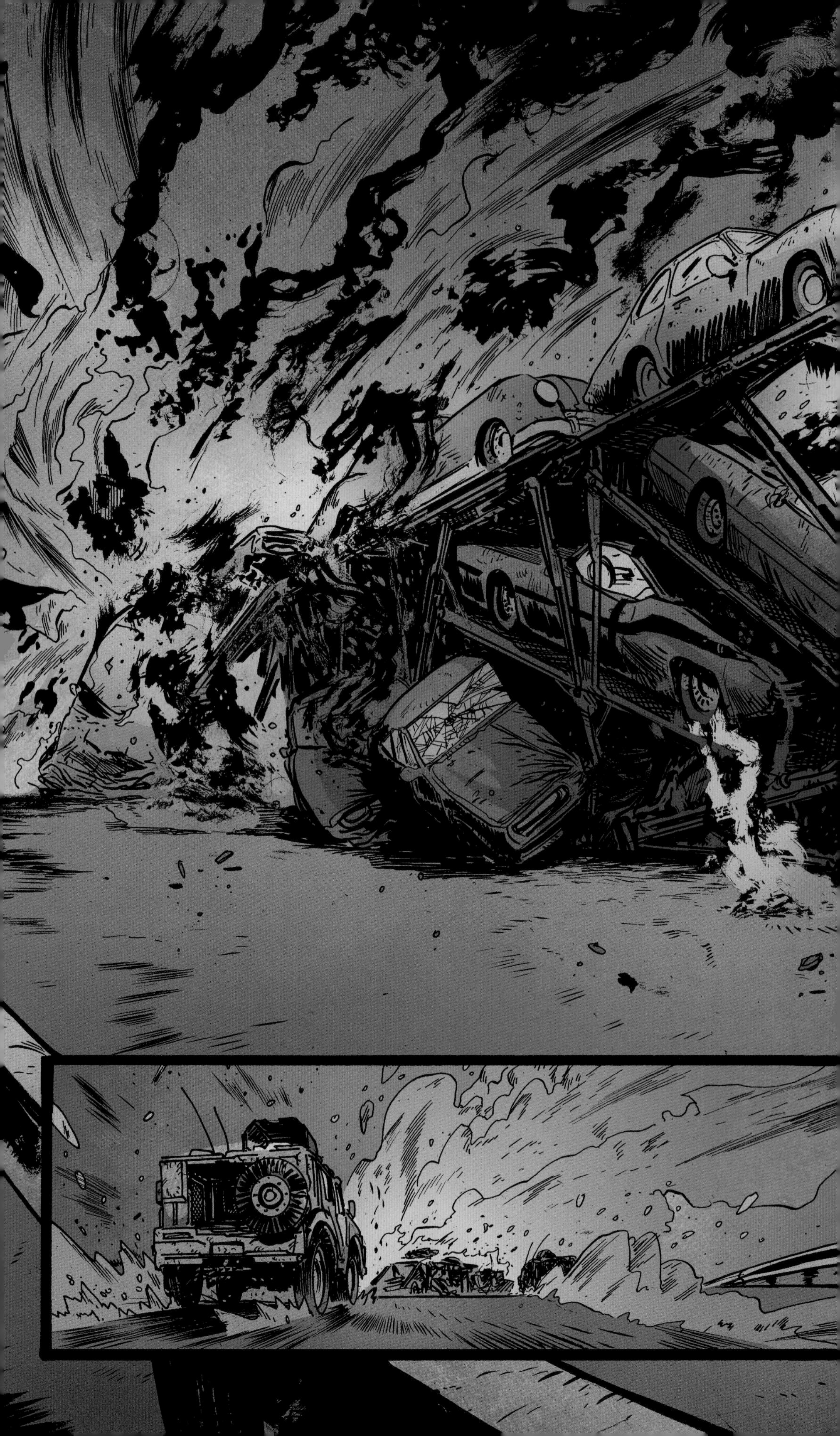

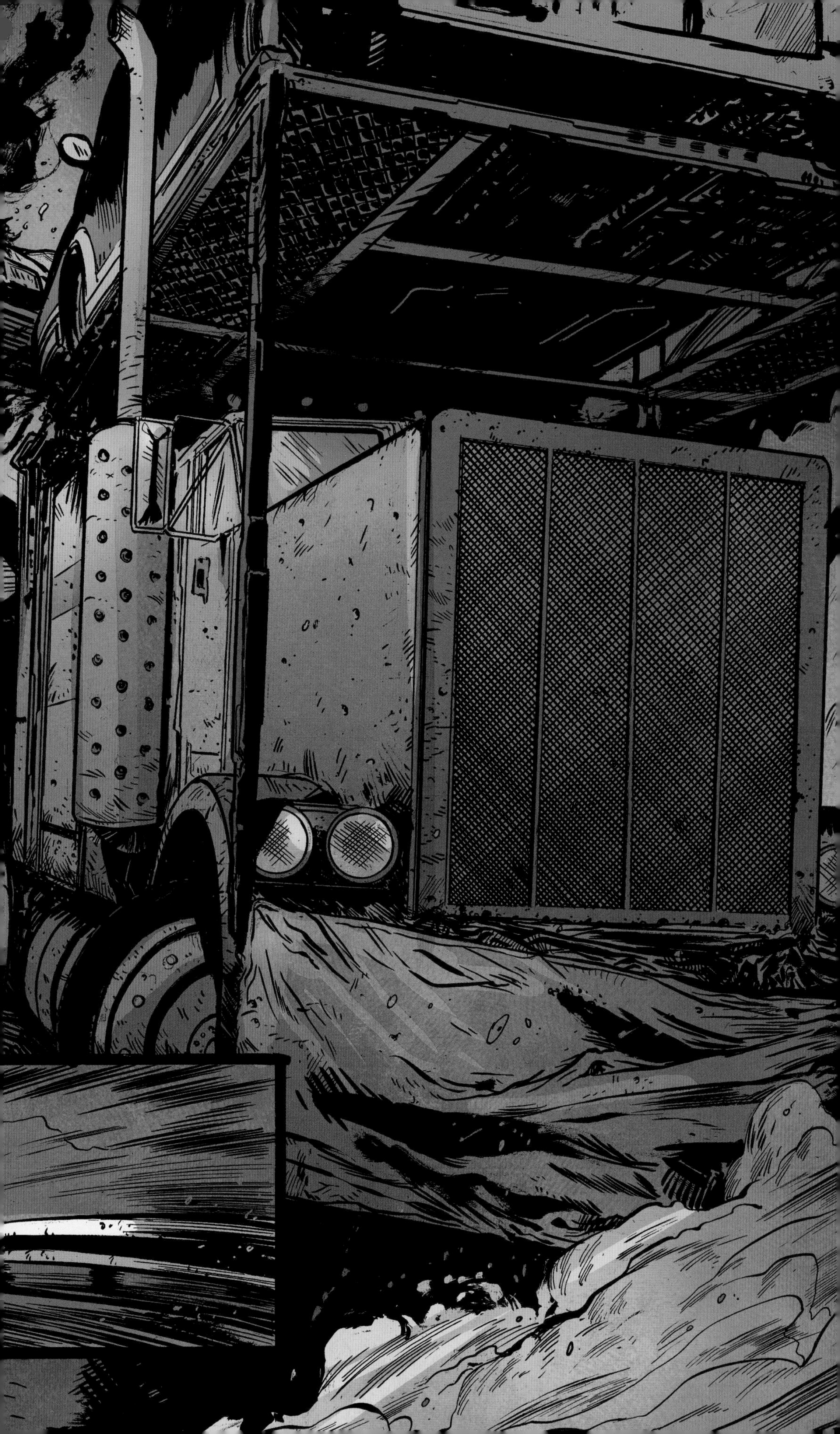

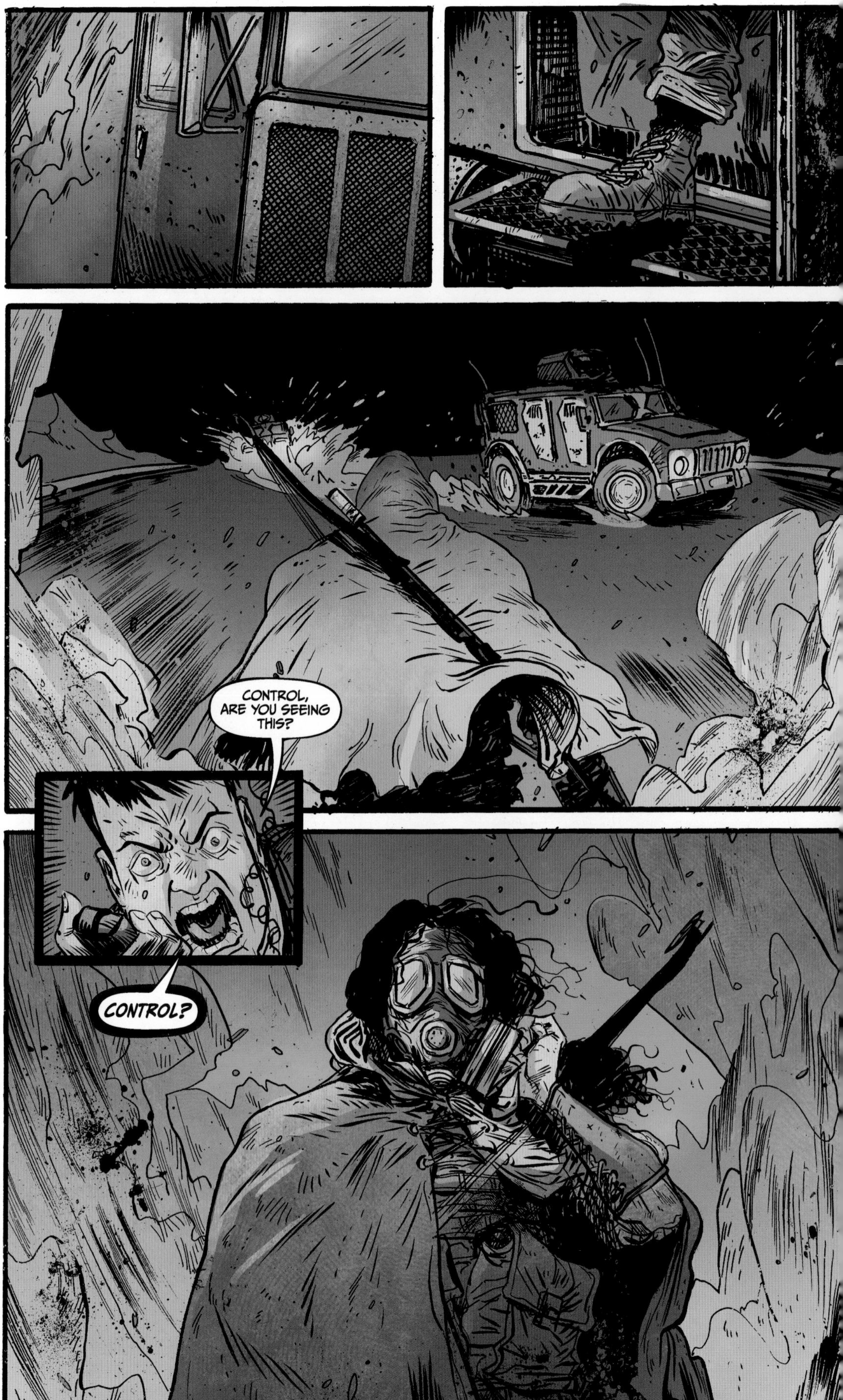
CONTROL, ARE YOU SEEING THIS?
CONTROL?

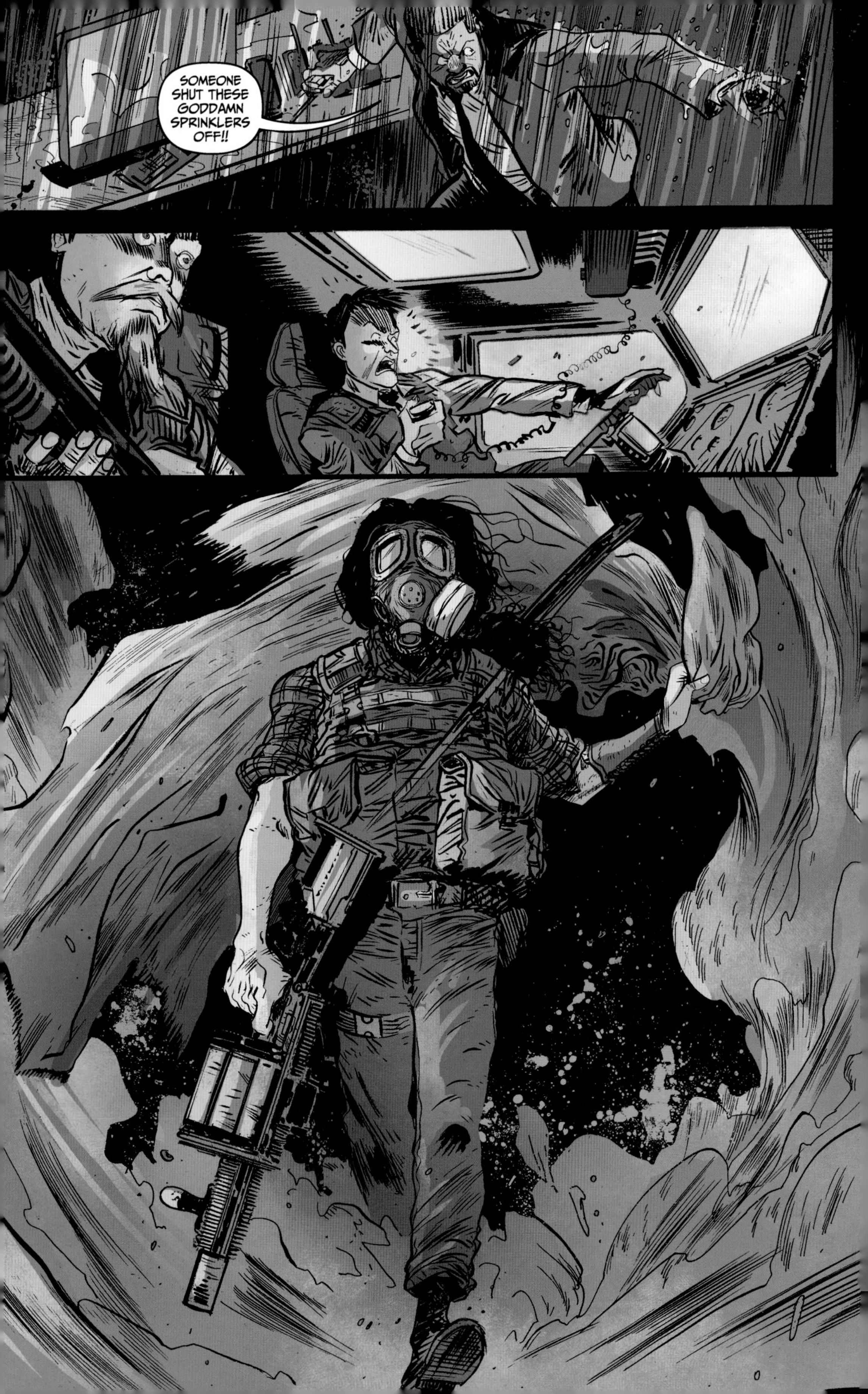
SOMEONE SHUT THESE GODDAMN SPRINKLERS OFF!!

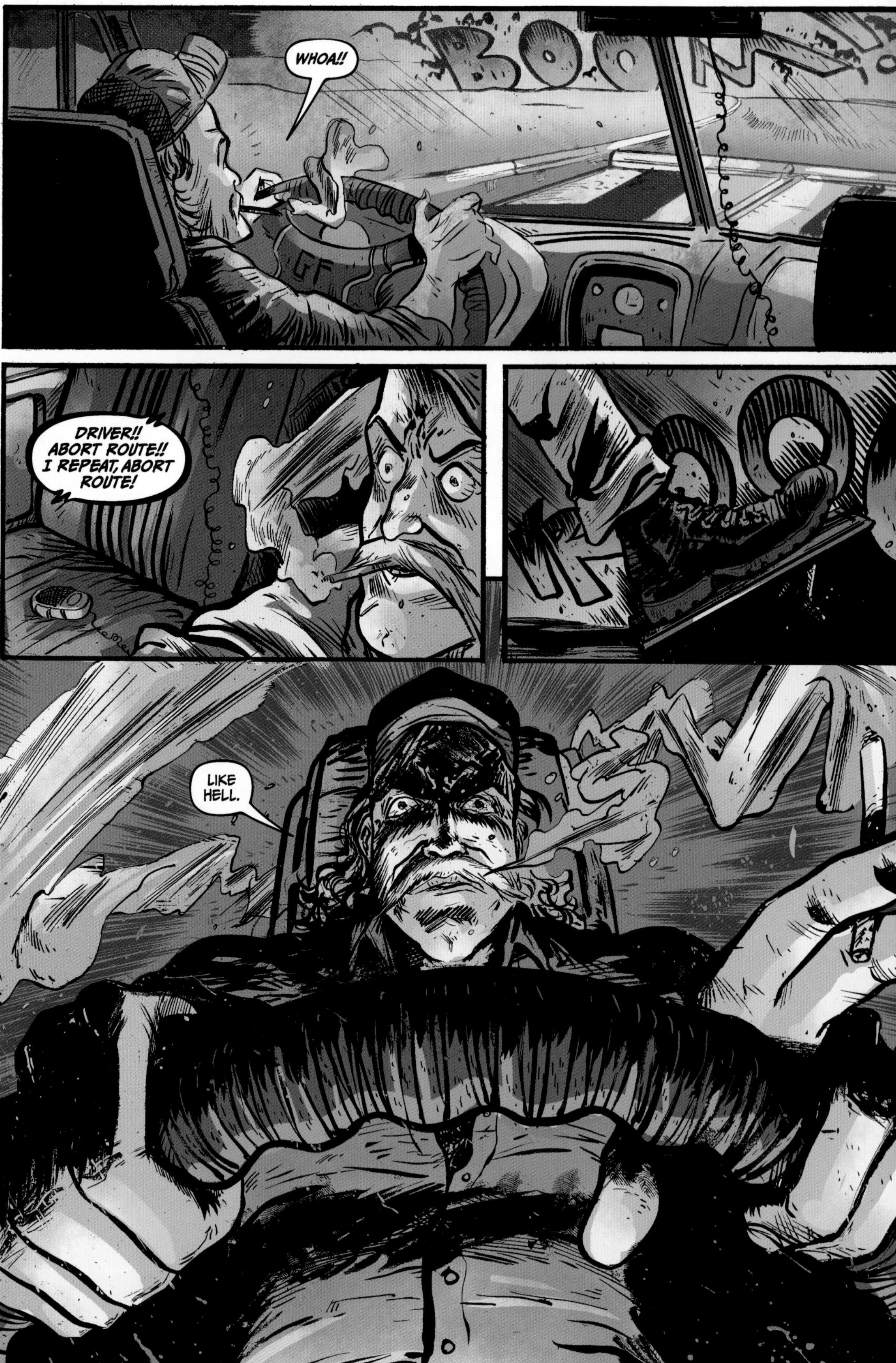
WHOA!!
DRIVER!! ABORT ROUTE!! I REPEAT, ABORT ROUTE!
LIKE HELL.

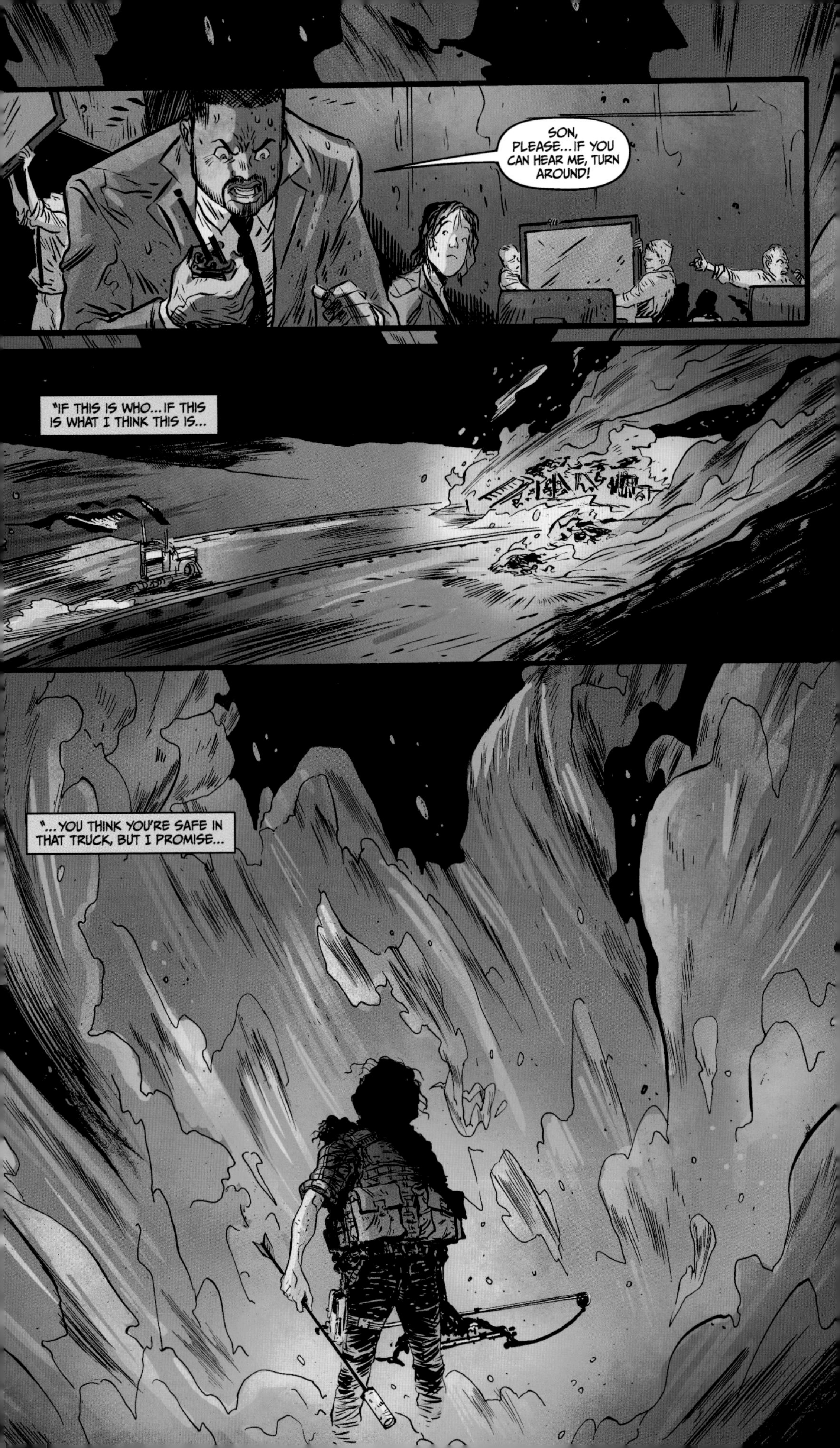
SON, PLEASE...IF YOU CAN HEAR ME, TURN AROUND!
"IF THIS IS WHO...IF THIS IS WHAT I THINK THIS IS...
"...YOU THINK YOU'RE SAFE IN THAT TRUCK, BUT I PROMISE...

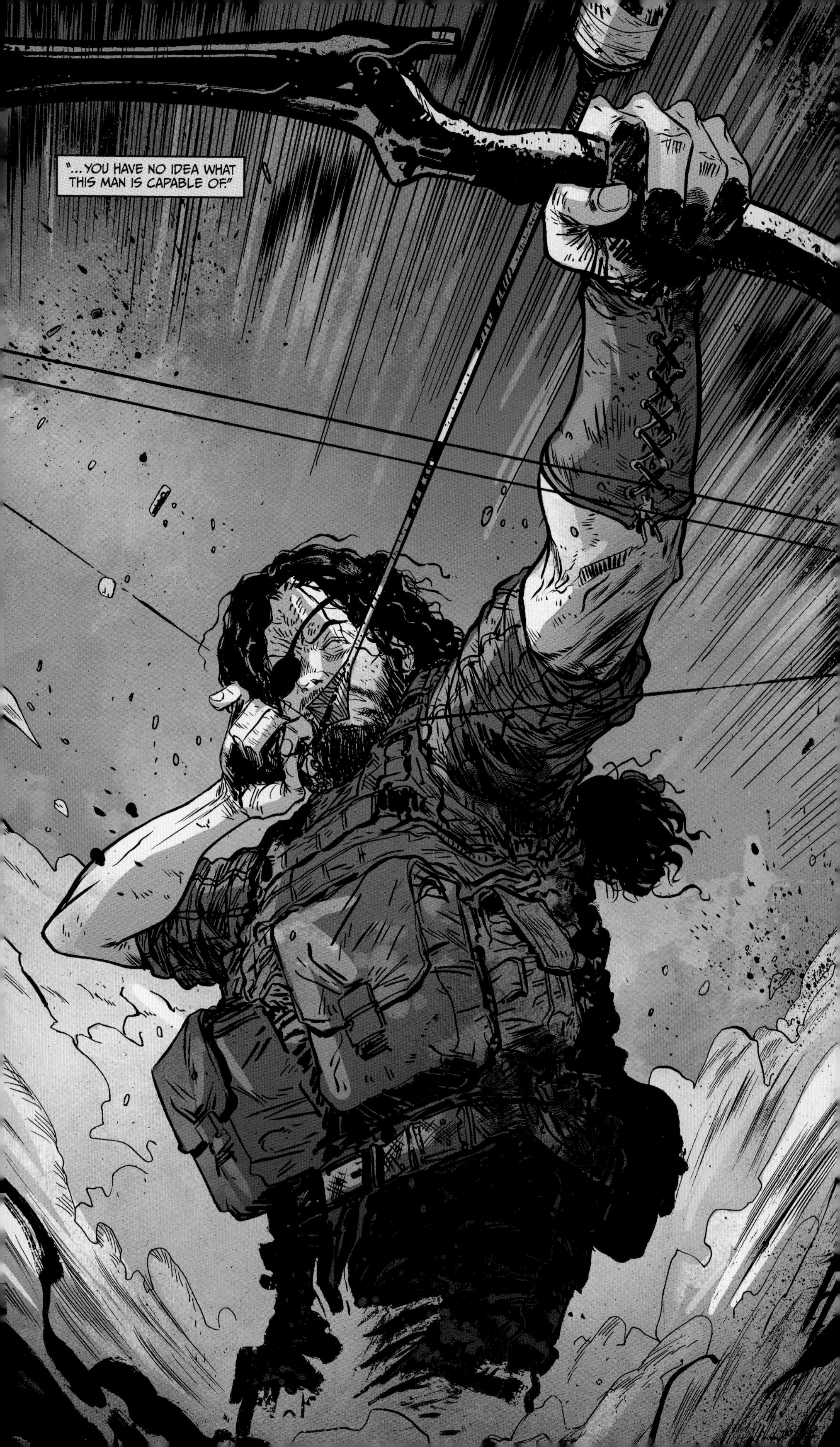
"...YOU HAVE NO IDEA WHAT THIS MAN IS CAPABLE OF."

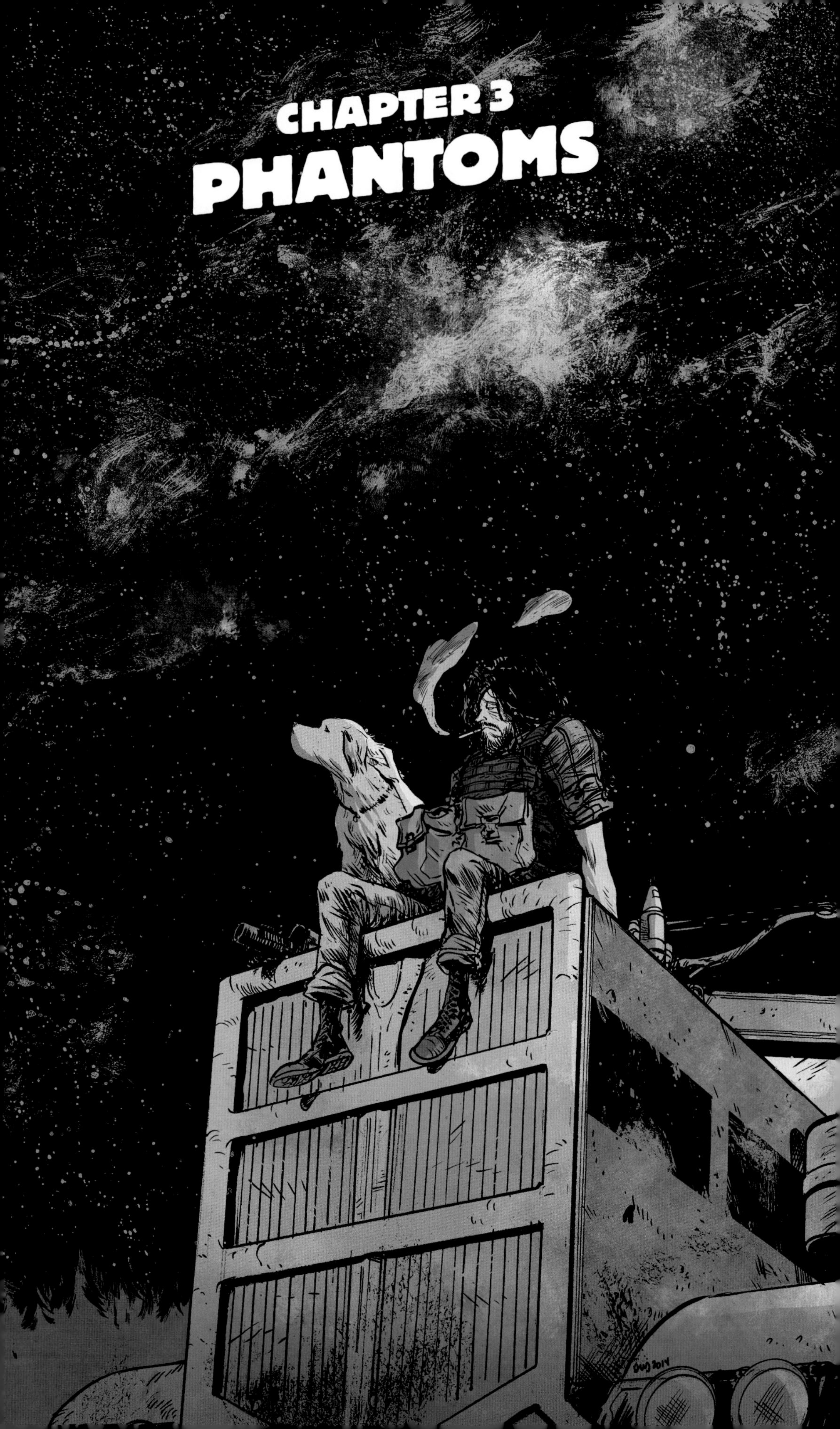
CHAPTER 3
PHANTOMS

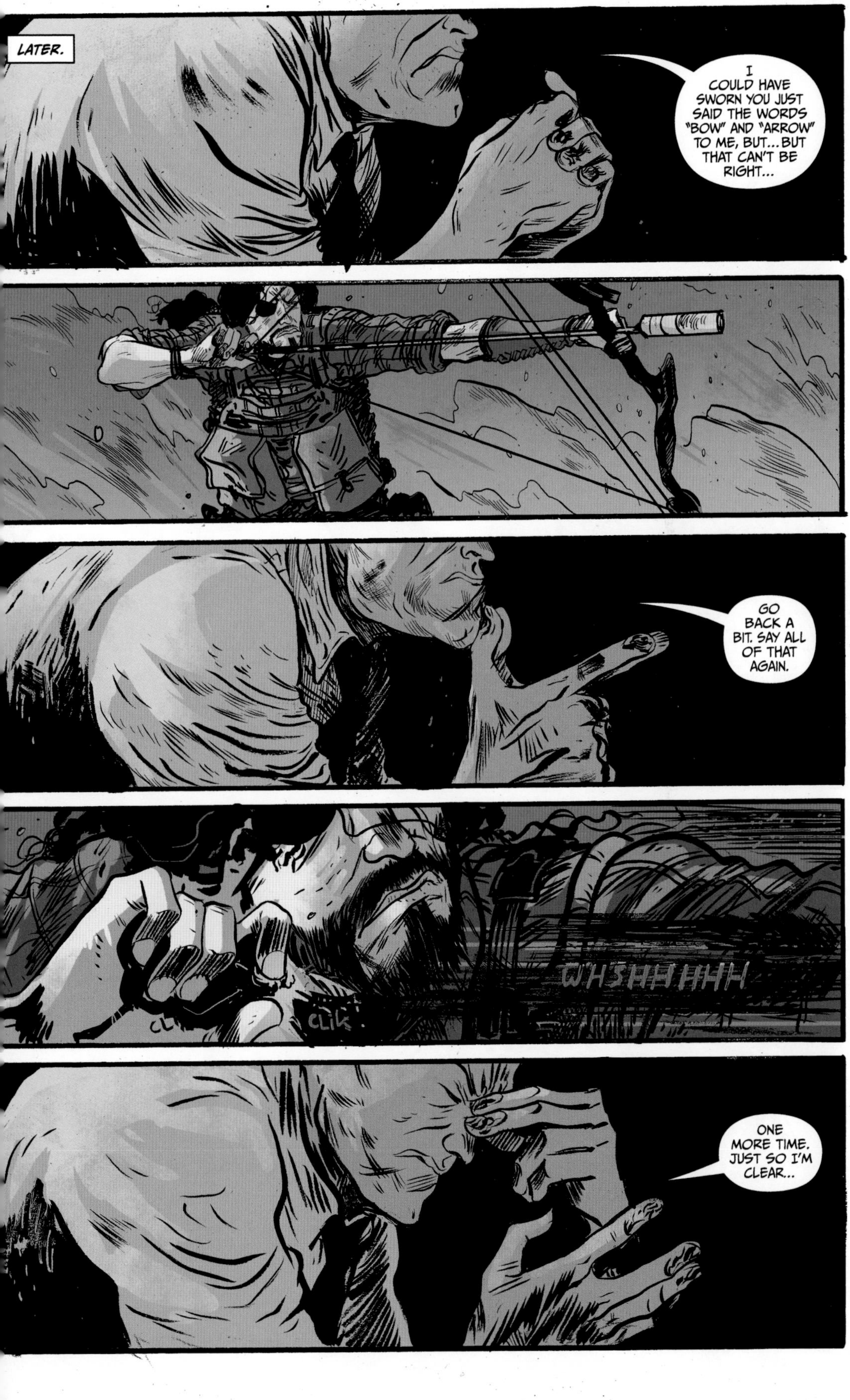
LATER.
I COULD HAVE SWORN YOU JUST SAID THE WORDS "BOW" AND "ARROW" TO ME, BUT... BUT THAT CAN'T BE RIGHT...
GO BACK A BIT. SAY ALL OF THAT AGAIN.
CLIK
CLIK
WHSHHHHHH
ONE MORE TIME. JUST SO I'M CLEAR...

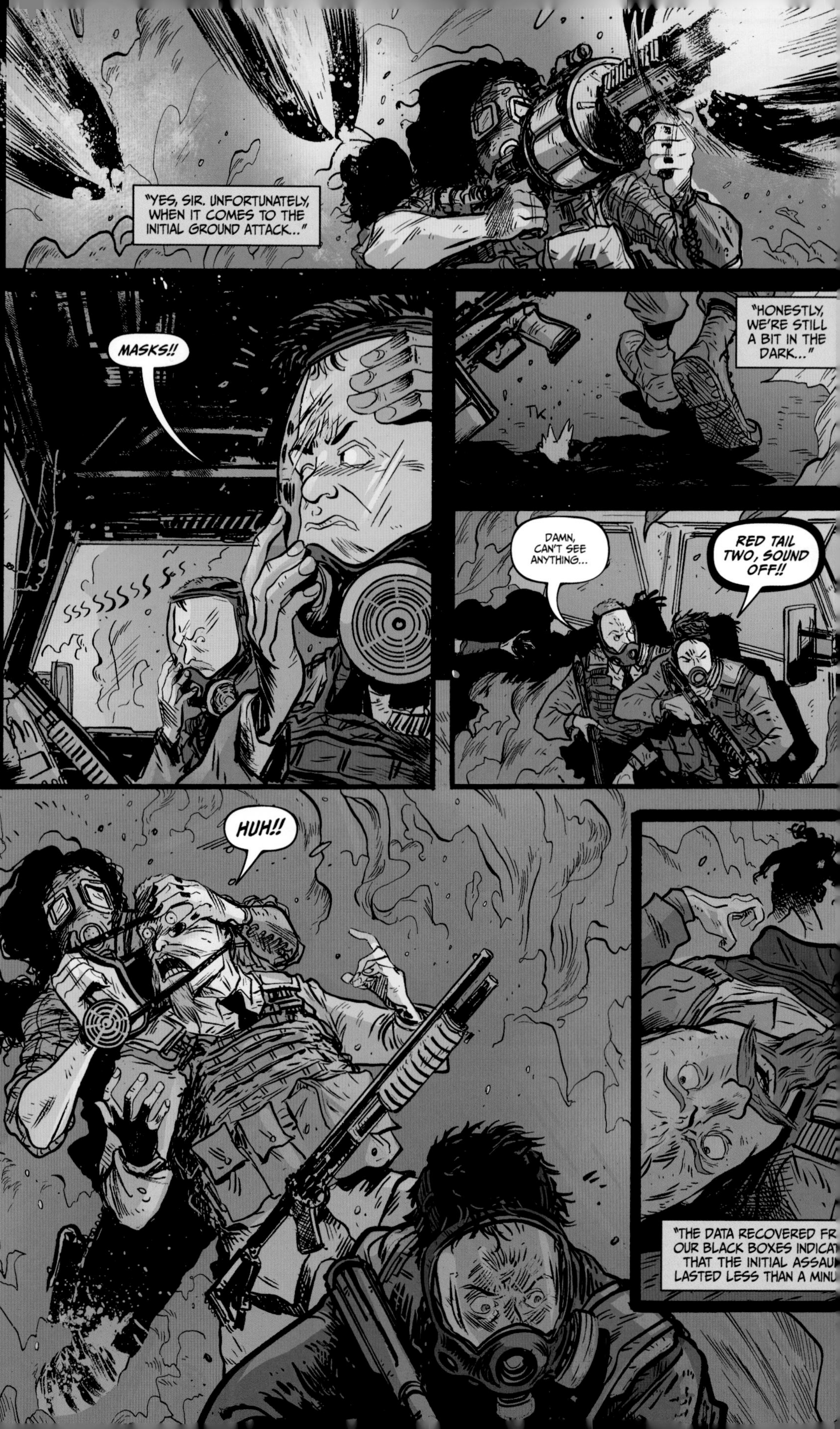
"YES, SIR. UNFORTUNATELY, WHEN IT COMES TO THE INITIAL GROUND ATTACK..."
MASKS!!
SSSSSSSS
"HONESTLY, WE'RE STILL A BIT IN THE DARK..."
TK
DAMN, CAN'T SEE ANYTHING...
RED TAIL TWO, SOUND OFF!!
HUH!!
"THE DATA RECOVERED FR
OUR BLACK BOXES INDICAT
THAT THE INITIAL ASSAU
LASTED LESS THAN A MINU

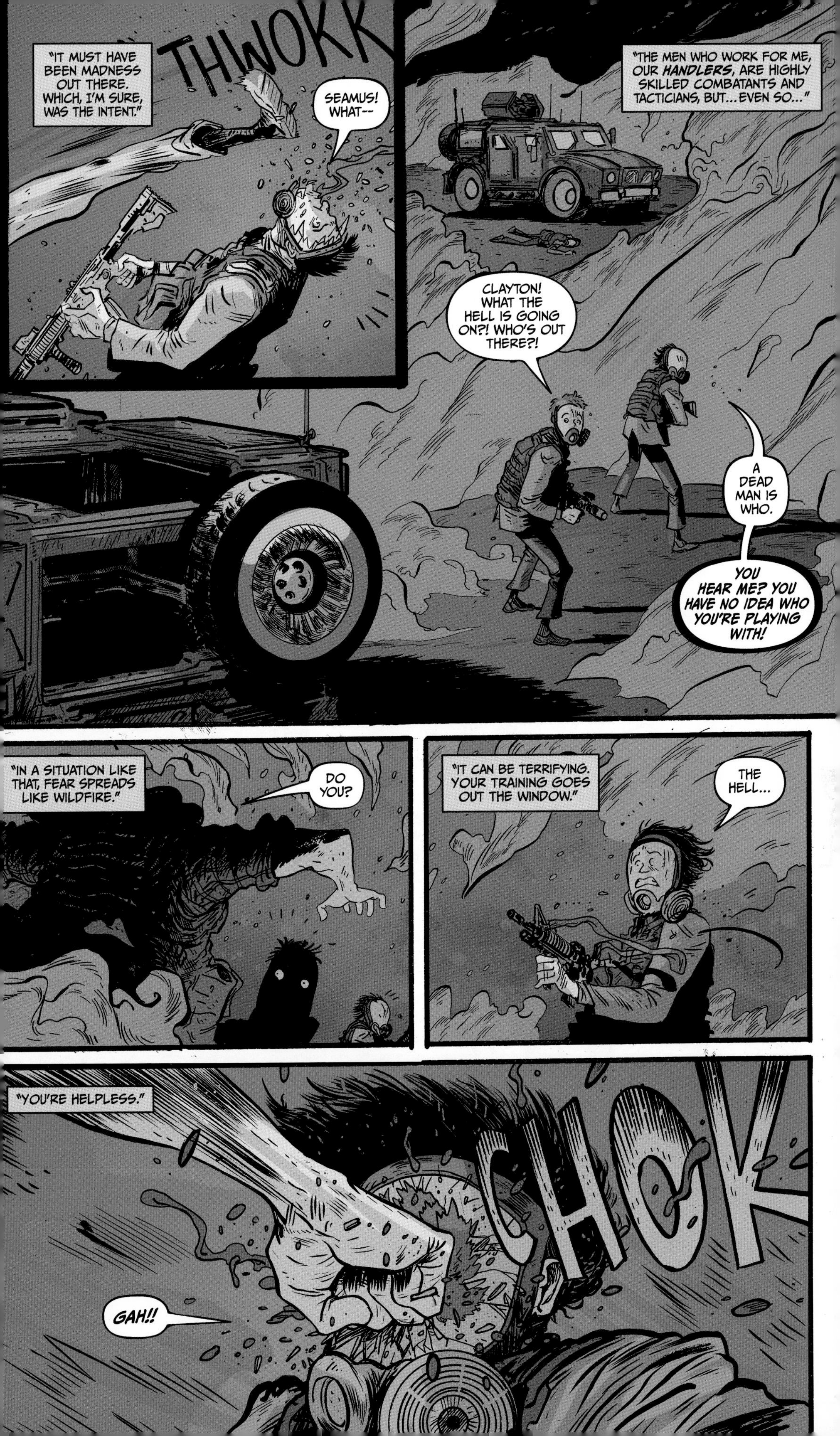
"IT MUST HAVE BEEN MADNESS OUT THERE. WHICH, I'M SURE, WAS THE INTENT."
THWOKK
SEAMUS! WHAT--
"THE MEN WHO WORK FOR ME, OUR HANDLERS, ARE HIGHLY SKILLED COMBATANTS AND TACTICIANS, BUT...EVEN SO..."
CLAYTON! WHAT THE HELL IS GOING ON?! WHO'S OUT THERE?!
A DEAD MAN IS WHO.
YOU HEAR ME? YOU HAVE NO IDEA WHO YOU'RE PLAYING WITH!
"IN A SITUATION LIKE THAT, FEAR SPREADS LIKE WILDFIRE."
DO YOU?
"IT CAN BE TERRIFYING. YOUR TRAINING GOES OUT THE WINDOW."
THE HELL...
"YOU'RE HELPLESS."
CHOK
GAH!!

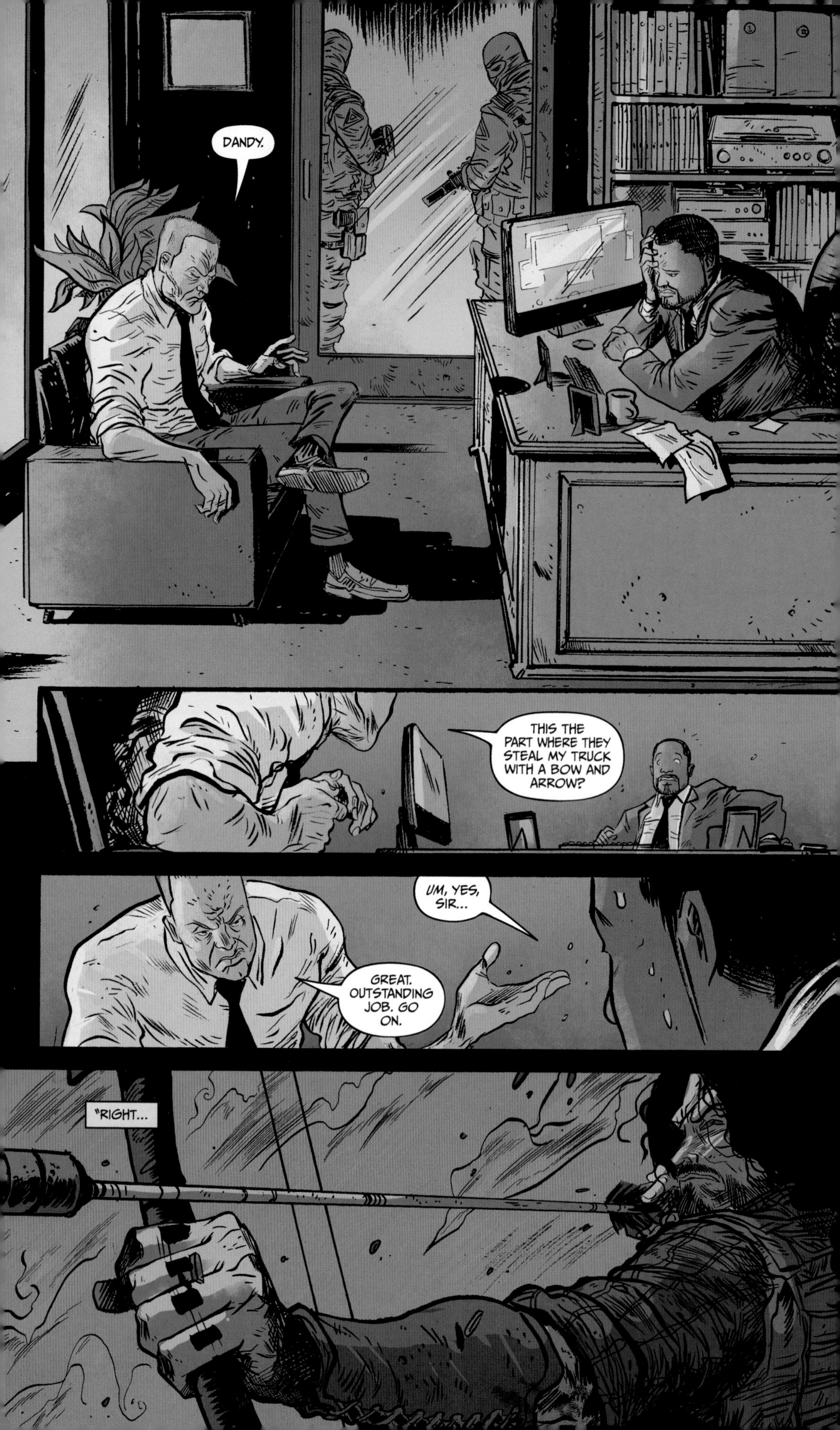
DANDY.
THIS THE PART WHERE THEY STEAL MY TRUCK WITH A BOW AND ARROW?
UM, YES, SIR...
GREAT. OUTSTANDING JOB. GO ON.
"RIGHT...

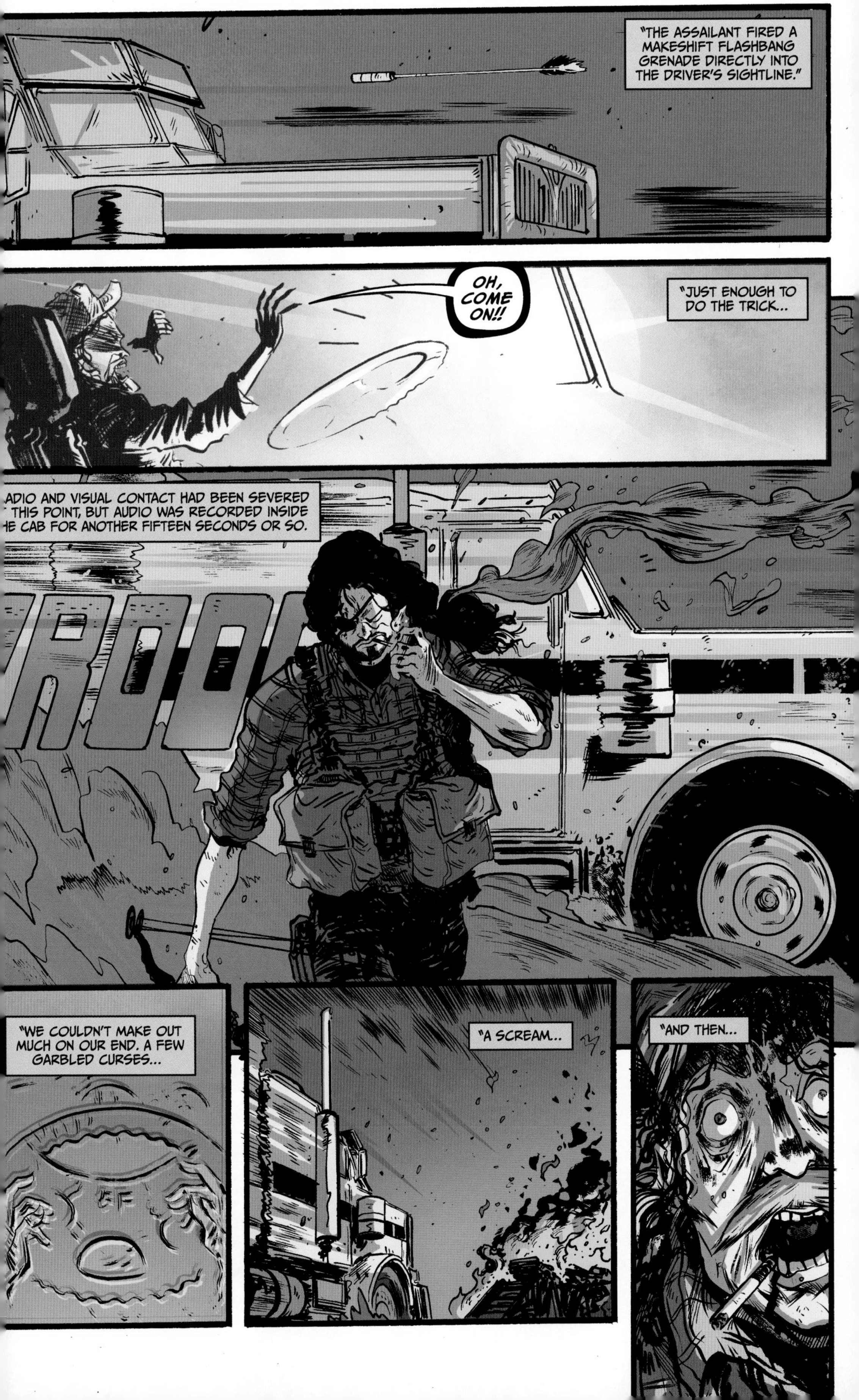
"THE ASSAILANT FIRED A MAKESHIFT FLASHBANG GRENADE DIRECTLY INTO THE DRIVER'S SIGHTLINE."
OH, COME ON!!
"JUST ENOUGH TO DO THE TRICK...
ADIO AND VISUAL CONTACT HAD BEEN SEVERED THIS POINT, BUT AUDIO WAS RECORDED INSIDE HE CAB FOR ANOTHER FIFTEEN SECONDS OR SO.
"WE COULDN'T MAKE OUT MUCH ON OUR END. A FEW GARBLED CURSES...
"A SCREAM...
"AND THEN...

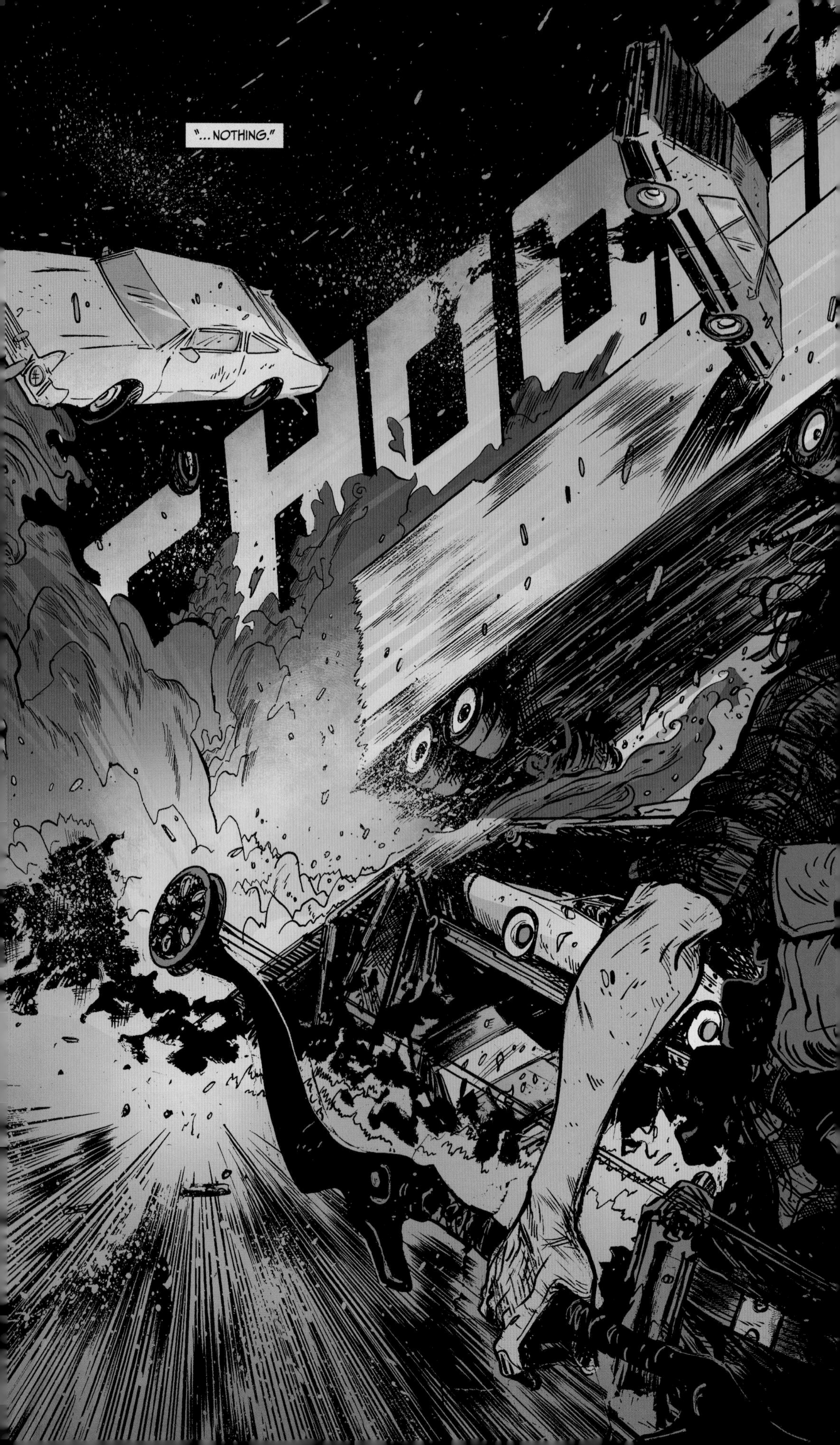
"... NOTHING."

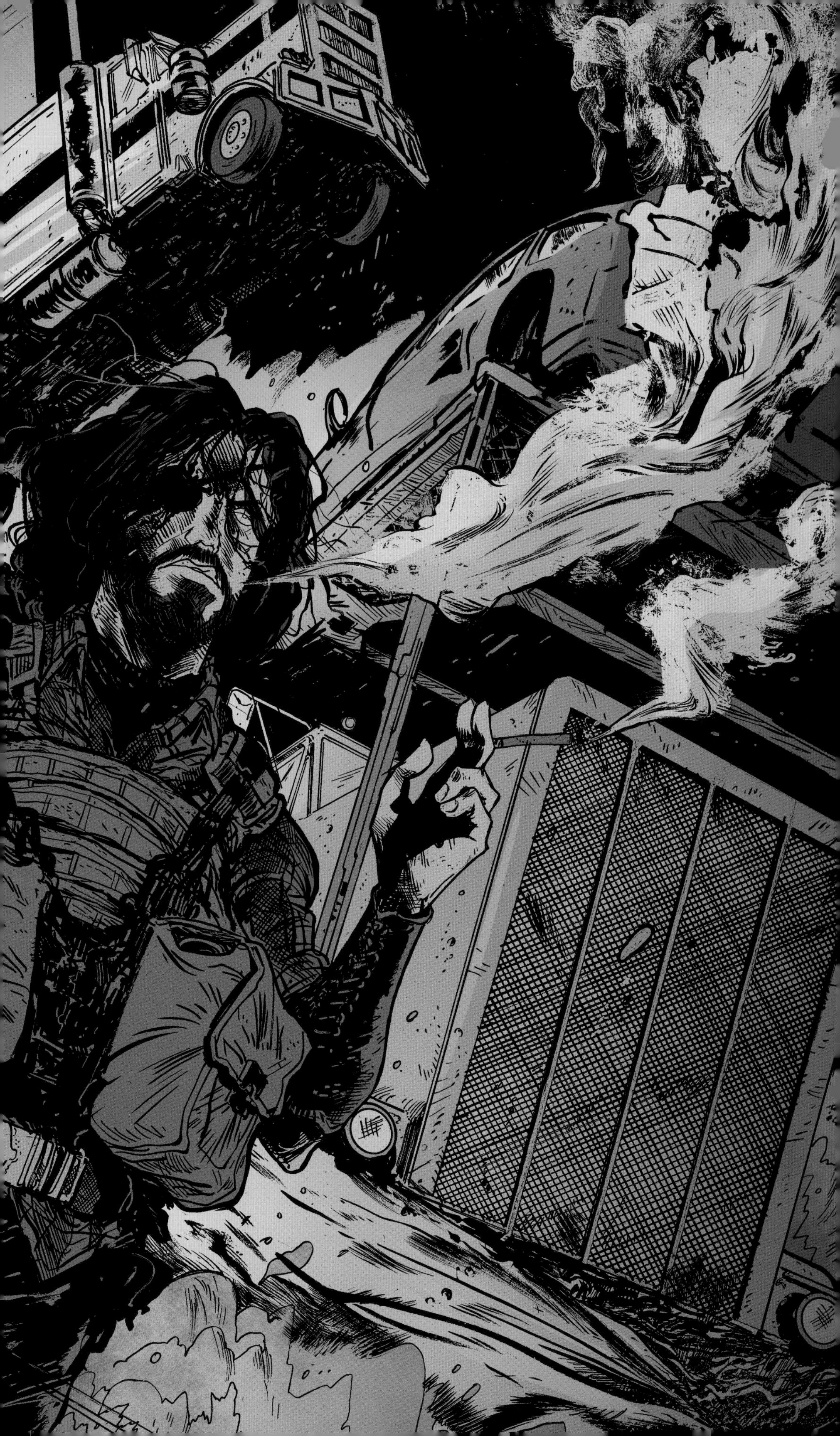

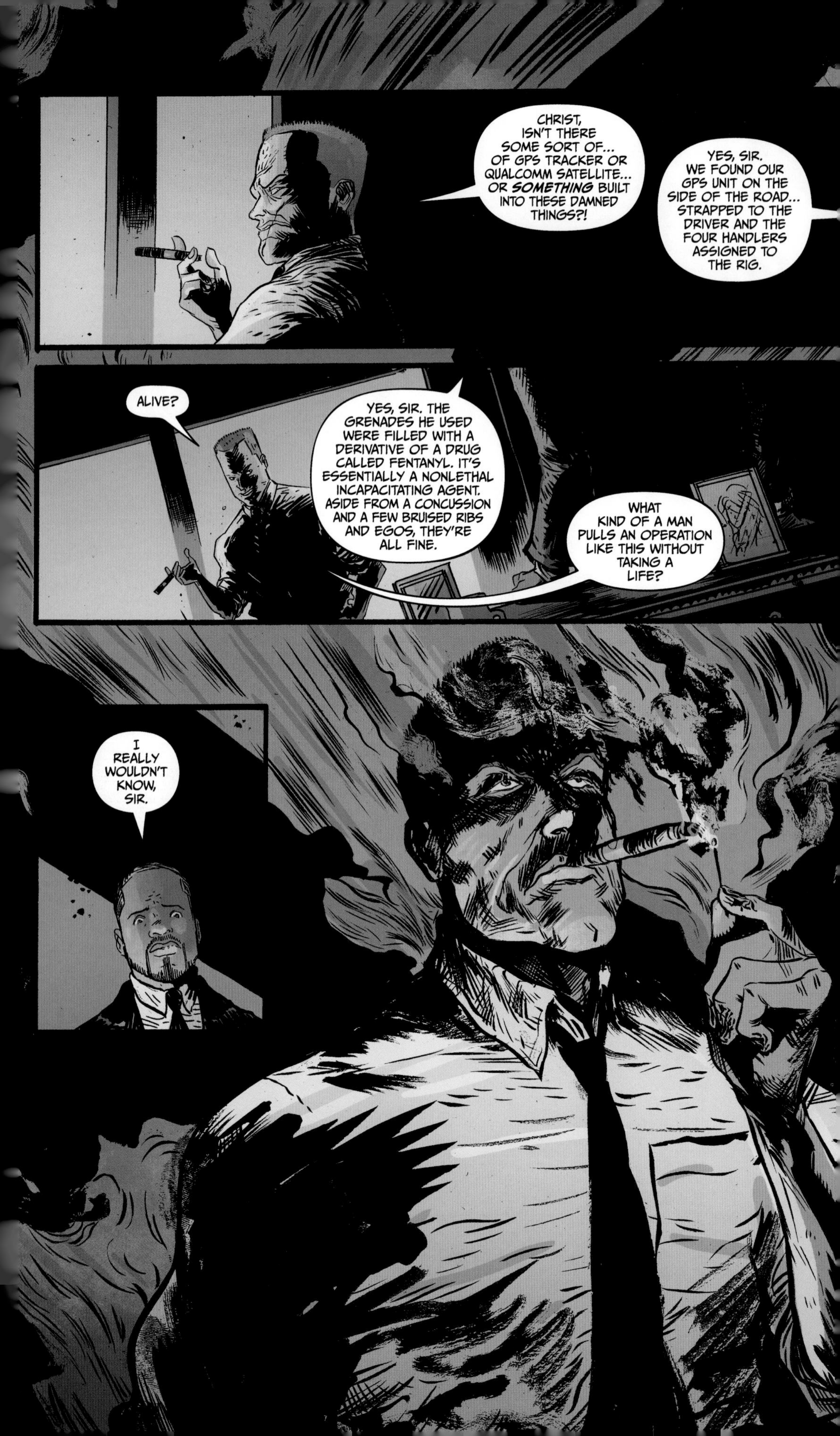
CHRIST, ISN'T THERE SOME SORT OF... OF GPS TRACKER OR QUALCOMM SATELLITE... OR *SOMETHING* BUILT INTO THESE DAMNED THINGS?!
YES, SIR. WE FOUND OUR GPS UNIT ON THE SIDE OF THE ROAD... STRAPPED TO THE DRIVER AND THE FOUR HANDLERS ASSIGNED TO THE RIG.
ALIVE?
YES, SIR. THE GRENADES HE USED WERE FILLED WITH A DERIVATIVE OF A DRUG CALLED FENTANYL. IT'S ESSENTIALLY A NONLETHAL INCAPACITATING AGENT. ASIDE FROM A CONCUSSION AND A FEW BRUISED RIBS AND EGOS, THEY'RE ALL FINE.
WHAT KIND OF A MAN PULLS AN OPERATION LIKE THIS WITHOUT TAKING A LIFE?
I REALLY WOULDN'T KNOW, SIR.

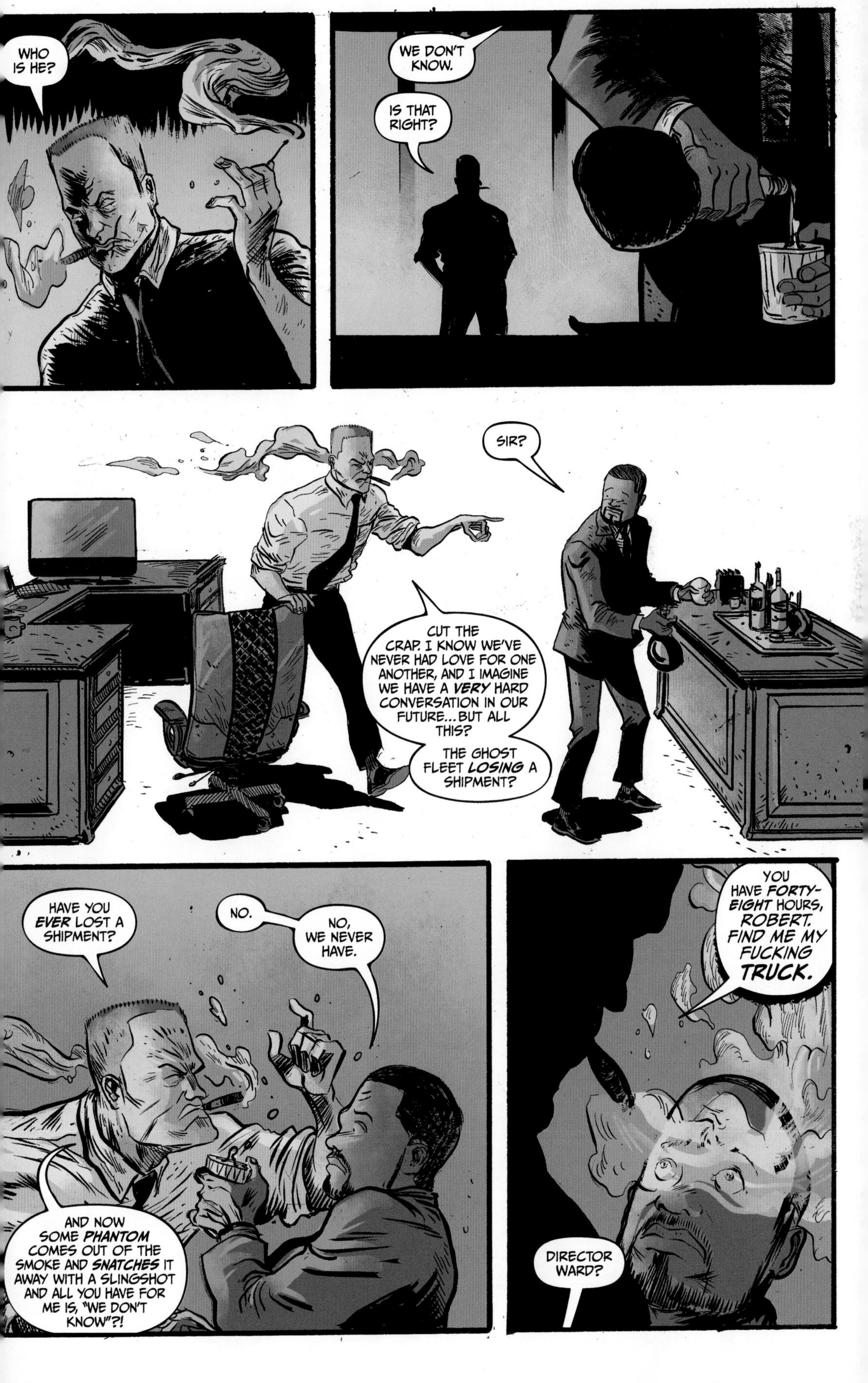
WHO IS HE?
WE DON'T KNOW.
IS THAT RIGHT?
SIR?
CUT THE CRAP. I KNOW WE'VE NEVER HAD LOVE FOR ONE ANOTHER, AND I IMAGINE WE HAVE A *VERY* HARD CONVERSATION IN OUR FUTURE... BUT ALL THIS?
THE GHOST FLEET *LOSING* A SHIPMENT?
HAVE YOU *EVER* LOST A SHIPMENT?
NO.
NO, WE NEVER HAVE.
AND NOW SOME *PHANTOM* COMES OUT OF THE SMOKE AND *SNATCHES* IT AWAY WITH A SLINGSHOT AND ALL YOU HAVE FOR ME IS, "WE DON'T KNOW"?!
YOU HAVE *FORTY-EIGHT* HOURS, *ROBERT. FIND ME MY FUCKING* **TRUCK.**
DIRECTOR WARD?

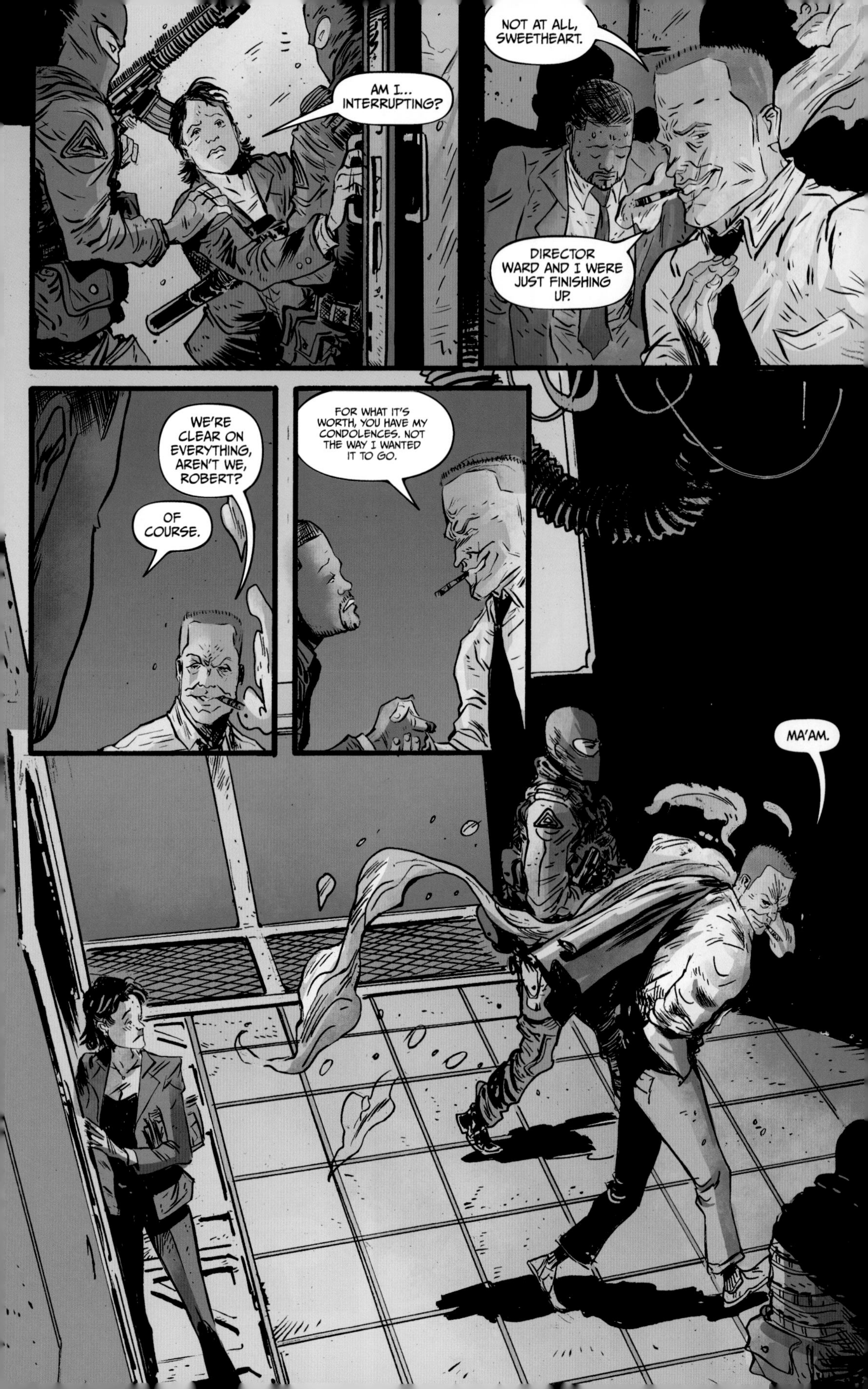
AM I... INTERRUPTING?
NOT AT ALL, SWEETHEART.
DIRECTOR WARD AND I WERE JUST FINISHING UP.
WE'RE CLEAR ON EVERYTHING, AREN'T WE, ROBERT?
OF COURSE.
FOR WHAT IT'S WORTH, YOU HAVE MY CONDOLENCES. NOT THE WAY I WANTED IT TO GO.
MA'AM.

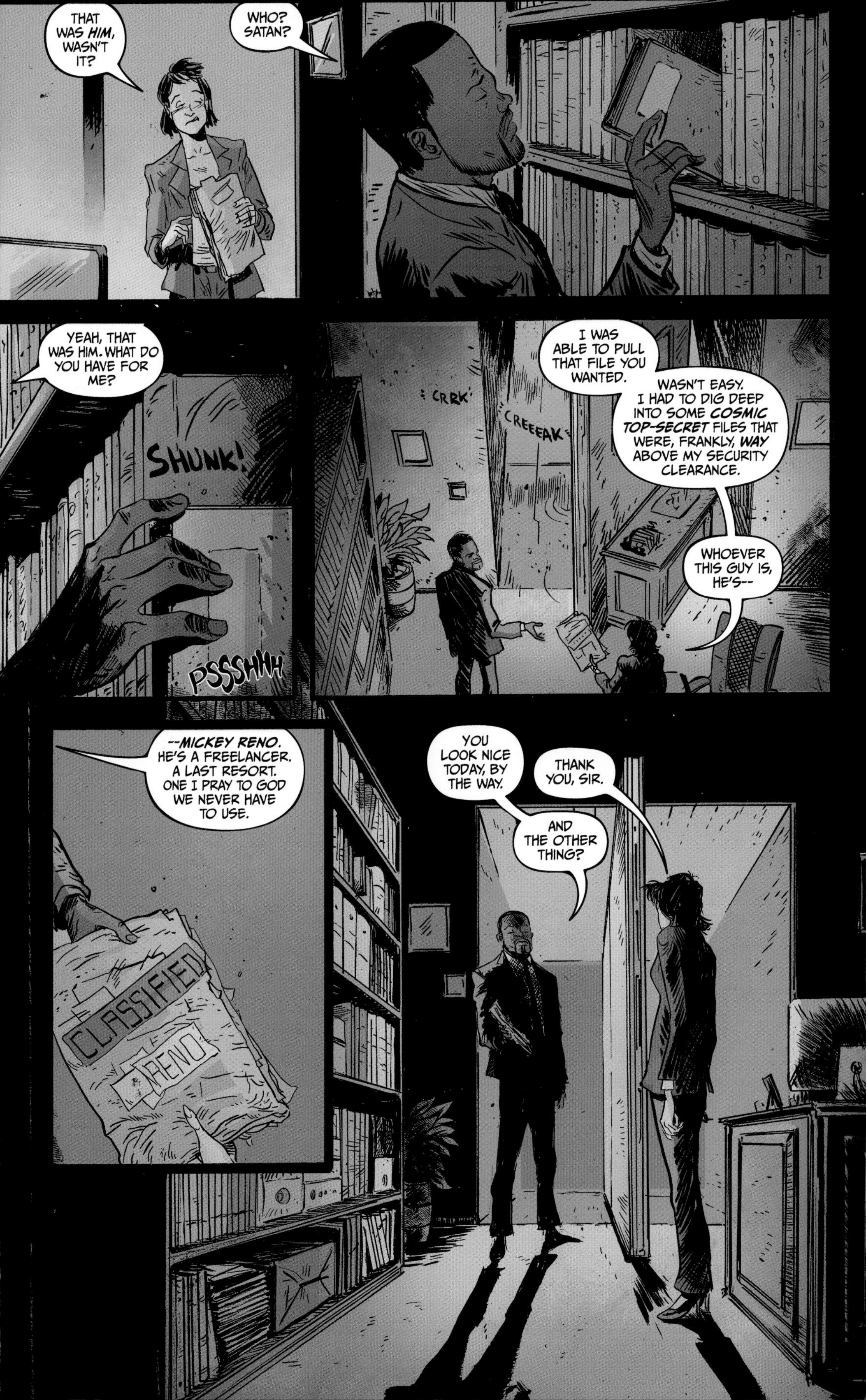
THAT WAS *HIM*, WASN'T IT?
WHO? SATAN?
YEAH, THAT WAS HIM. WHAT DO YOU HAVE FOR ME?
SHUNK!
PSSSHHH
CRRK
CREEEAK
I WAS ABLE TO PULL THAT FILE YOU WANTED.
WASN'T EASY. I HAD TO DIG DEEP INTO SOME ***COSMIC TOP-SECRET*** FILES THAT WERE, FRANKLY, ***WAY*** ABOVE MY SECURITY CLEARANCE.
WHOEVER THIS GUY IS, HE'S--
--***MICKEY RENO***. HE'S A FREELANCER. A LAST RESORT. ONE I PRAY TO GOD WE NEVER HAVE TO USE.
CLASSIFIED
RENO
YOU LOOK NICE TODAY, BY THE WAY.
THANK YOU, SIR.
AND THE OTHER THING?

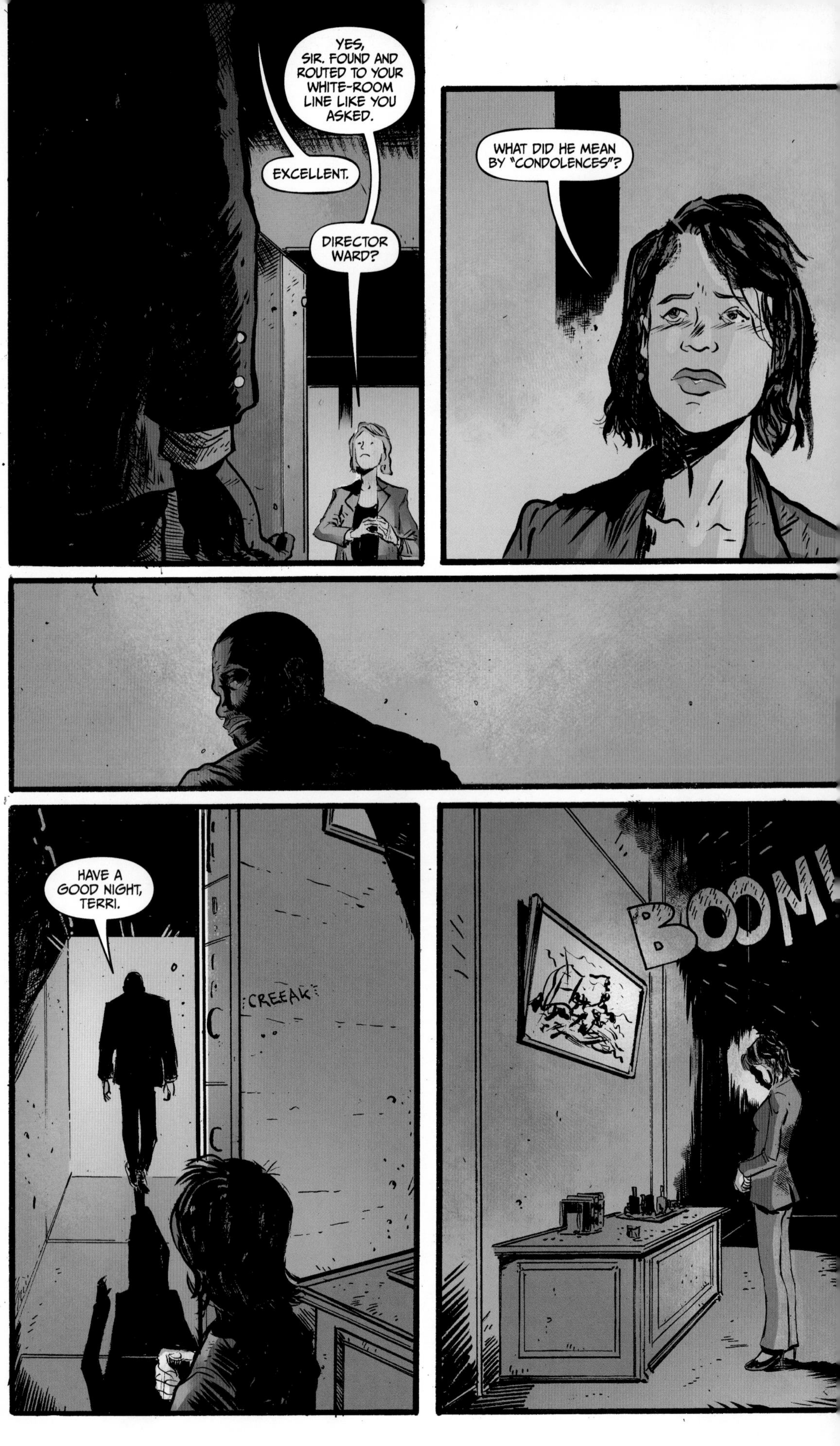
YES, SIR. FOUND AND ROUTED TO YOUR WHITE-ROOM LINE LIKE YOU ASKED.
EXCELLENT.
DIRECTOR WARD?
WHAT DID HE MEAN BY "CONDOLENCES"?
HAVE A GOOD NIGHT, TERRI.
CREEAK
BOOM

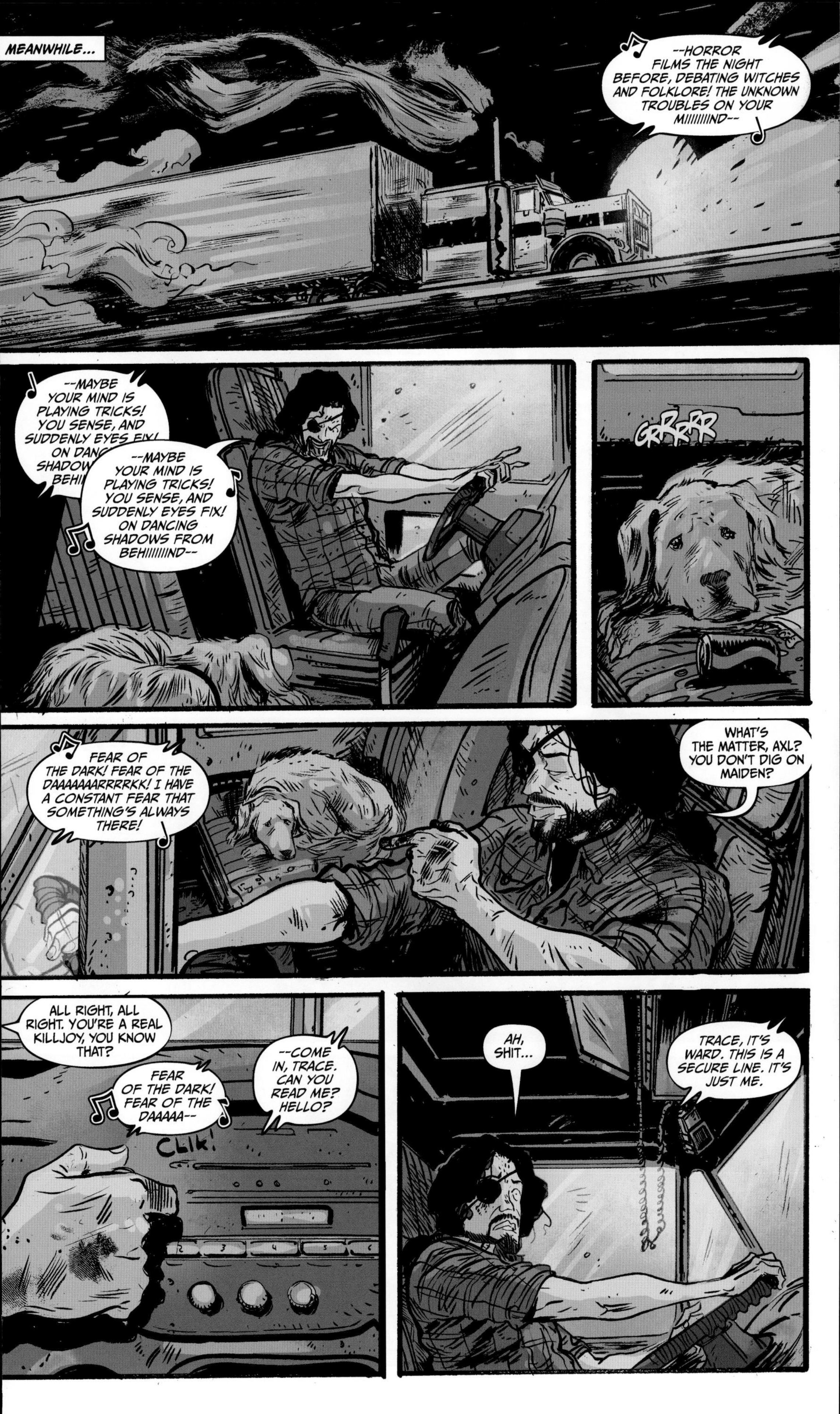

MEANWHILE...
--HORROR FILMS THE NIGHT BEFORE, DEBATING WITCHES AND FOLKLORE! THE UNKNOWN TROUBLES ON YOUR MIIIIIIIND--
--MAYBE YOUR MIND IS PLAYING TRICKS! YOU SENSE, AND SUDDENLY EYES FIX! ON DANCING SHADOWS FROM BEHIIIIIIIND--
GRRRRR
FEAR OF THE DARK! FEAR OF THE DAAAAAAARRRRKK! I HAVE A CONSTANT FEAR THAT SOMETHING'S ALWAYS THERE!
WHAT'S THE MATTER, AXL? YOU DON'T DIG ON MAIDEN?
ALL RIGHT, ALL RIGHT. YOU'RE A REAL KILLJOY, YOU KNOW THAT?
FEAR OF THE DARK! FEAR OF THE DAAAAA--
CLIK!
--COME IN, TRACE. CAN YOU READ ME? HELLO?
AH, SHIT...
TRACE, IT'S WARD. THIS IS A SECURE LINE. IT'S JUST ME.

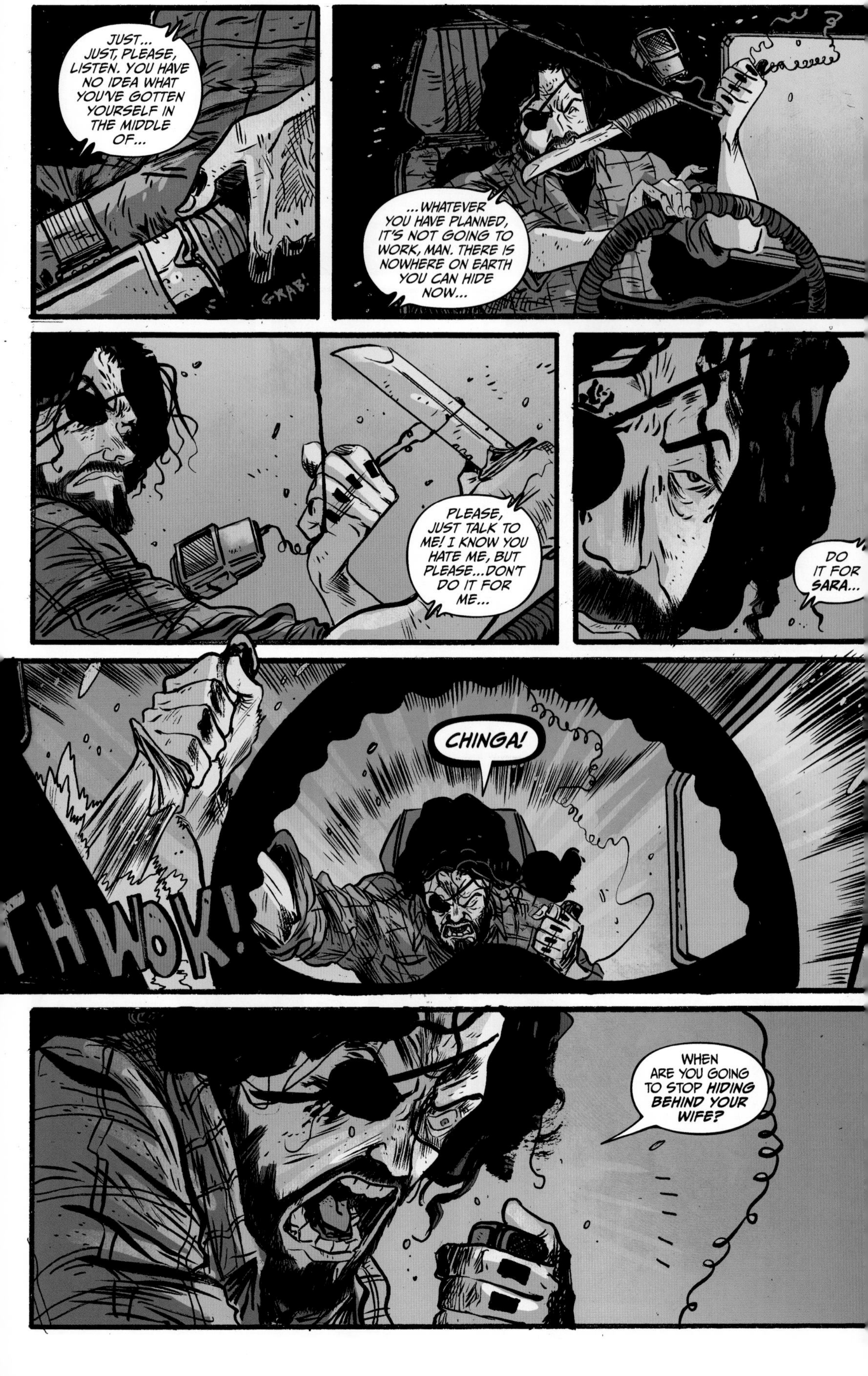
JUST... JUST, PLEASE, LISTEN. YOU HAVE NO IDEA WHAT YOU'VE GOTTEN YOURSELF IN THE MIDDLE OF...
GRAB!
...WHATEVER YOU HAVE PLANNED, IT'S NOT GOING TO WORK, MAN. THERE IS NOWHERE ON EARTH YOU CAN HIDE NOW...
PLEASE, JUST TALK TO ME! I KNOW YOU HATE ME, BUT PLEASE...DON'T DO IT FOR ME...
DO IT FOR SARA...
CHINGA!
THWOK!
WHEN ARE YOU GOING TO STOP HIDING BEHIND YOUR WIFE?

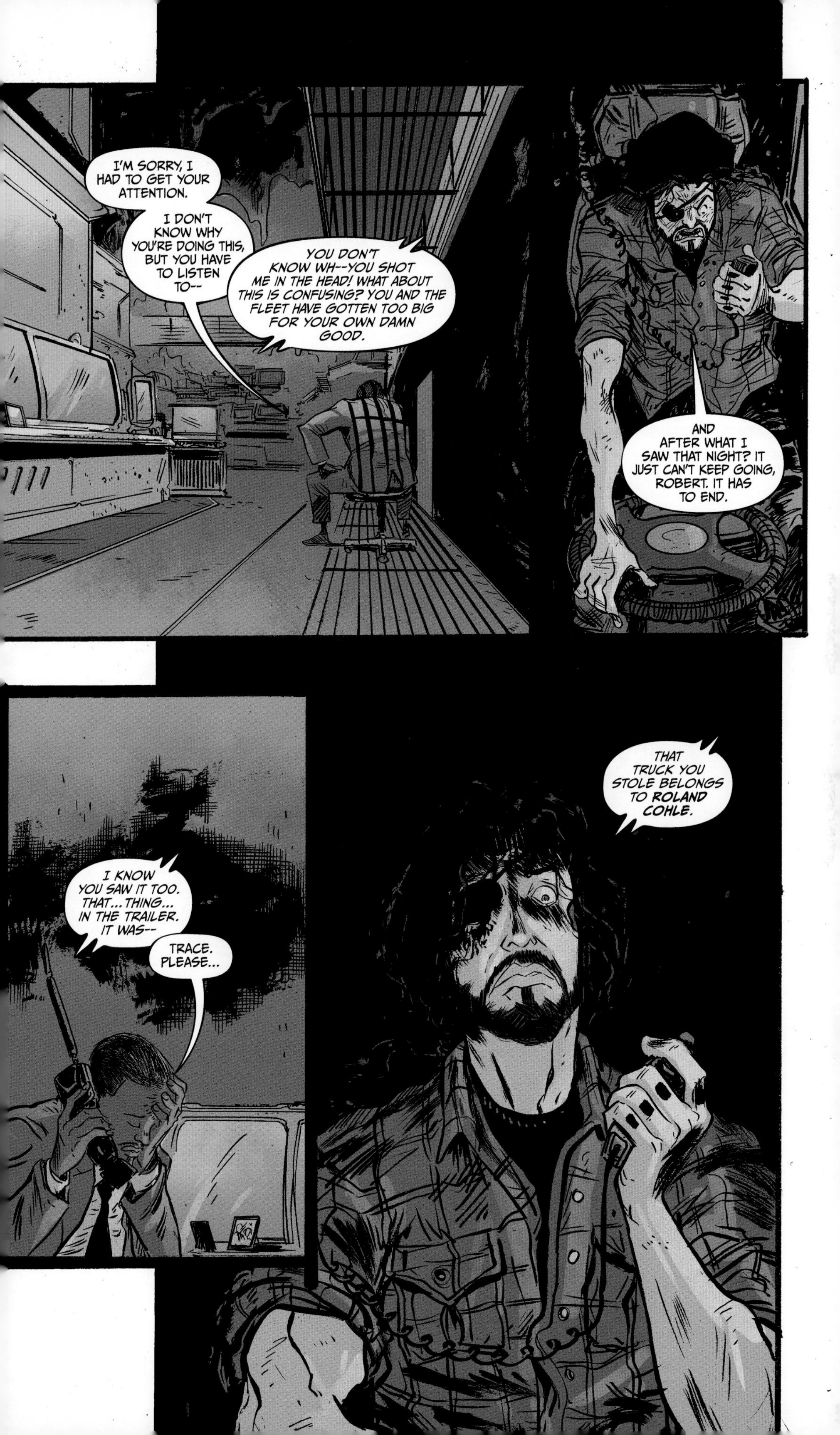
I'M SORRY, I HAD TO GET YOUR ATTENTION.
I DON'T KNOW WHY YOU'RE DOING THIS, BUT YOU HAVE TO LISTEN TO--
YOU DON'T KNOW WH--YOU SHOT ME IN THE HEAD! WHAT ABOUT THIS IS CONFUSING? YOU AND THE FLEET HAVE GOTTEN TOO BIG FOR YOUR OWN DAMN GOOD.
AND AFTER WHAT I SAW THAT NIGHT? IT JUST CAN'T KEEP GOING, ROBERT. IT HAS TO END.
I KNOW YOU SAW IT TOO. THAT... THING... IN THE TRAILER. IT WAS--
TRACE. PLEASE...
THAT TRUCK YOU STOLE BELONGS TO ROLAND COHLE.

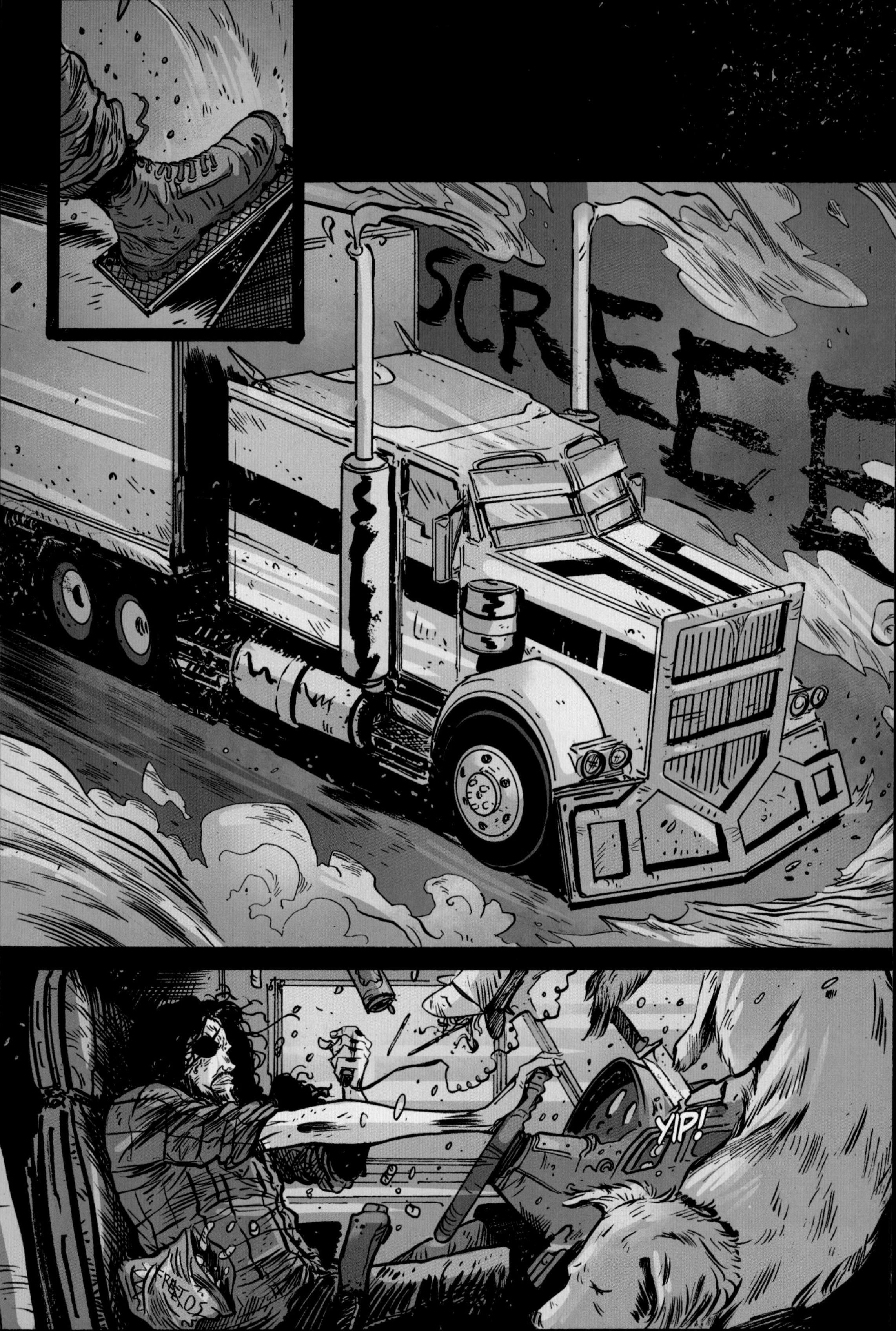
SCREEE
YIP!

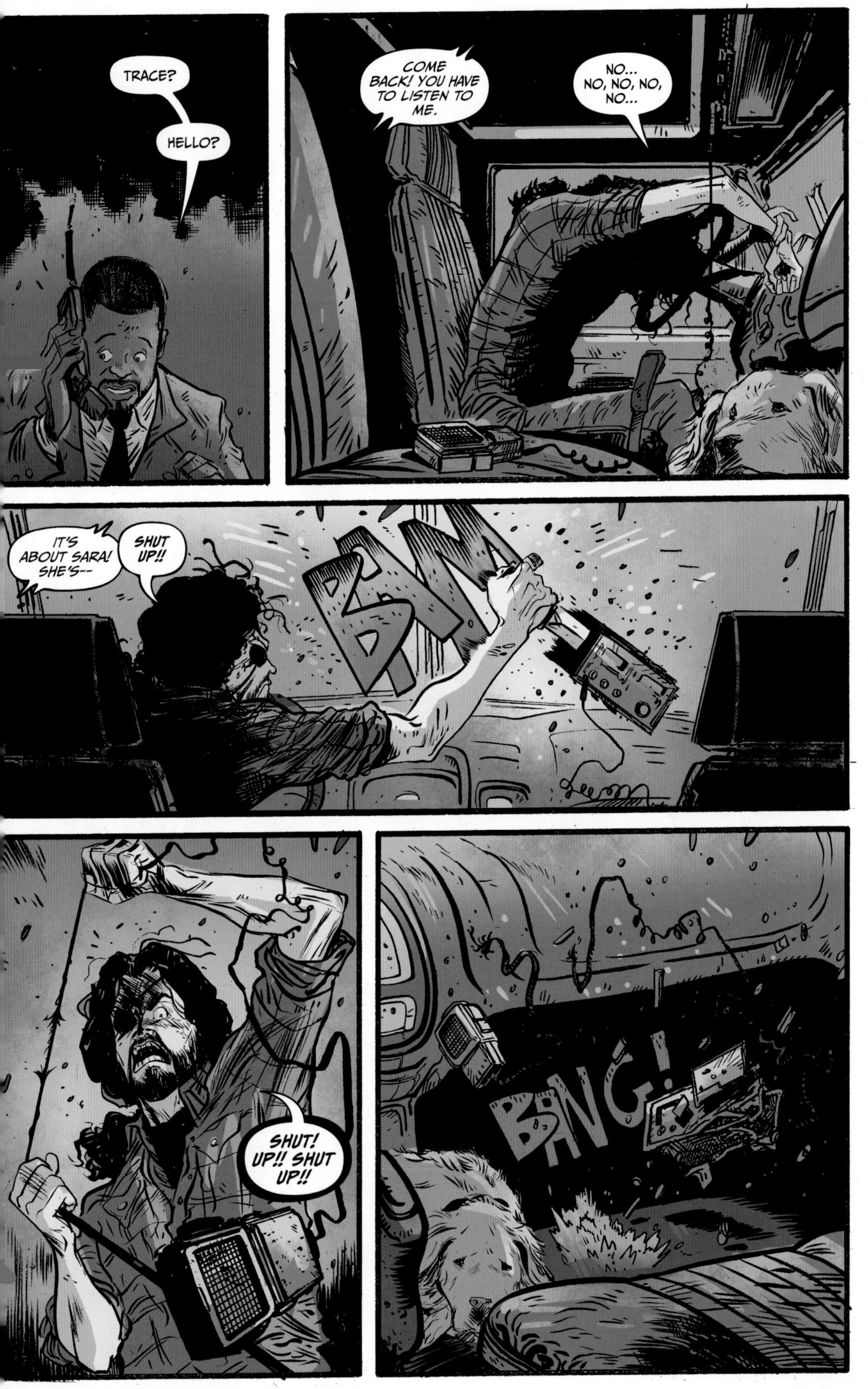
TRACE?
HELLO?
COME BACK! YOU HAVE TO LISTEN TO ME.
NO... NO, NO, NO, NO...
IT'S ABOUT SARA! SHE'S--
SHUT UP!!
BAM
SHUT! UP!! SHUT UP!!
BANG!

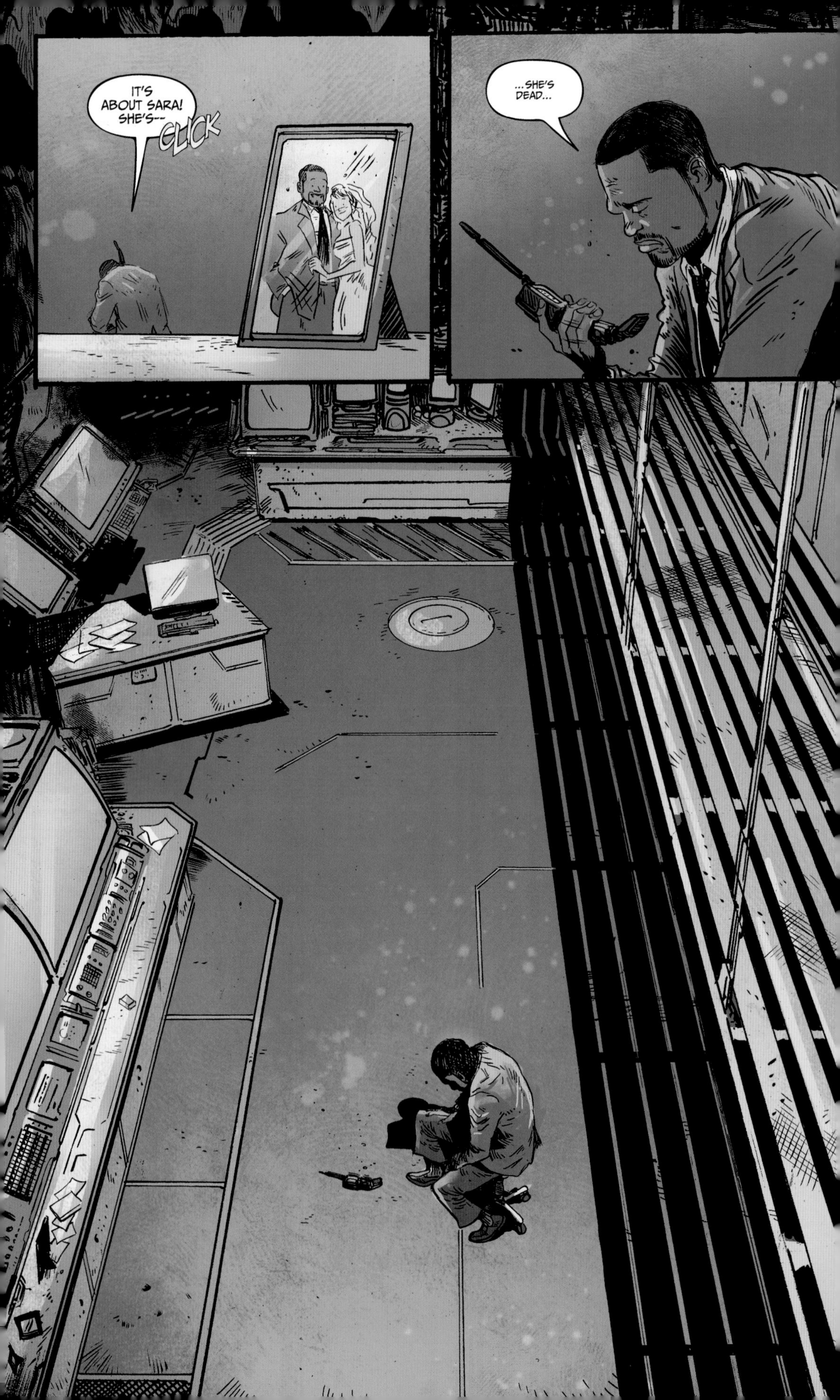
IT'S ABOUT SARA! SHE'S--
CLICK
...SHE'S DEAD...

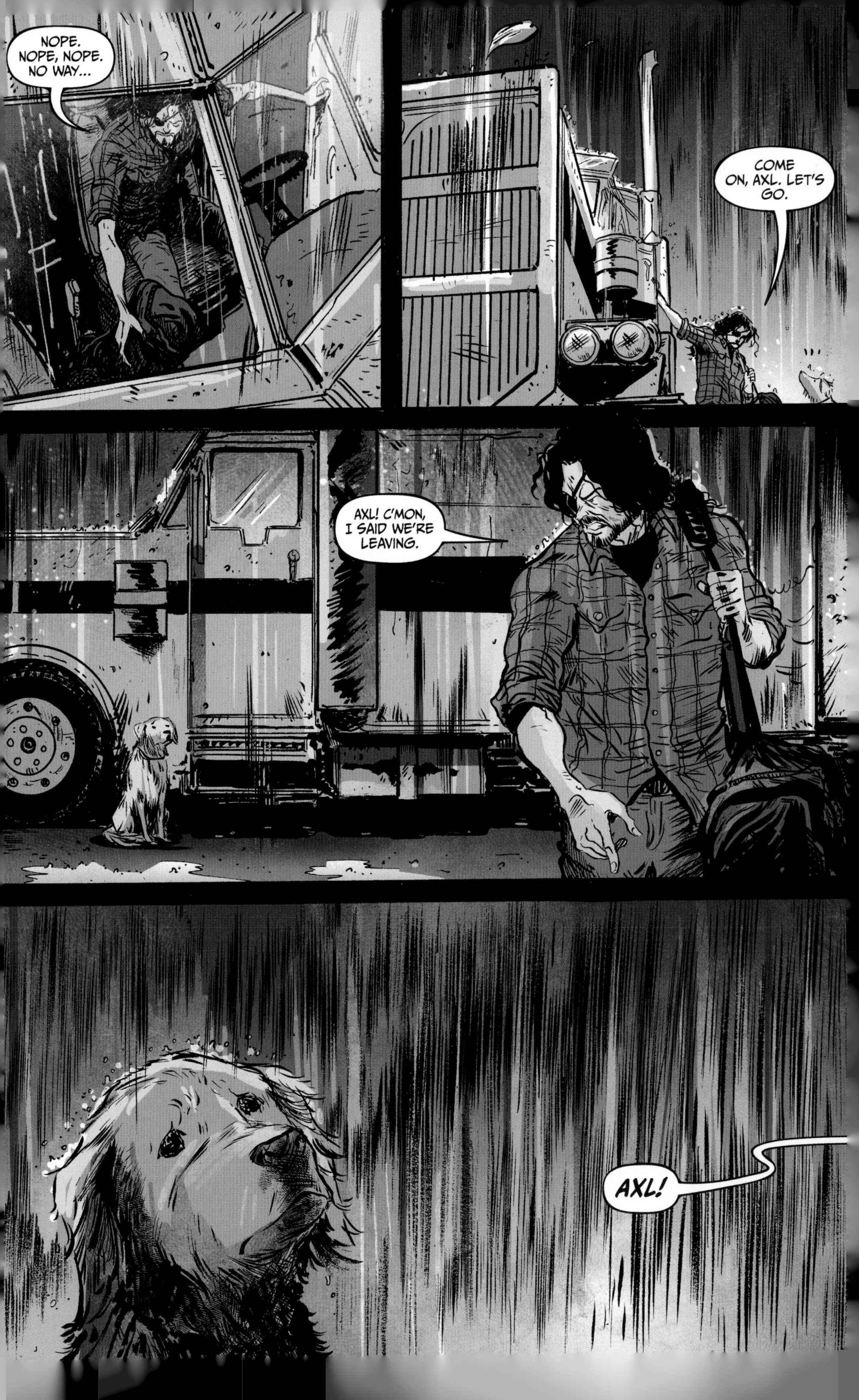
NOPE. NOPE, NOPE. NO WAY...
COME ON, AXL. LET'S GO.
AXL! C'MON, I SAID WE'RE LEAVING.
AXL!

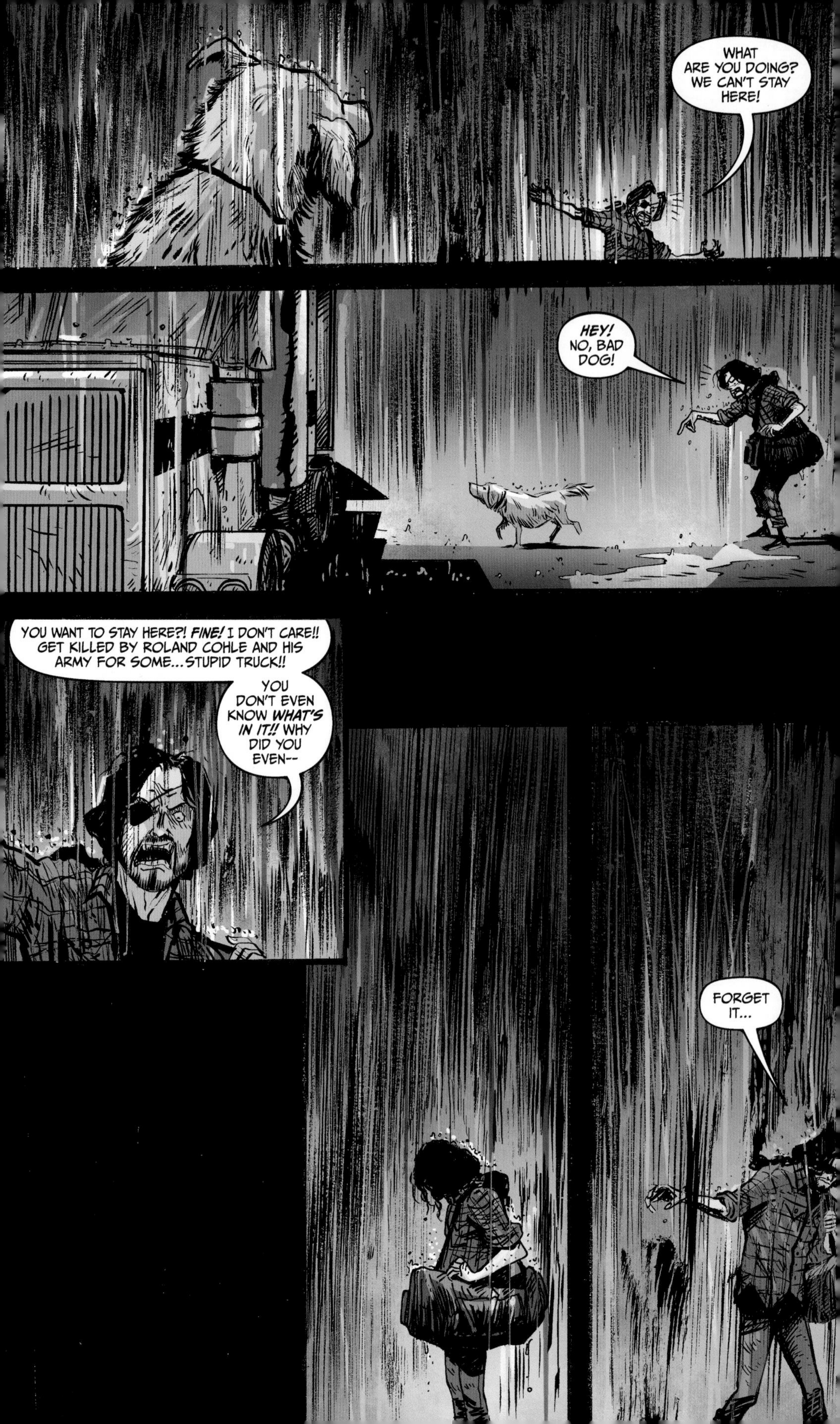
WHAT ARE YOU DOING? WE CAN'T STAY HERE!
HEY! NO, BAD DOG!
YOU WANT TO STAY HERE?! FINE! I DON'T CARE!! GET KILLED BY ROLAND COHLE AND HIS ARMY FOR SOME...STUPID TRUCK!!
YOU DON'T EVEN KNOW WHAT'S IN IT!! WHY DID YOU EVEN--
FORGET IT...

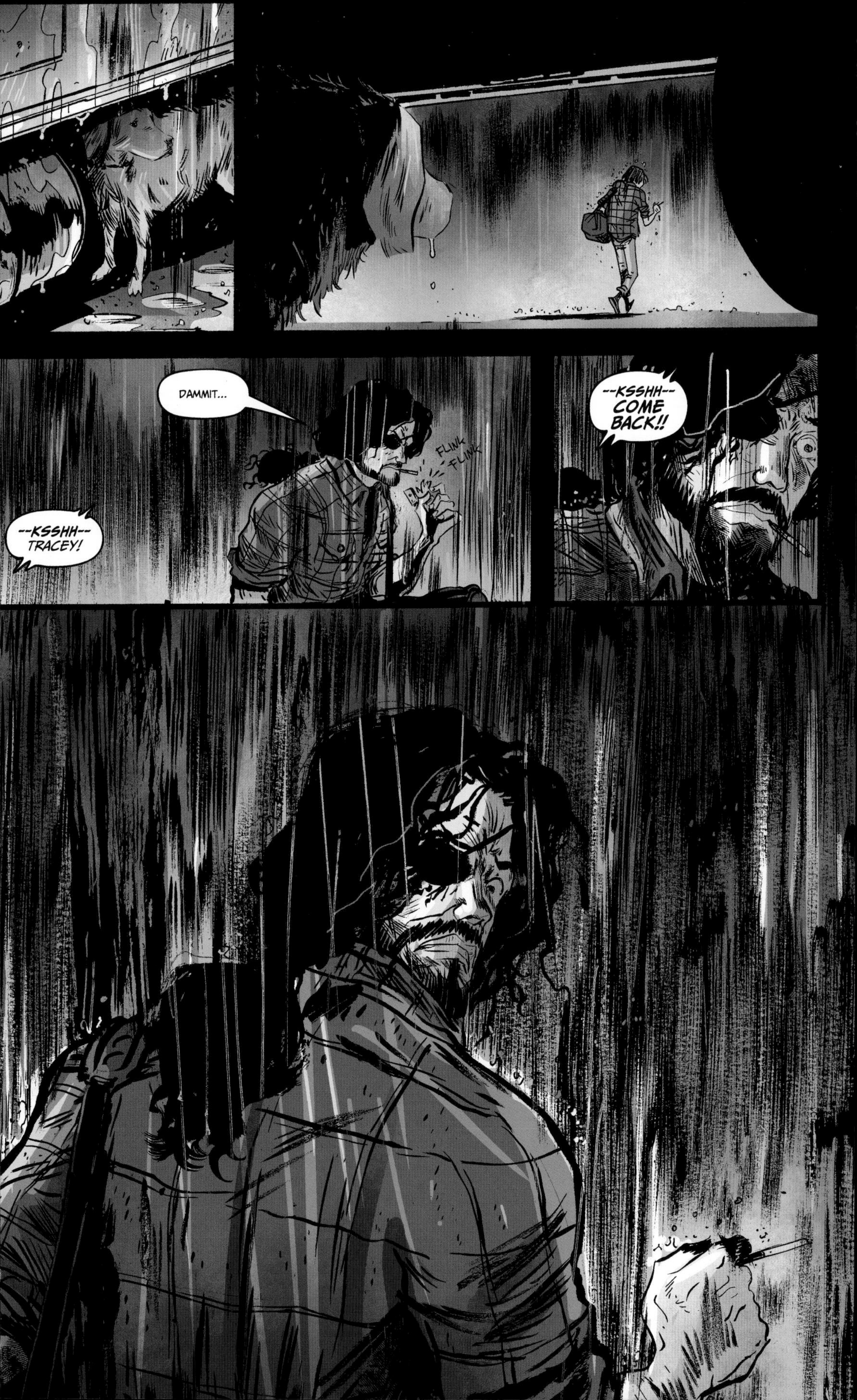
DAMMIT...
FLINK FLINK
--KSSHH-- TRACEY!
--KSSHH-- COME BACK!!

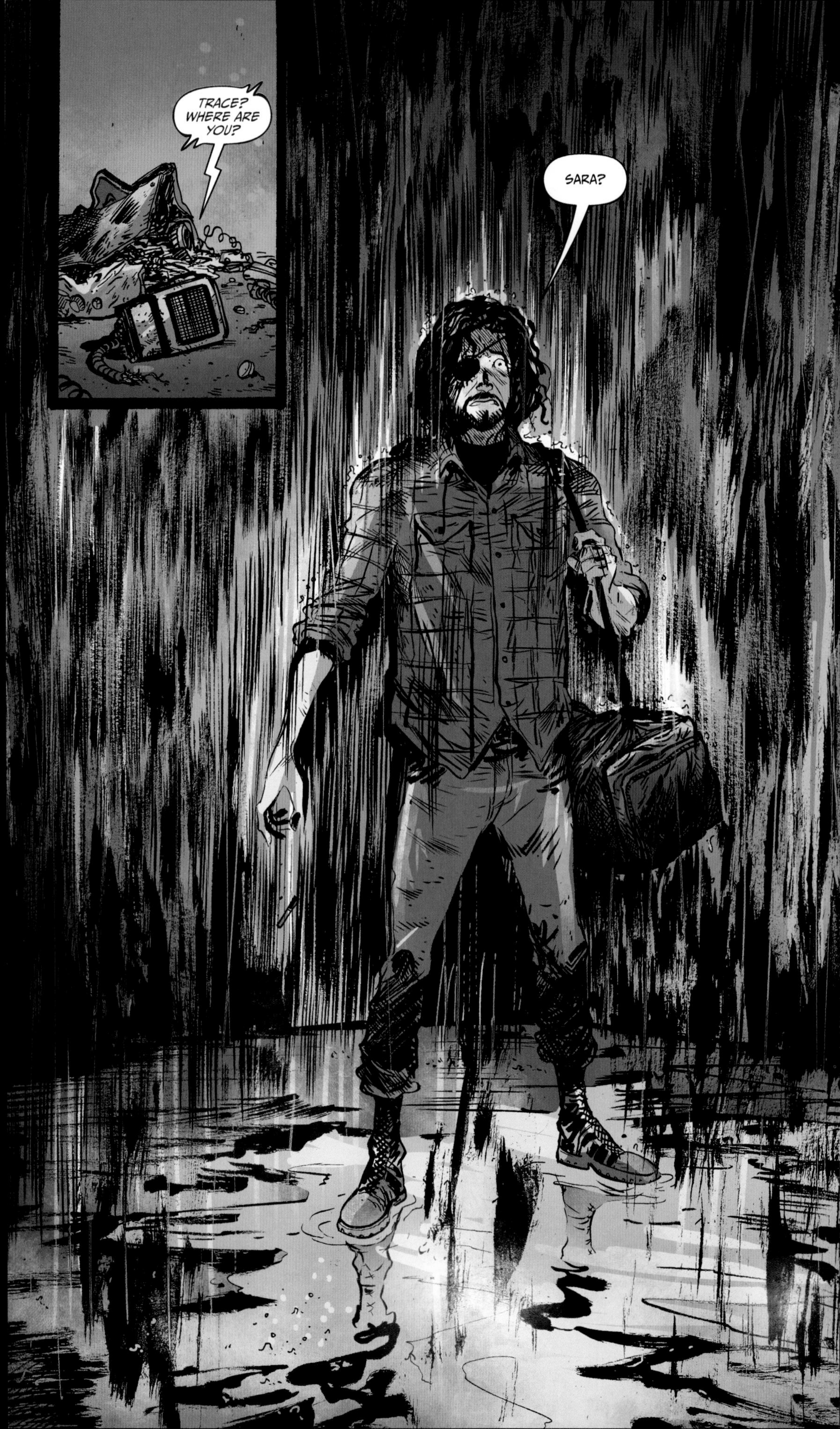
TRACE? WHERE ARE YOU?
SARA?

CHAPTER 4
THE WHEEL

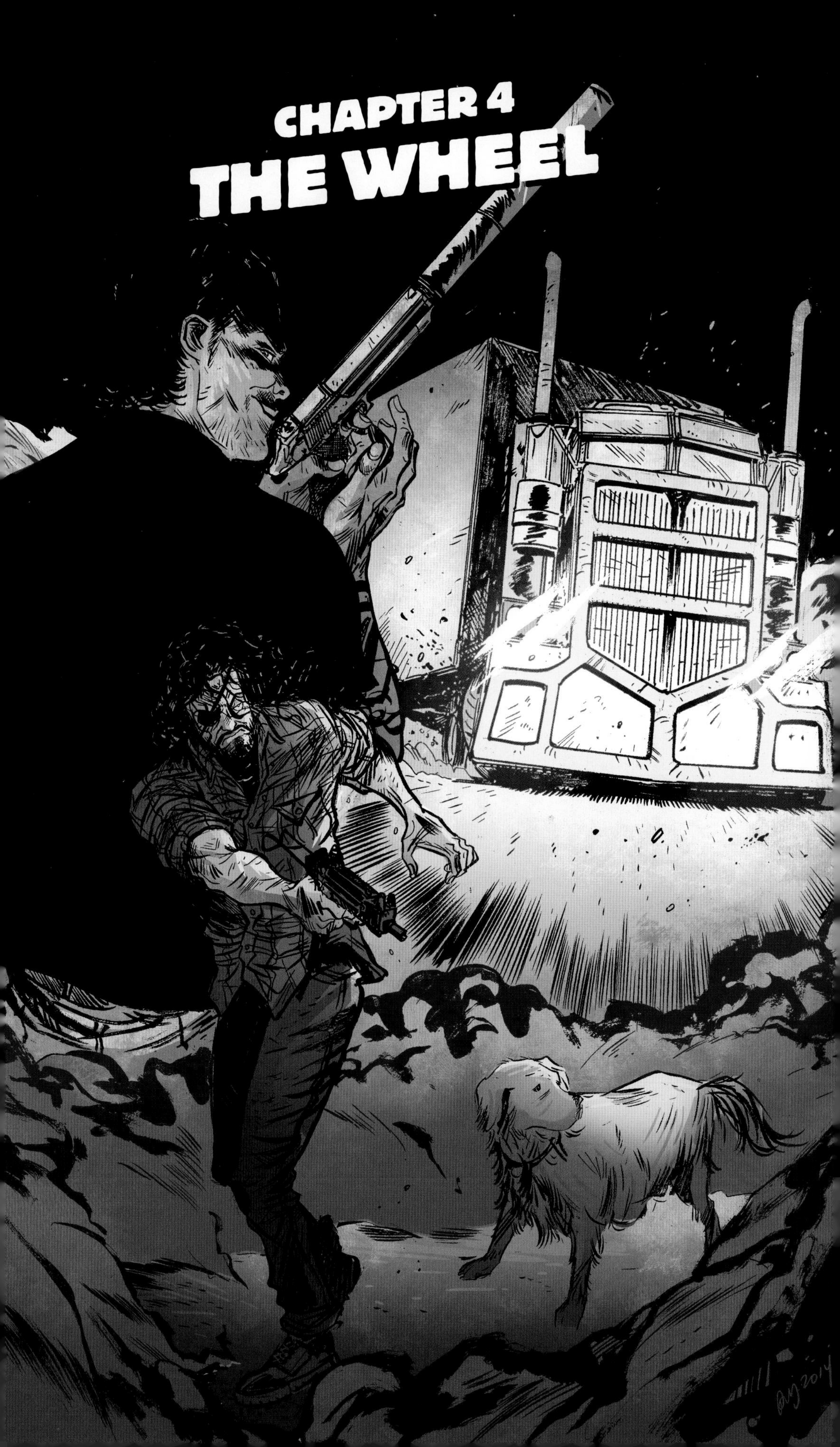

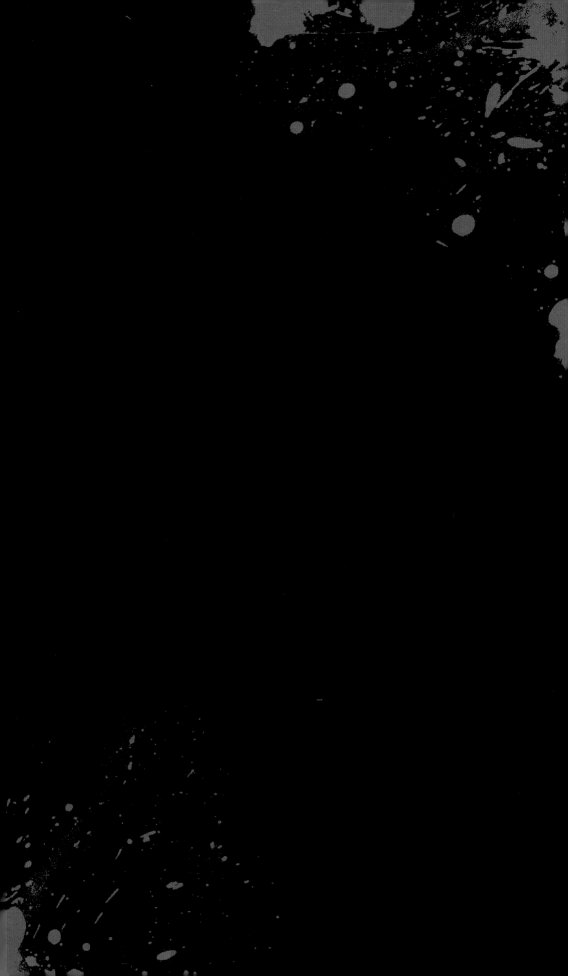

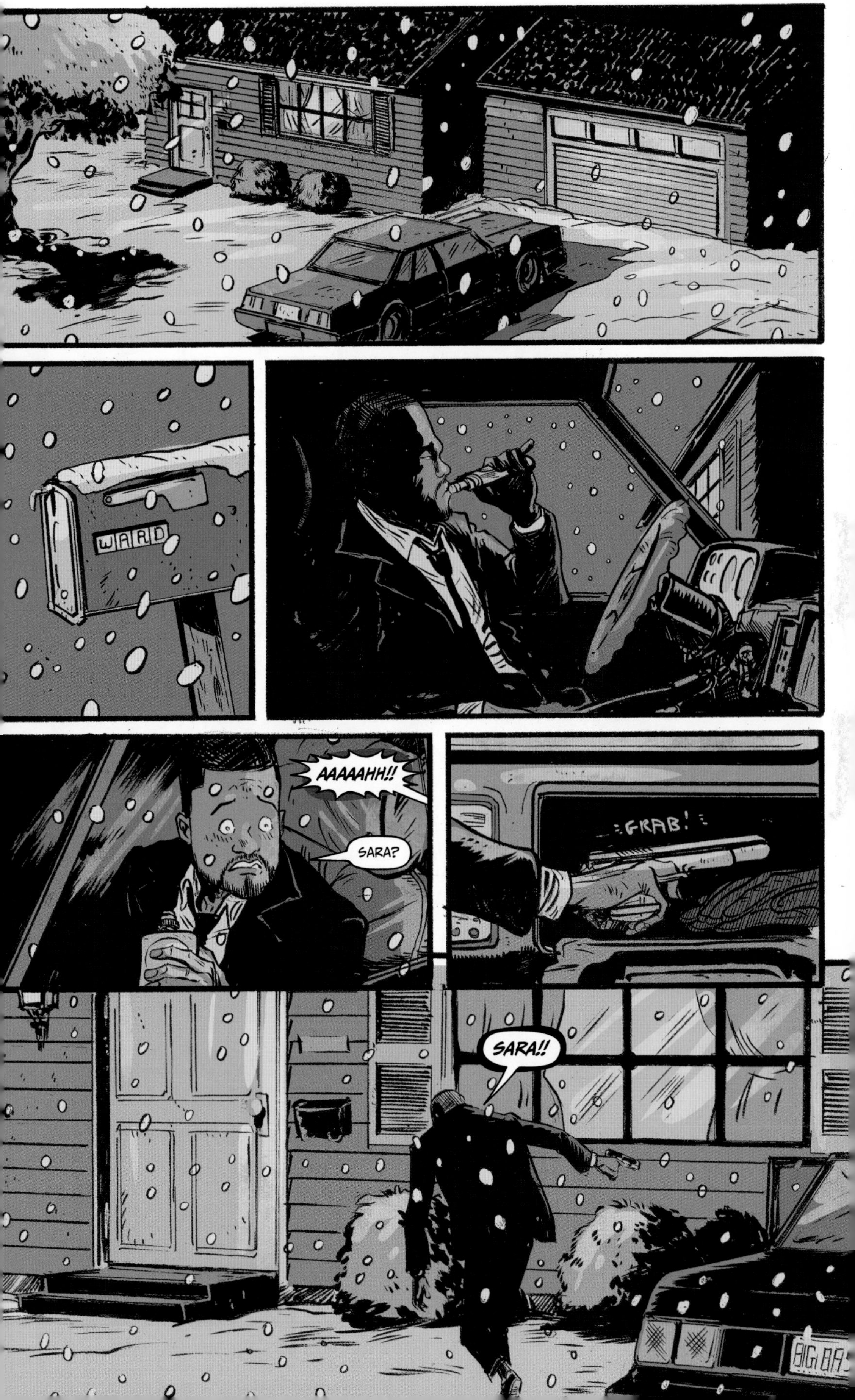
WARD
AAAAAHH!!
SARA?
GRAB!
SARA!!
BIG BA

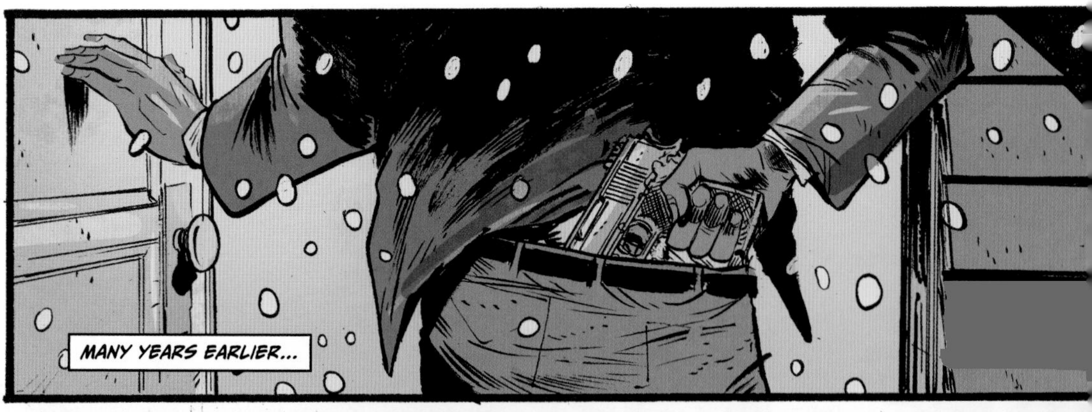
MANY YEARS EARLIER...

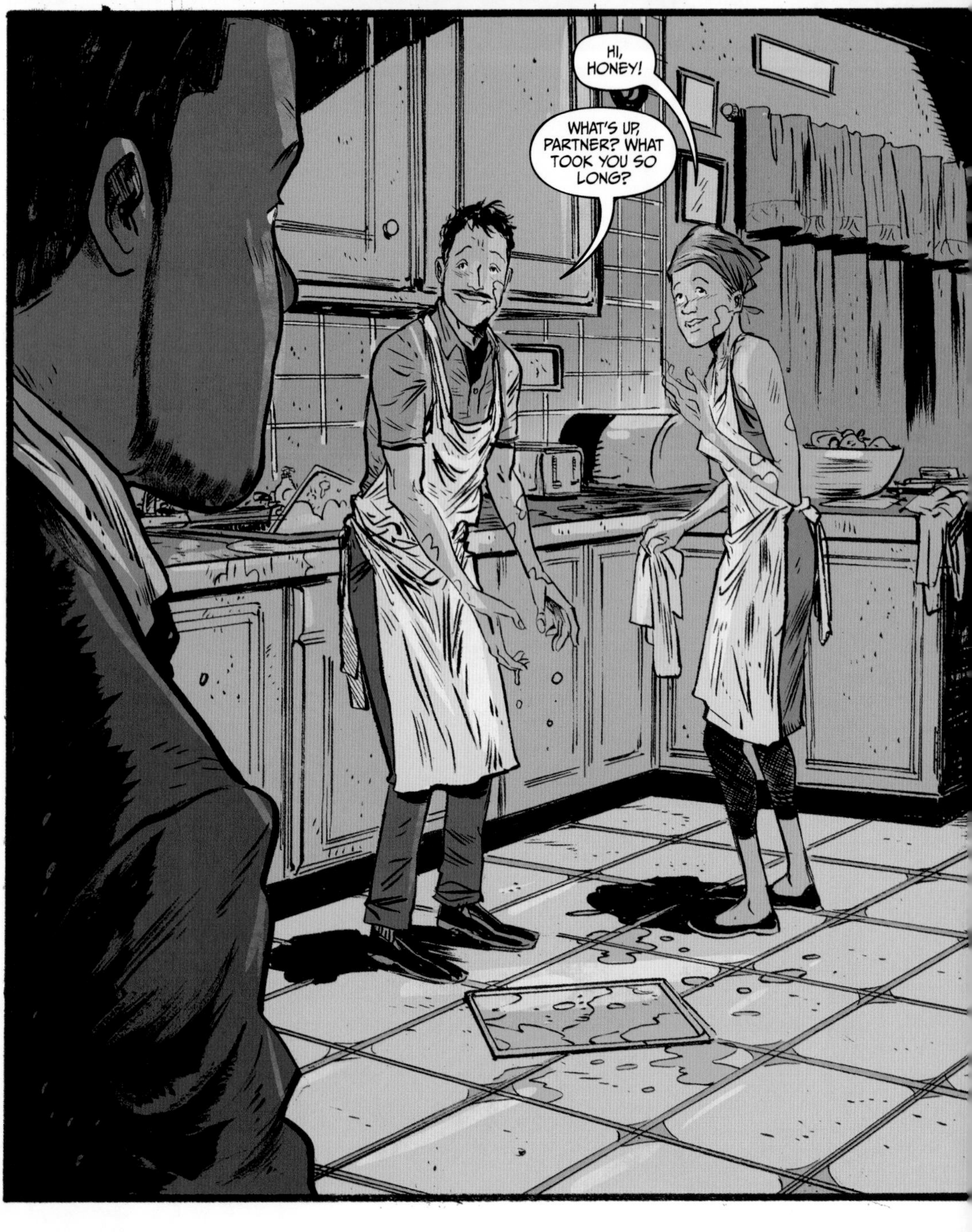
HI, HONEY!
WHAT'S UP, PARTNER? WHAT TOOK YOU SO LONG?

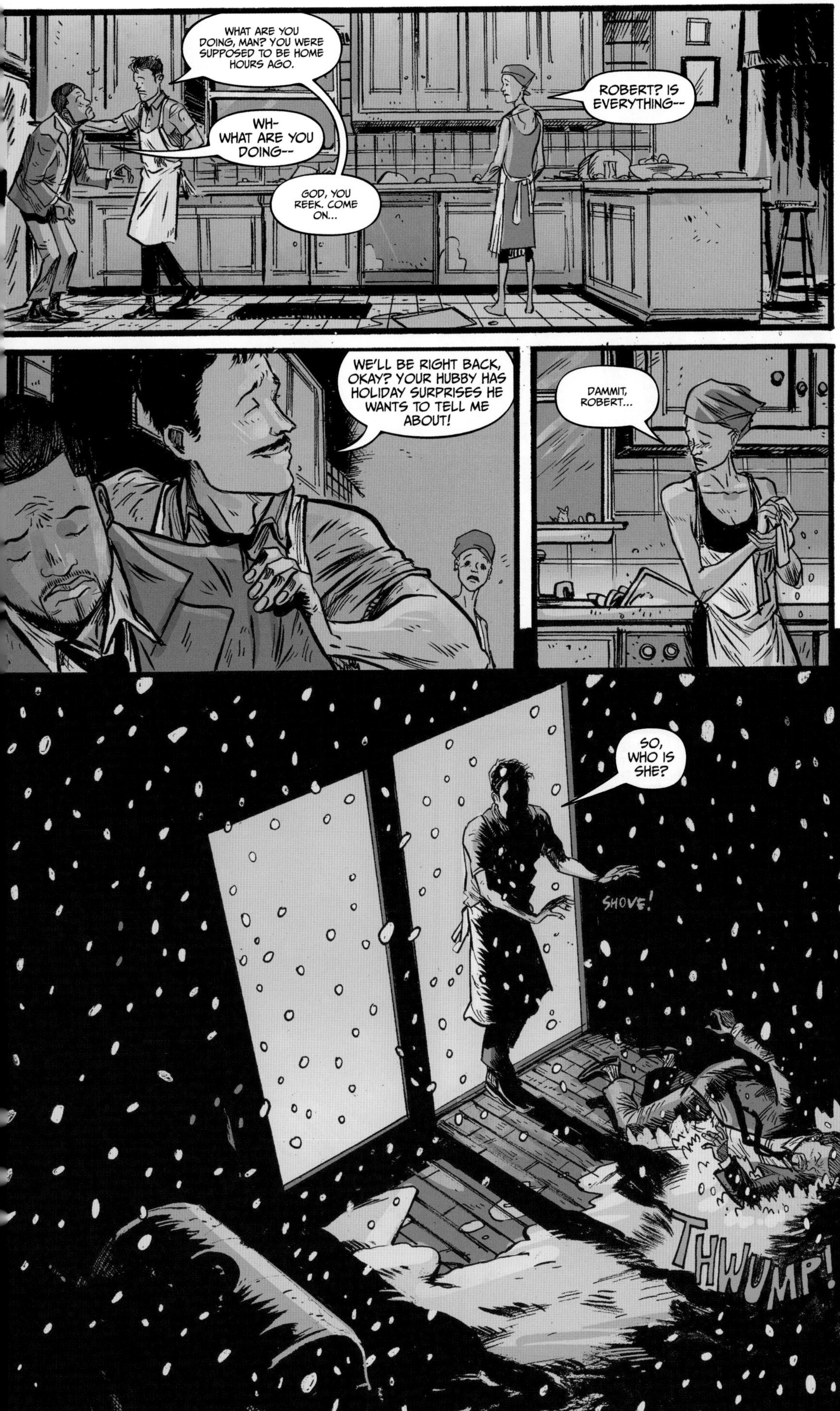
WHAT ARE YOU DOING, MAN? YOU WERE SUPPOSED TO BE HOME HOURS AGO.
WH- WHAT ARE YOU DOING--
GOD, YOU REEK. COME ON...
ROBERT? IS EVERYTHING--
WE'LL BE RIGHT BACK, OKAY? YOUR HUBBY HAS HOLIDAY SURPRISES HE WANTS TO TELL ME ABOUT!
DAMMIT, ROBERT...
SO, WHO IS SHE?
SHOVE!
THWUMP!

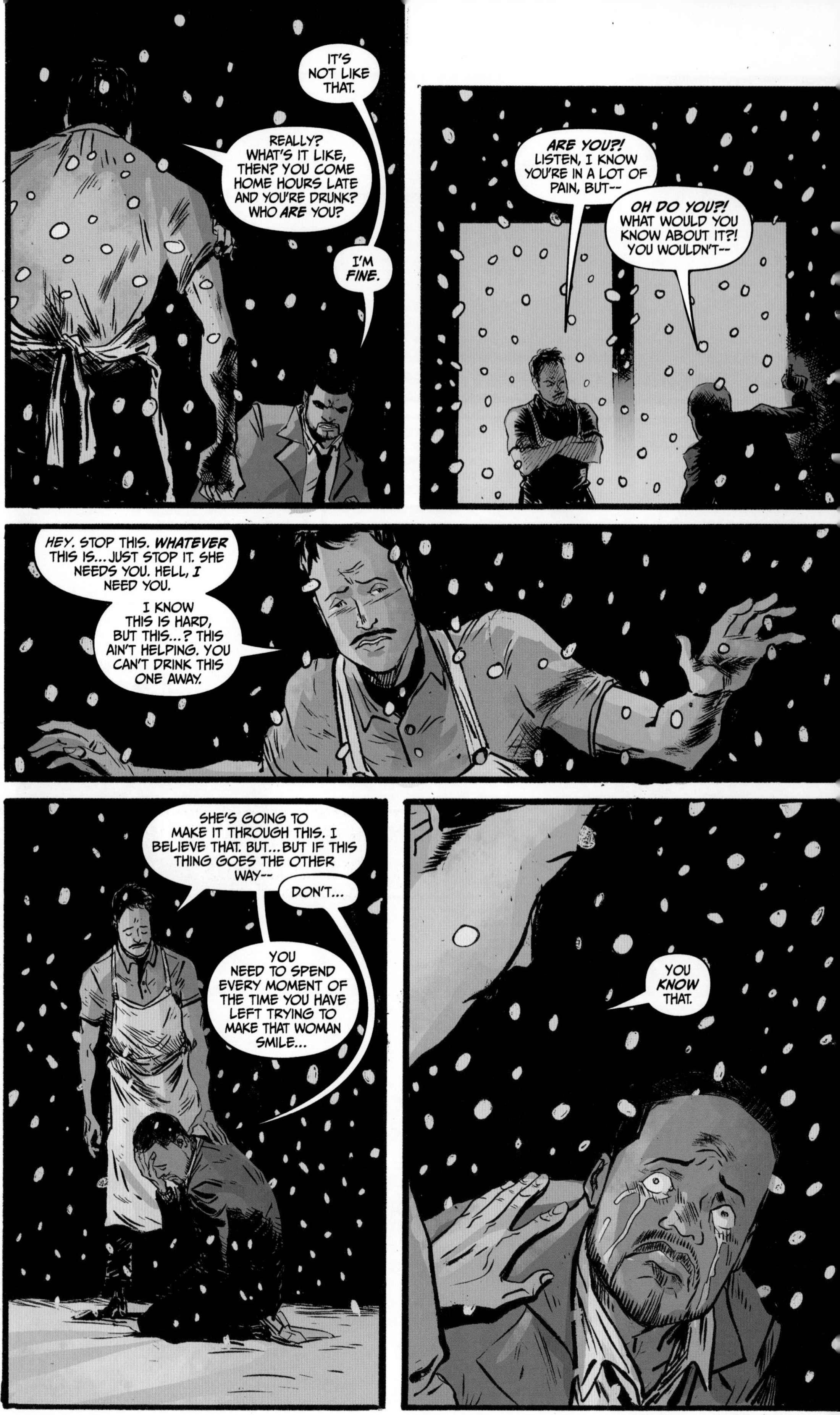
IT'S NOT LIKE THAT.
REALLY? WHAT'S IT LIKE, THEN? YOU COME HOME HOURS LATE AND YOU'RE DRUNK? WHO ARE YOU?
I'M FINE.
ARE YOU?! LISTEN, I KNOW YOU'RE IN A LOT OF PAIN, BUT--
OH DO YOU?! WHAT WOULD YOU KNOW ABOUT IT?! YOU WOULDN'T--
HEY. STOP THIS. WHATEVER THIS IS... JUST STOP IT. SHE NEEDS YOU. HELL, I NEED YOU.
I KNOW THIS IS HARD, BUT THIS...? THIS AIN'T HELPING. YOU CAN'T DRINK THIS ONE AWAY.
SHE'S GOING TO MAKE IT THROUGH THIS. I BELIEVE THAT. BUT... BUT IF THIS THING GOES THE OTHER WAY--
DON'T...
YOU NEED TO SPEND EVERY MOMENT OF THE TIME YOU HAVE LEFT TRYING TO MAKE THAT WOMAN SMILE...
YOU KNOW THAT.

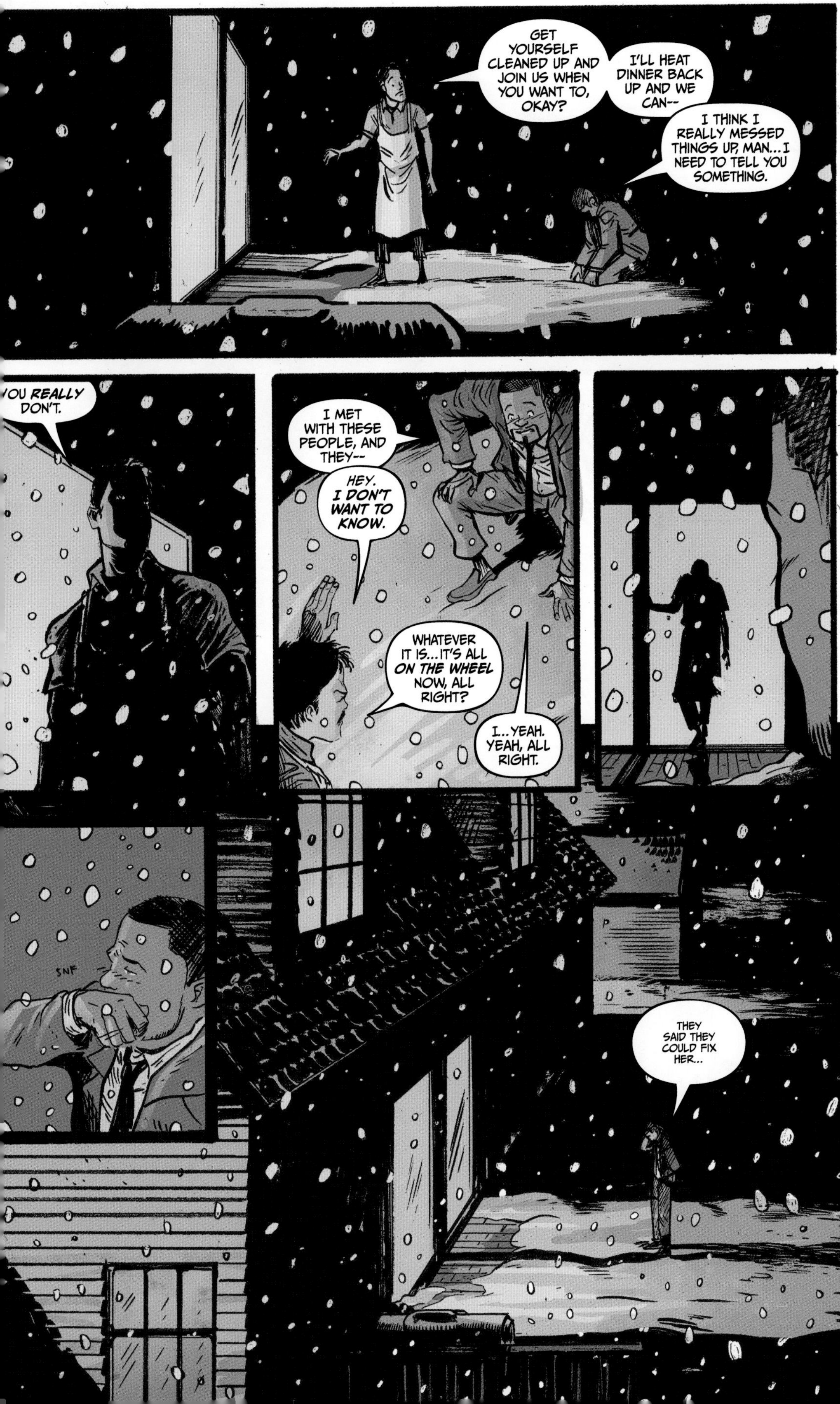
GET YOURSELF CLEANED UP AND JOIN US WHEN YOU WANT TO, OKAY?
I'LL HEAT DINNER BACK UP AND WE CAN--
I THINK I REALLY MESSED THINGS UP, MAN... I NEED TO TELL YOU SOMETHING.
YOU REALLY DON'T.
I MET WITH THESE PEOPLE, AND THEY--
HEY. I DON'T WANT TO KNOW.
WHATEVER IT IS... IT'S ALL ON THE WHEEL NOW, ALL RIGHT?
I... YEAH. YEAH, ALL RIGHT.
SNF
THEY SAID THEY COULD FIX HER...

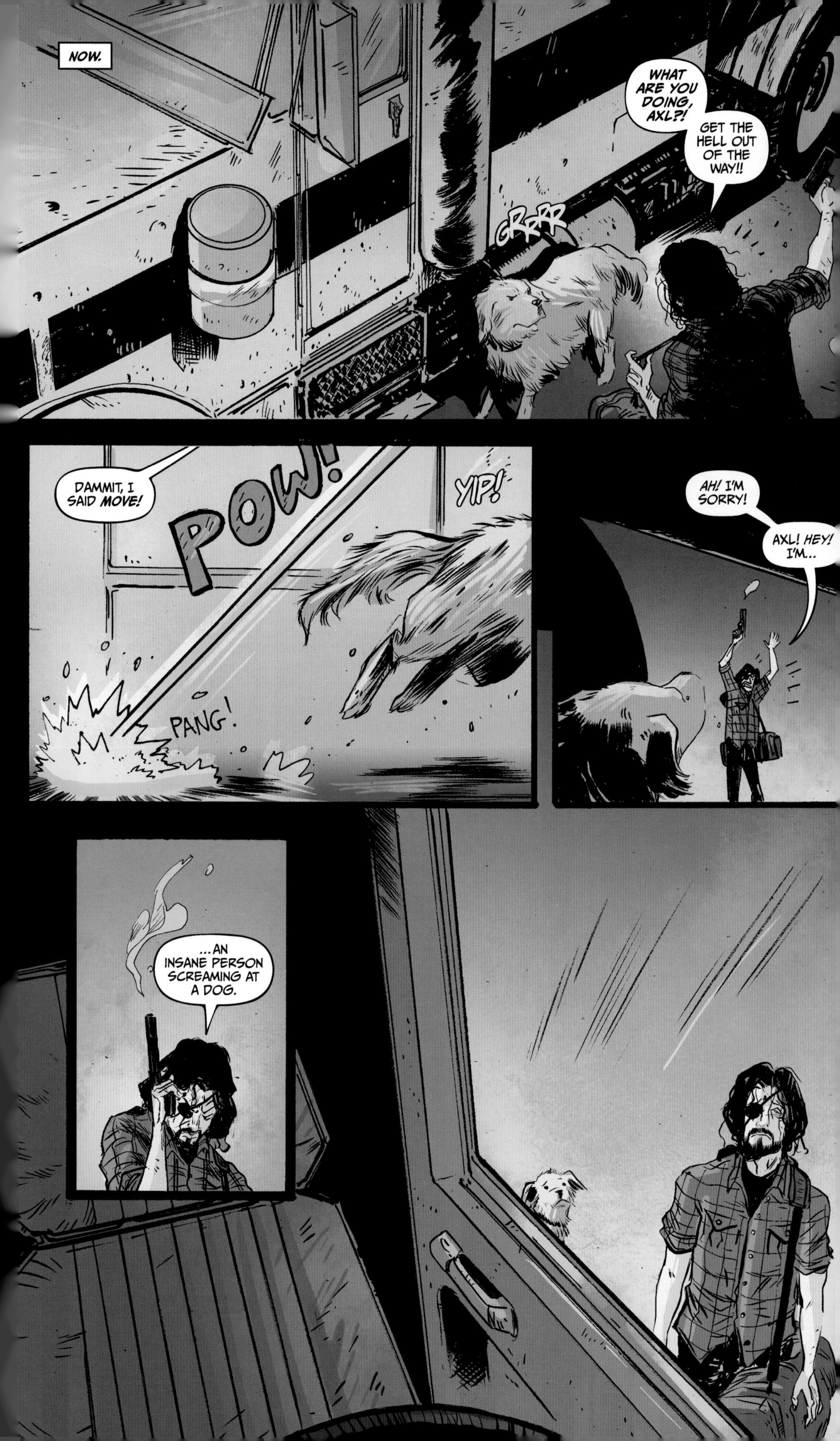
NOW.
WHAT ARE YOU DOING, AXL?!
GET THE HELL OUT OF THE WAY!!
GRRRR
DAMMIT, I SAID MOVE!
POW!
YIP!
PANG!
AH! I'M SORRY!
AXL! HEY! I'M...
...AN INSANE PERSON SCREAMING AT A DOG.

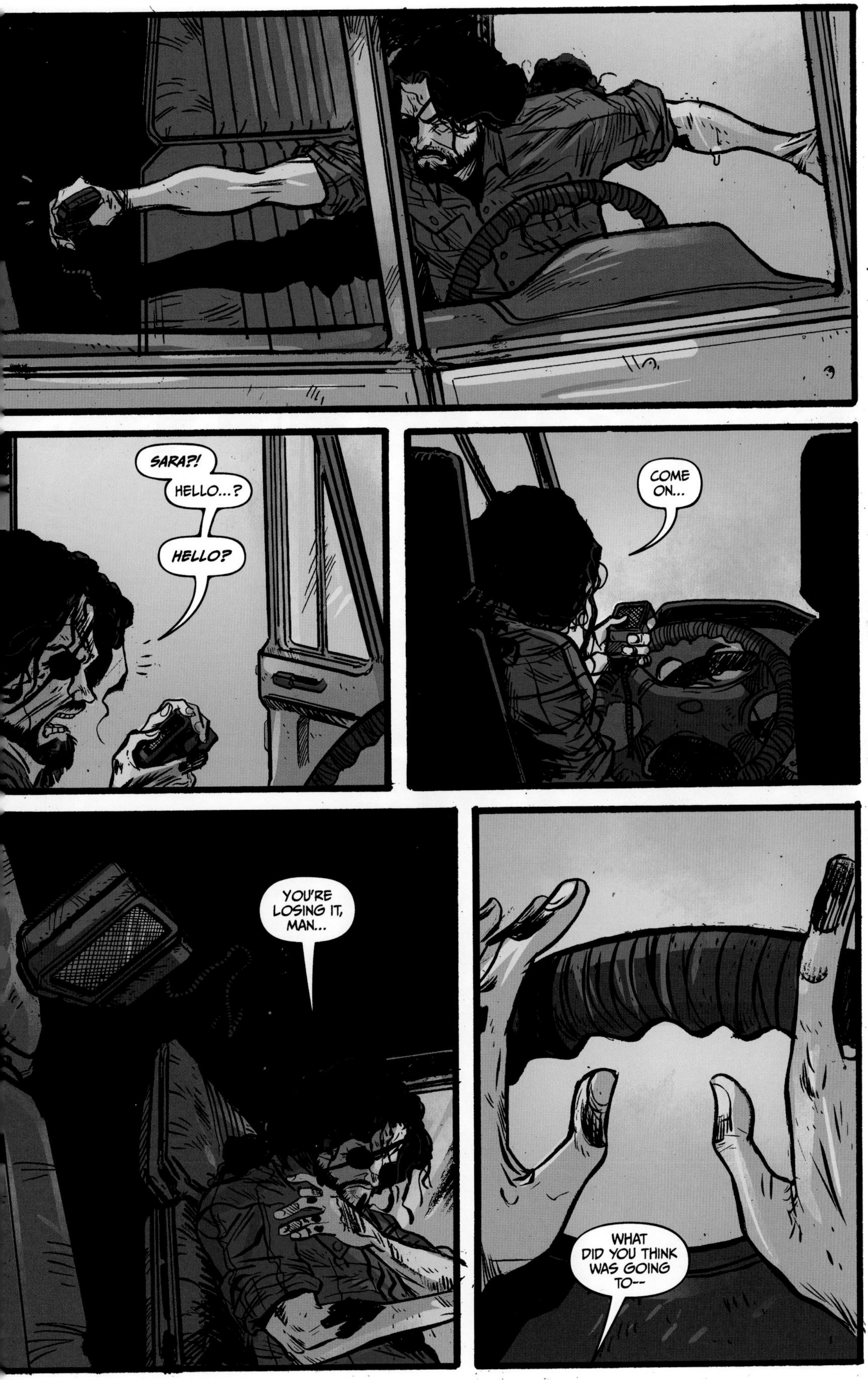
SARA?!
HELLO...?
HELLO?
COME ON...
YOU'RE LOSING IT, MAN...
WHAT DID YOU THINK WAS GOING TO--

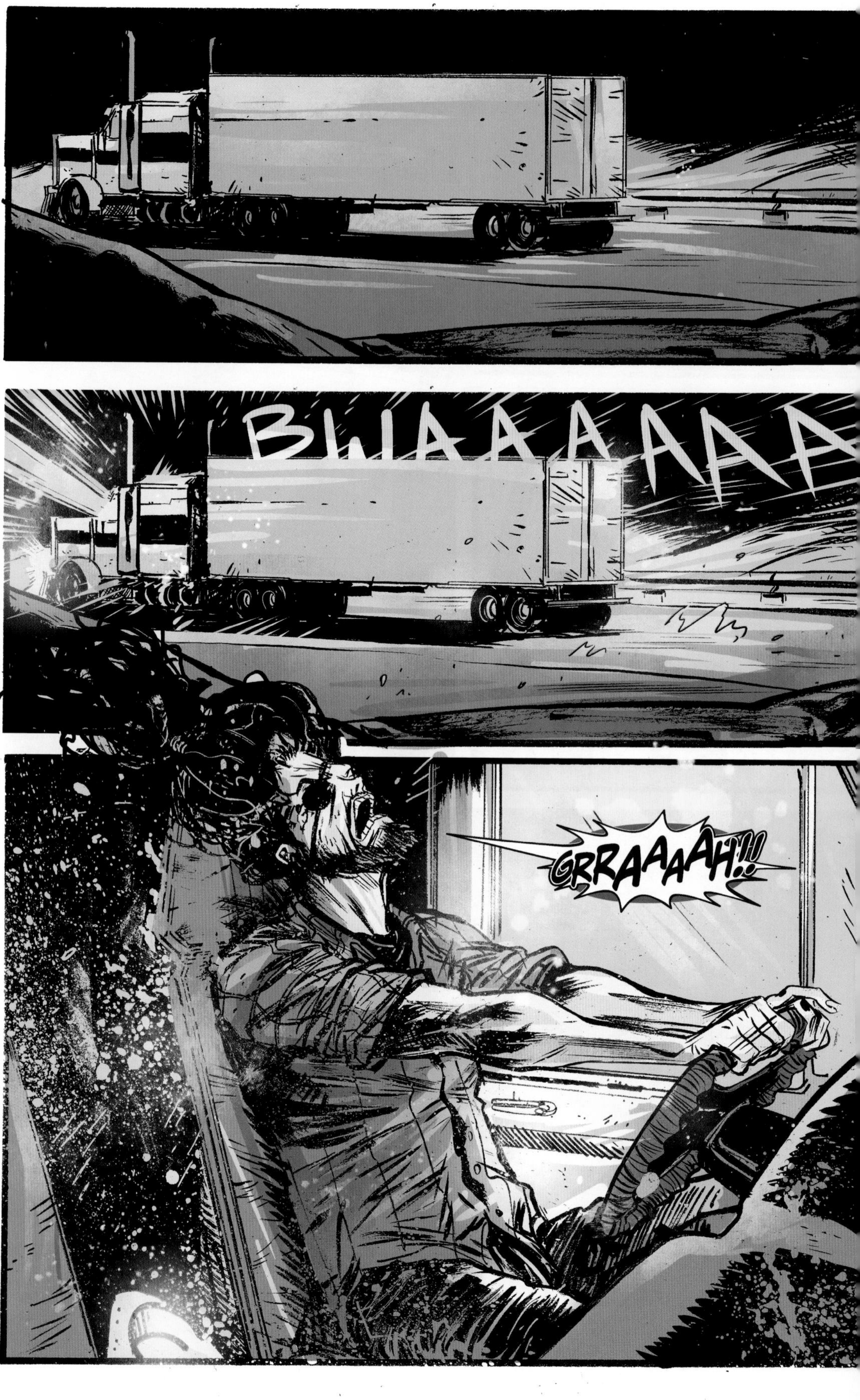
BWAAAAAAA
GRRAAAAAH!!!

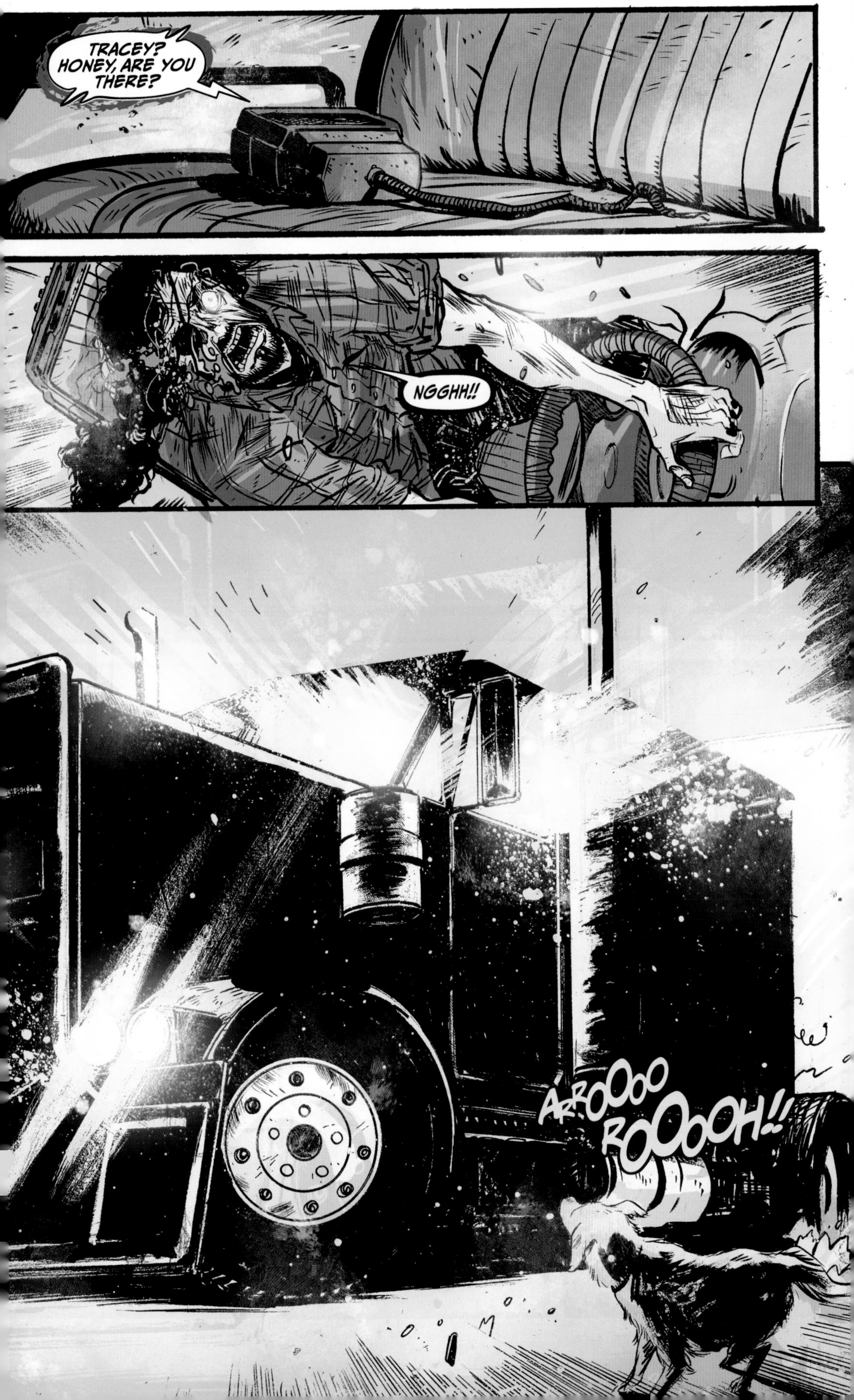
TRACEY? HONEY, ARE YOU THERE?
NGGHH!!
ARROOOO ROOOOOH!!

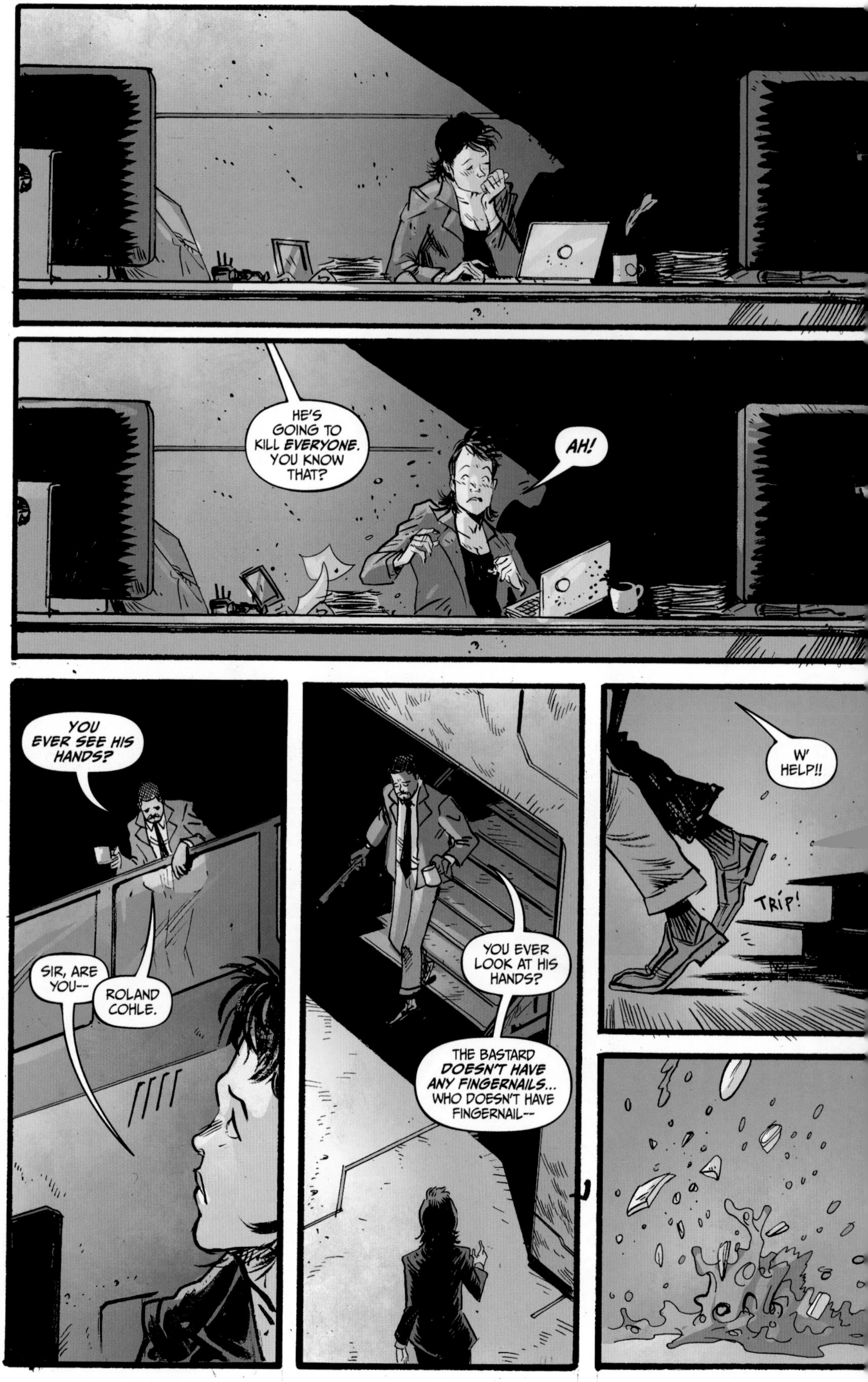
HE'S GOING TO KILL EVERYONE. YOU KNOW THAT?
AH!
YOU EVER SEE HIS HANDS?
SIR, ARE YOU--
ROLAND COHLE.
YOU EVER LOOK AT HIS HANDS?
THE BASTARD DOESN'T HAVE ANY FINGERNAILS... WHO DOESN'T HAVE FINGERNAIL--
W' HELP!!
TRIP!

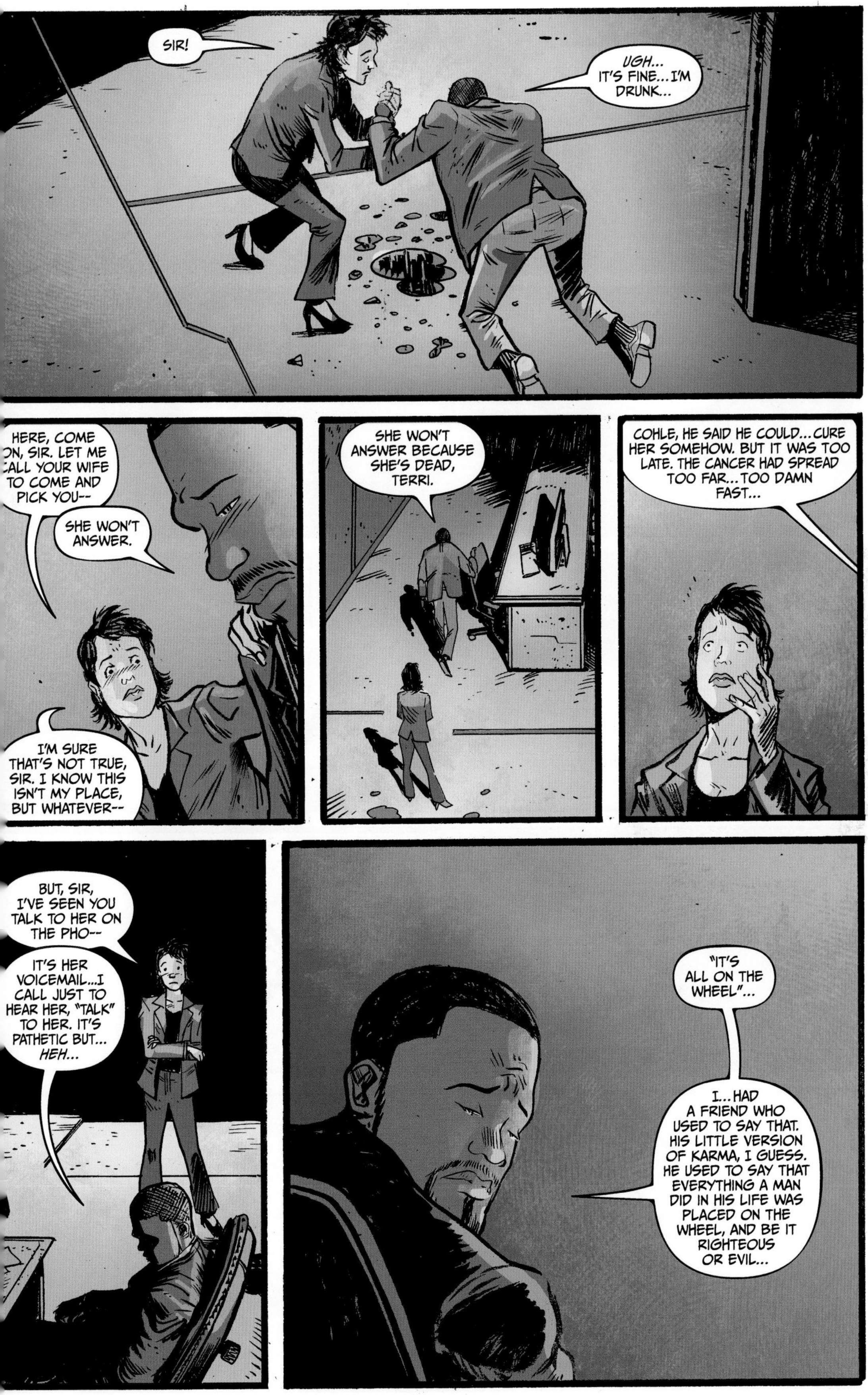
SIR!
UGH... IT'S FINE...I'M DRUNK...
HERE, COME ON, SIR. LET ME CALL YOUR WIFE TO COME AND PICK YOU--
SHE WON'T ANSWER.
I'M SURE THAT'S NOT TRUE, SIR. I KNOW THIS ISN'T MY PLACE, BUT WHATEVER--
SHE WON'T ANSWER BECAUSE SHE'S DEAD, TERRI.
COHLE, HE SAID HE COULD...CURE HER SOMEHOW. BUT IT WAS TOO LATE. THE CANCER HAD SPREAD TOO FAR...TOO DAMN FAST...
BUT, SIR, I'VE SEEN YOU TALK TO HER ON THE PHO--
IT'S HER VOICEMAIL...I CALL JUST TO HEAR HER, "TALK" TO HER. IT'S PATHETIC BUT... HEH...
"IT'S ALL ON THE WHEEL"...
I...HAD A FRIEND WHO USED TO SAY THAT. HIS LITTLE VERSION OF KARMA, I GUESS. HE USED TO SAY THAT EVERYTHING A MAN DID IN HIS LIFE WAS PLACED ON THE WHEEL, AND BE IT RIGHTEOUS OR EVIL...

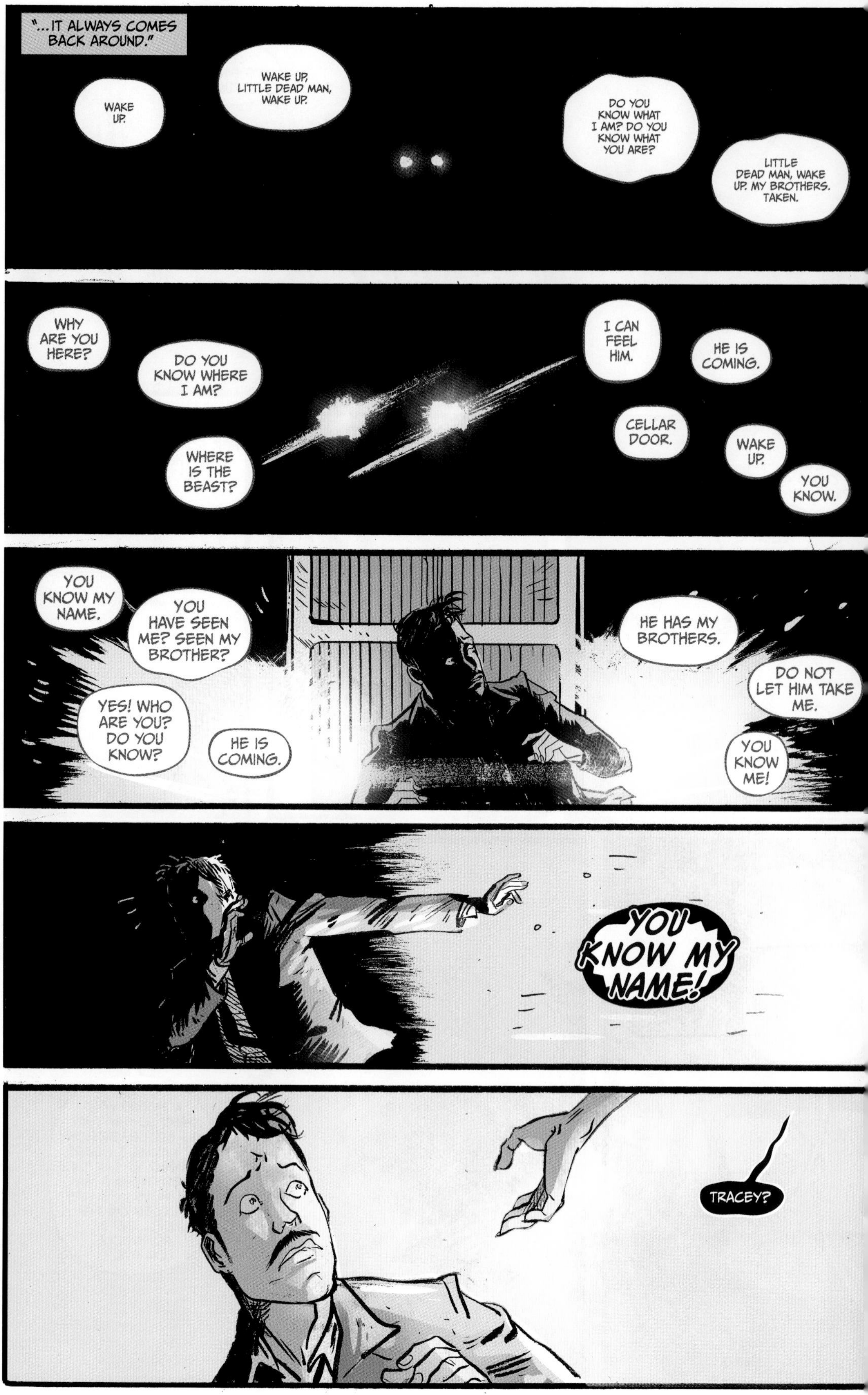
"...IT ALWAYS COMES BACK AROUND."
WAKE UP.
WAKE UP, LITTLE DEAD MAN, WAKE UP.
DO YOU KNOW WHAT I AM? DO YOU KNOW WHAT YOU ARE?
LITTLE DEAD MAN, WAKE UP. MY BROTHERS. TAKEN.
WHY ARE YOU HERE?
DO YOU KNOW WHERE I AM?
WHERE IS THE BEAST?
I CAN FEEL HIM.
HE IS COMING.
CELLAR DOOR.
WAKE UP.
YOU KNOW.
YOU KNOW MY NAME.
YOU HAVE SEEN ME? SEEN MY BROTHER?
YES! WHO ARE YOU? DO YOU KNOW?
HE IS COMING.
HE HAS MY BROTHERS.
DO NOT LET HIM TAKE ME.
YOU KNOW ME!
YOU KNOW MY NAME!
TRACEY?

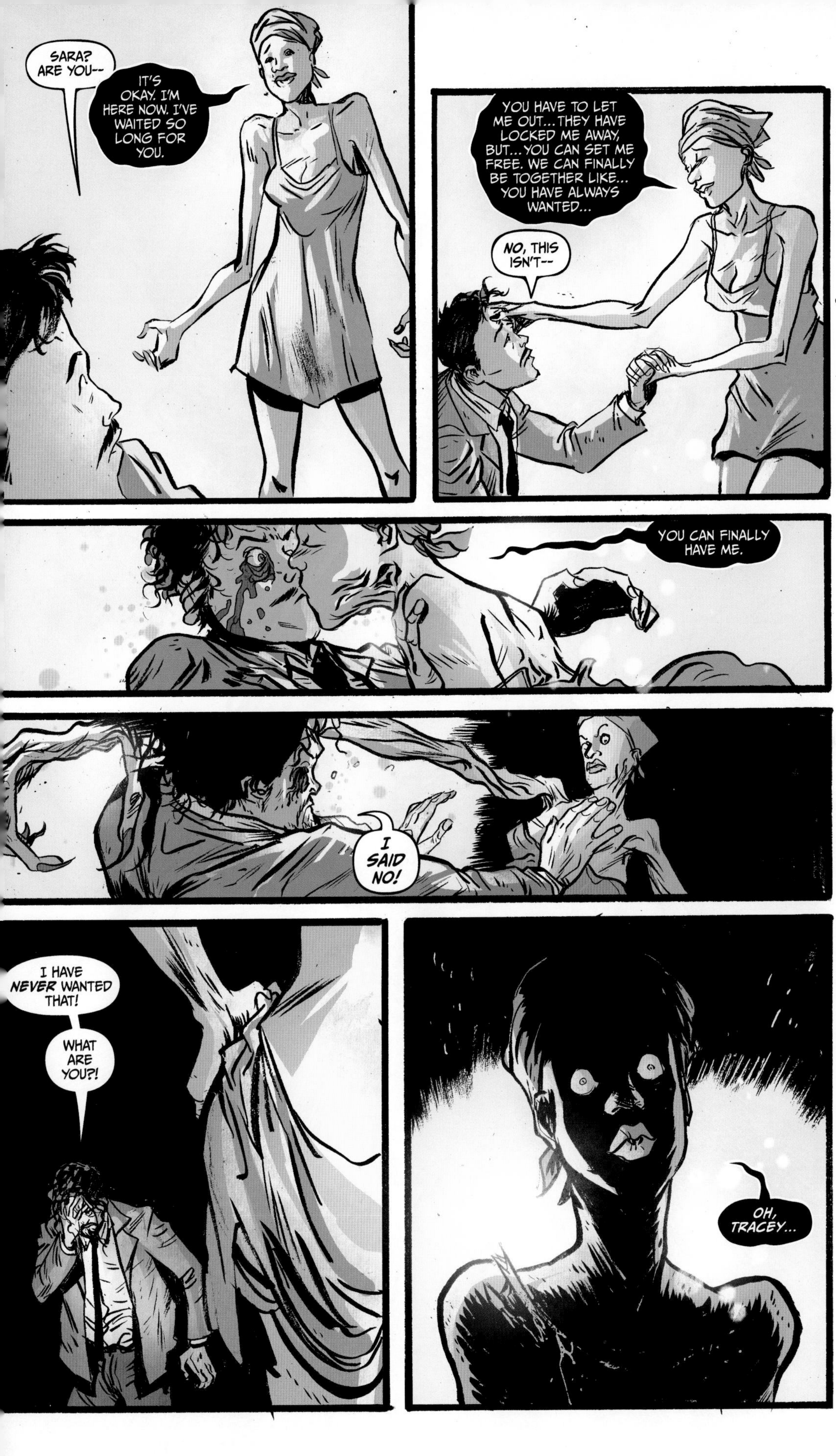
SARA? ARE YOU--
IT'S OKAY. I'M HERE NOW. I'VE WAITED SO LONG FOR YOU.
YOU HAVE TO LET ME OUT...THEY HAVE LOCKED ME AWAY, BUT...YOU CAN SET ME FREE. WE CAN FINALLY BE TOGETHER LIKE... YOU HAVE ALWAYS WANTED...
NO, THIS ISN'T--
YOU CAN FINALLY HAVE ME.
I SAID NO!
I HAVE NEVER WANTED THAT!
WHAT ARE YOU?!
OH, TRACEY...

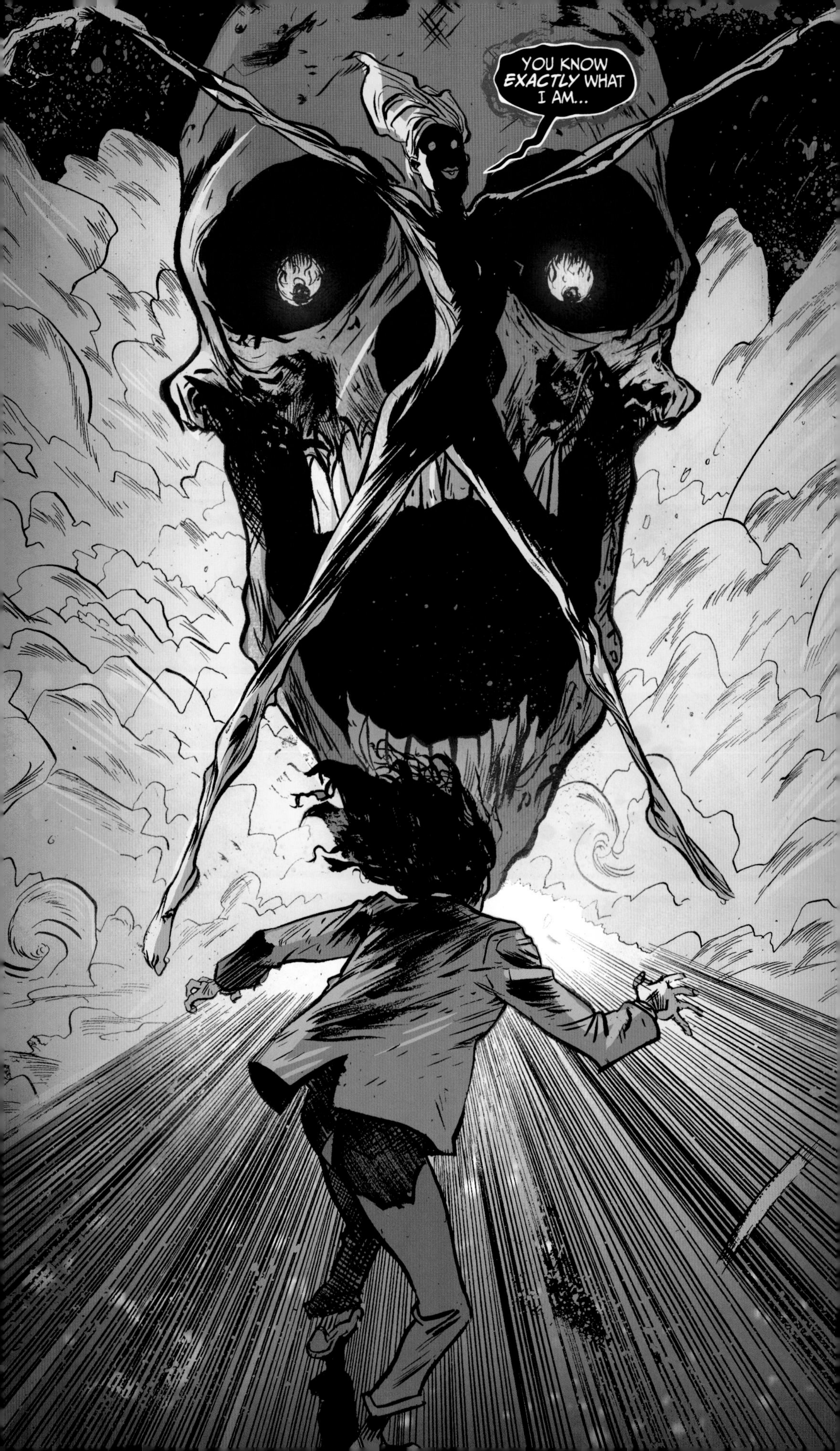
YOU KNOW EXACTLY WHAT I AM...

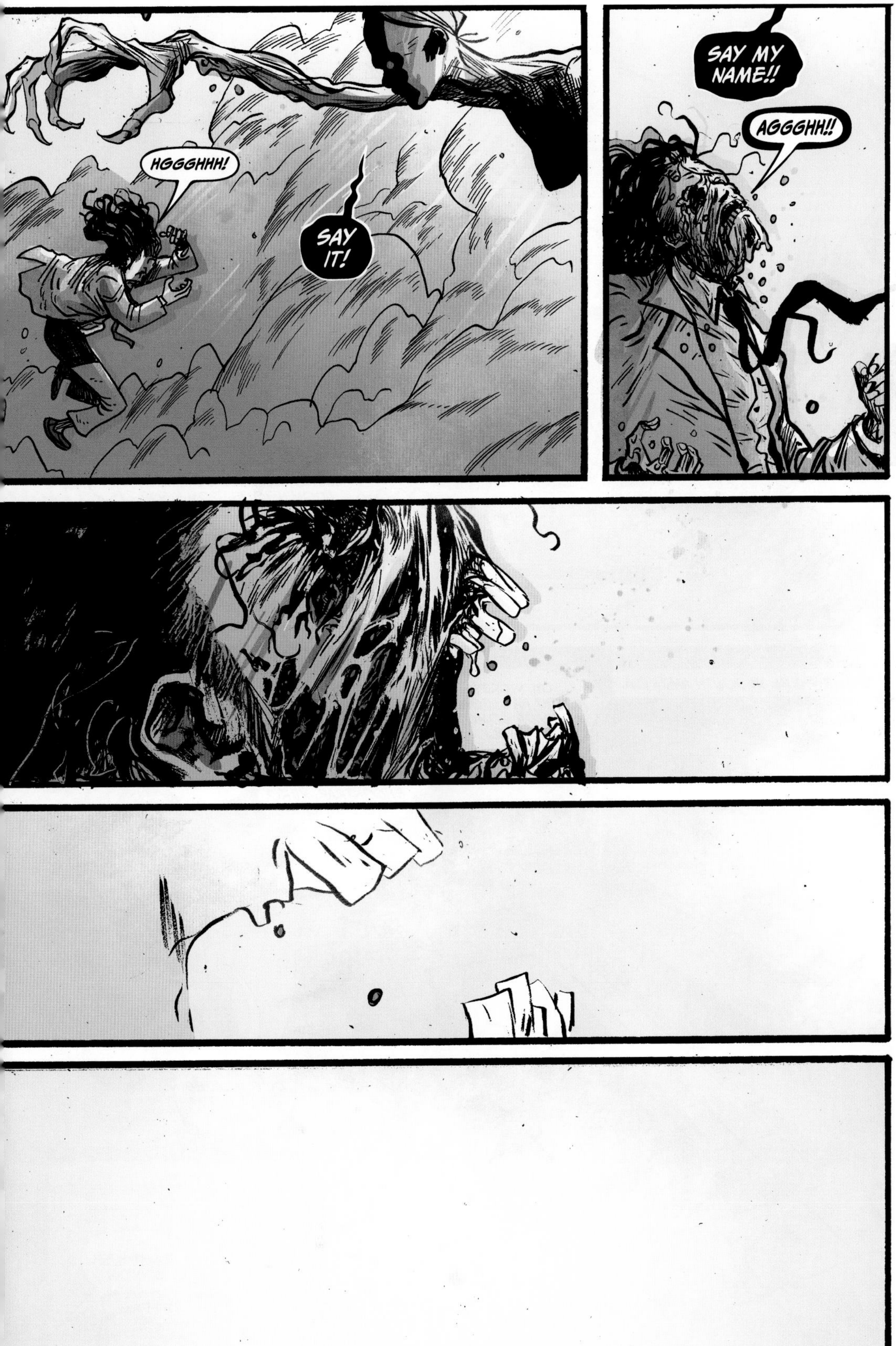
HGGGHHH!
SAY IT!
SAY MY NAME!!
AGGGHH!!

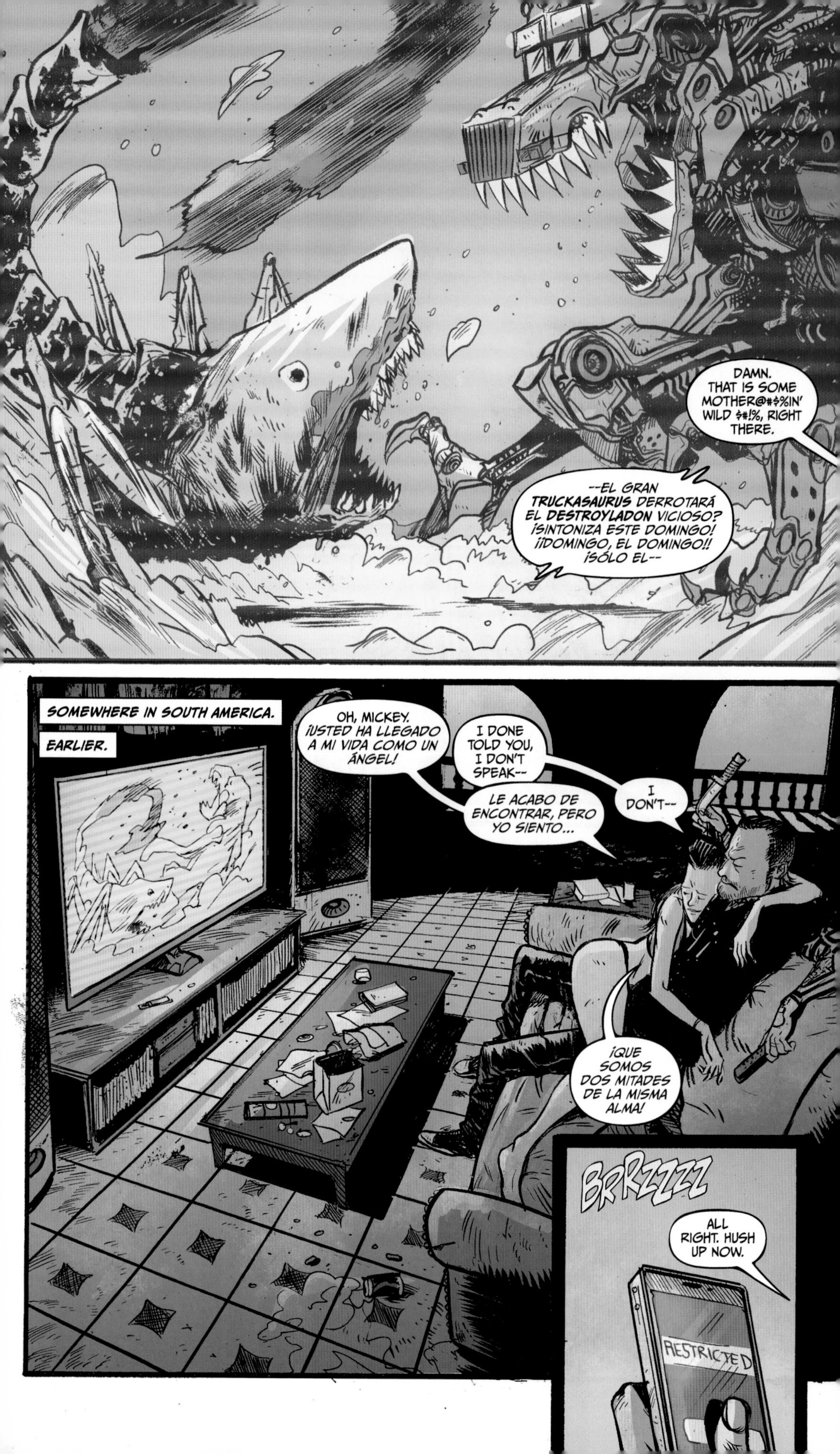

DAMN. THAT IS SOME MOTHER@#$%IN' WILD $#!%, RIGHT THERE.
--EL GRAN TRUCKASAURUS DERROTARÁ EL DESTROYLADON VICIOSO? ¡SINTONIZA ESTE DOMINGO! ¡¡DOMINGO, EL DOMINGO!! ¡SÓLO EL--
SOMEWHERE IN SOUTH AMERICA.
EARLIER.
OH, MICKEY. ¡USTED HA LLEGADO A MI VIDA COMO UN ÁNGEL!
I DONE TOLD YOU, I DON'T SPEAK--
LE ACABO DE ENCONTRAR, PERO YO SIENTO...
I DON'T--
¡QUE SOMOS DOS MITADES DE LA MISMA ALMA!
BRRZZZZ
ALL RIGHT. HUSH UP NOW.
RESTRICTED

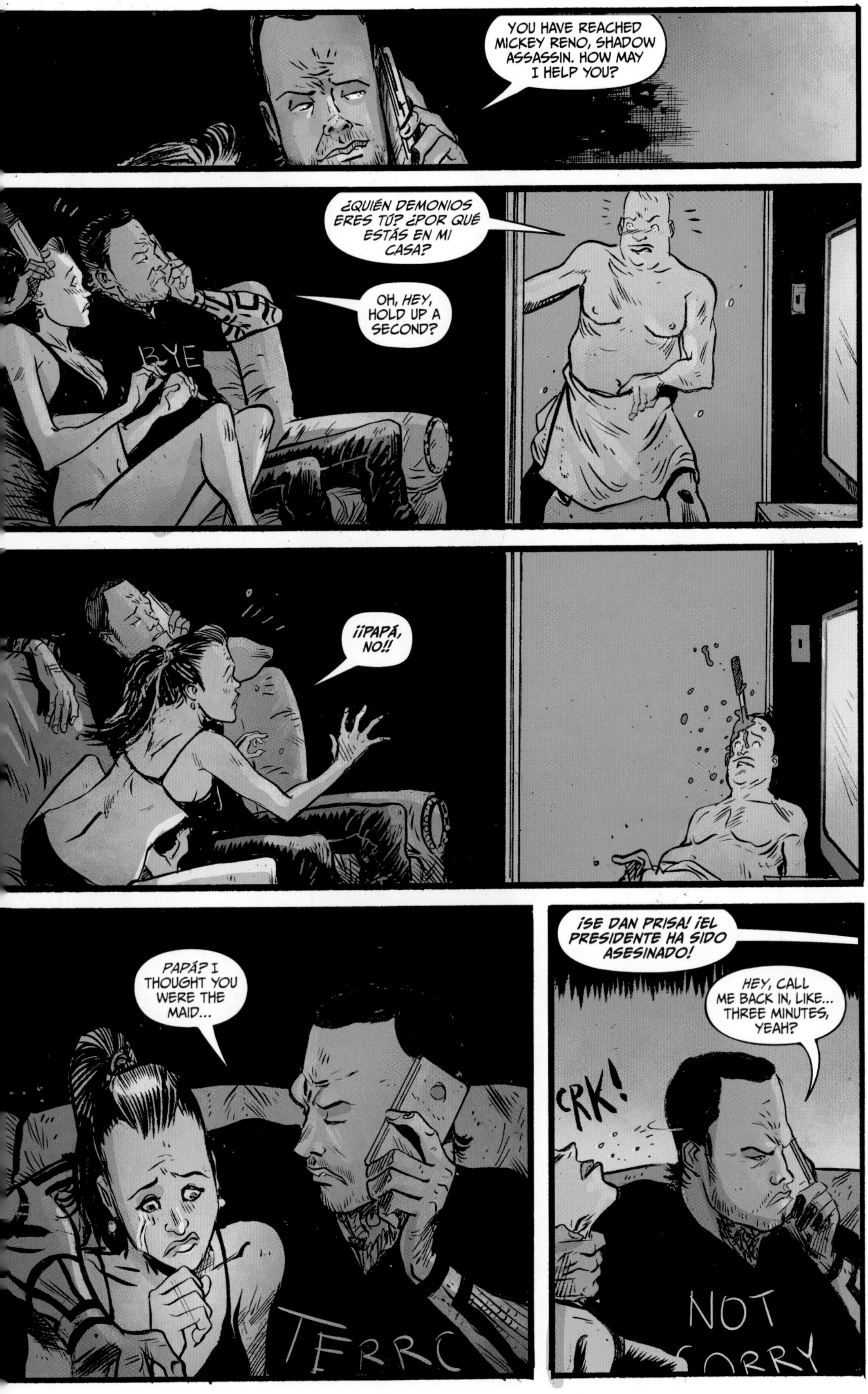
YOU HAVE REACHED MICKEY RENO, SHADOW ASSASSIN. HOW MAY I HELP YOU?
¿QUIÉN DEMONIOS ERES TÚ? ¿POR QUÉ ESTÁS EN MI CASA?
OH, HEY, HOLD UP A SECOND?
BYE
¡¡PAPÁ, NO!!
PAPÁ? I THOUGHT YOU WERE THE MAID...
TERRC
¡SE DAN PRISA! ¡EL PRESIDENTE HA SIDO ASESINADO!
HEY, CALL ME BACK IN, LIKE... THREE MINUTES, YEAH?
CRK!
NOT
ORRY

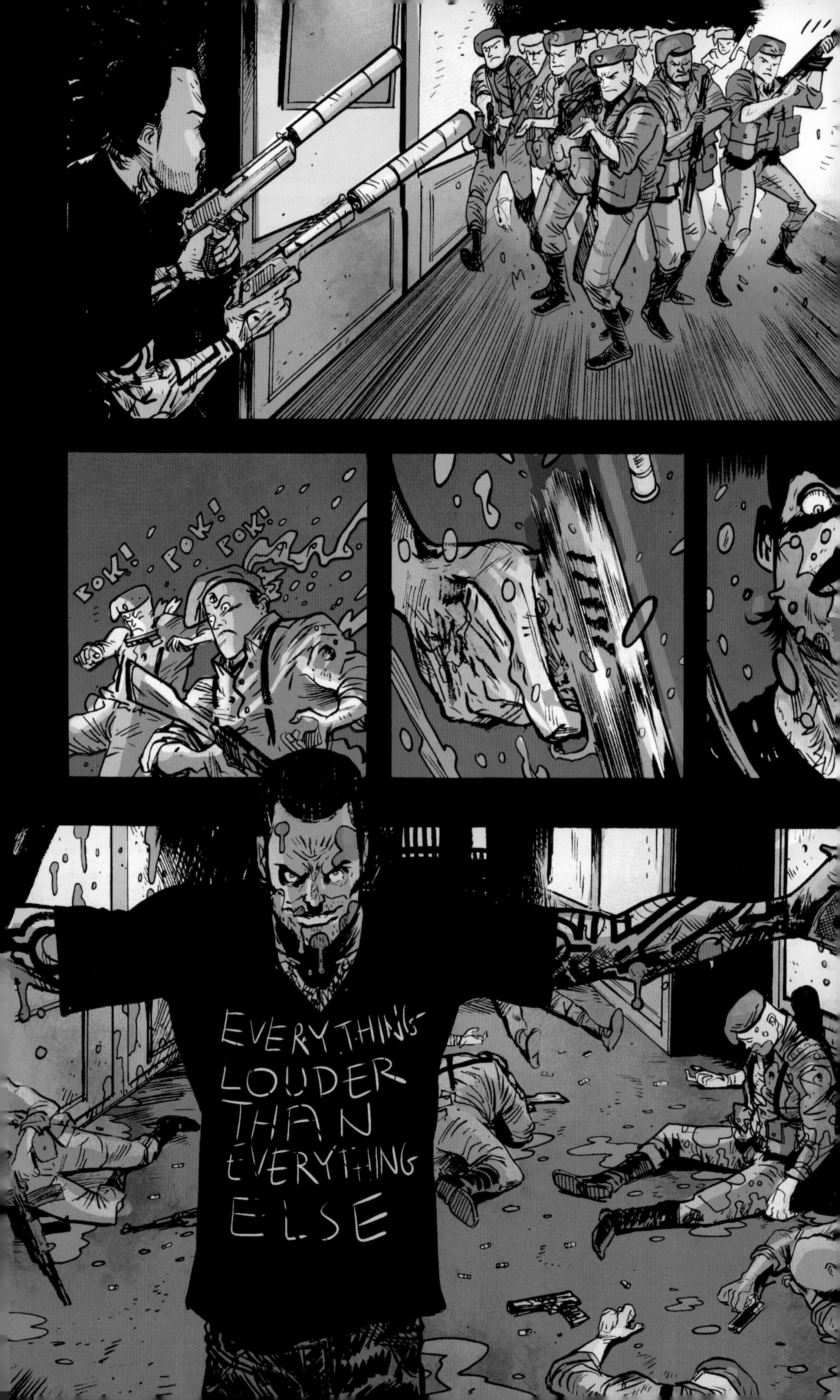
POK! POK! POK!
EVERYTHING LOUDER THAN EVERYTHING ELSE

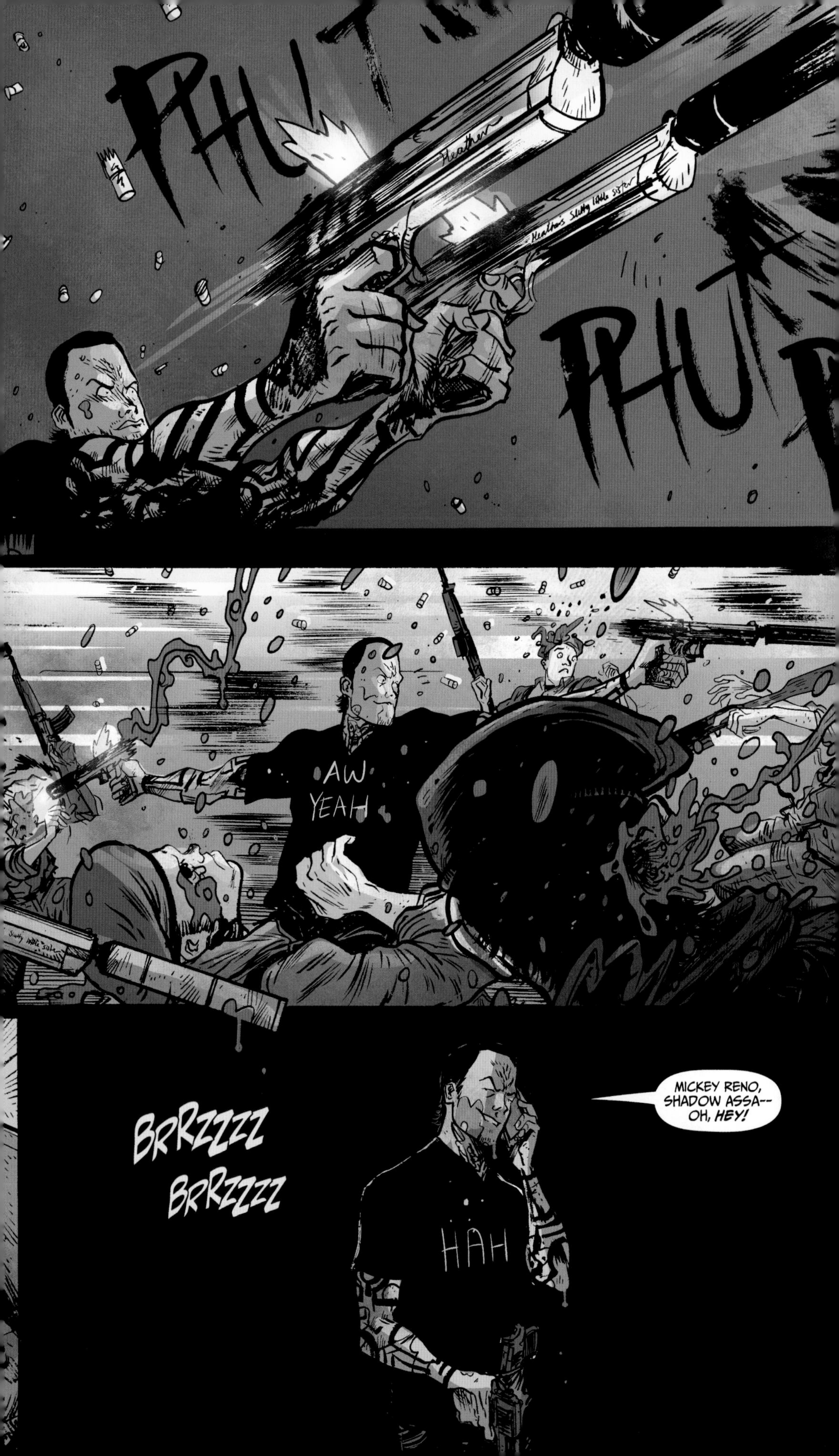
PHUT
Heather
Heather's slutty little sister
PHUT
AW YEAH
BRRZZZZ
BRRZZZZ
MICKEY RENO, SHADOW ASSA-- OH, HEY!
HAH

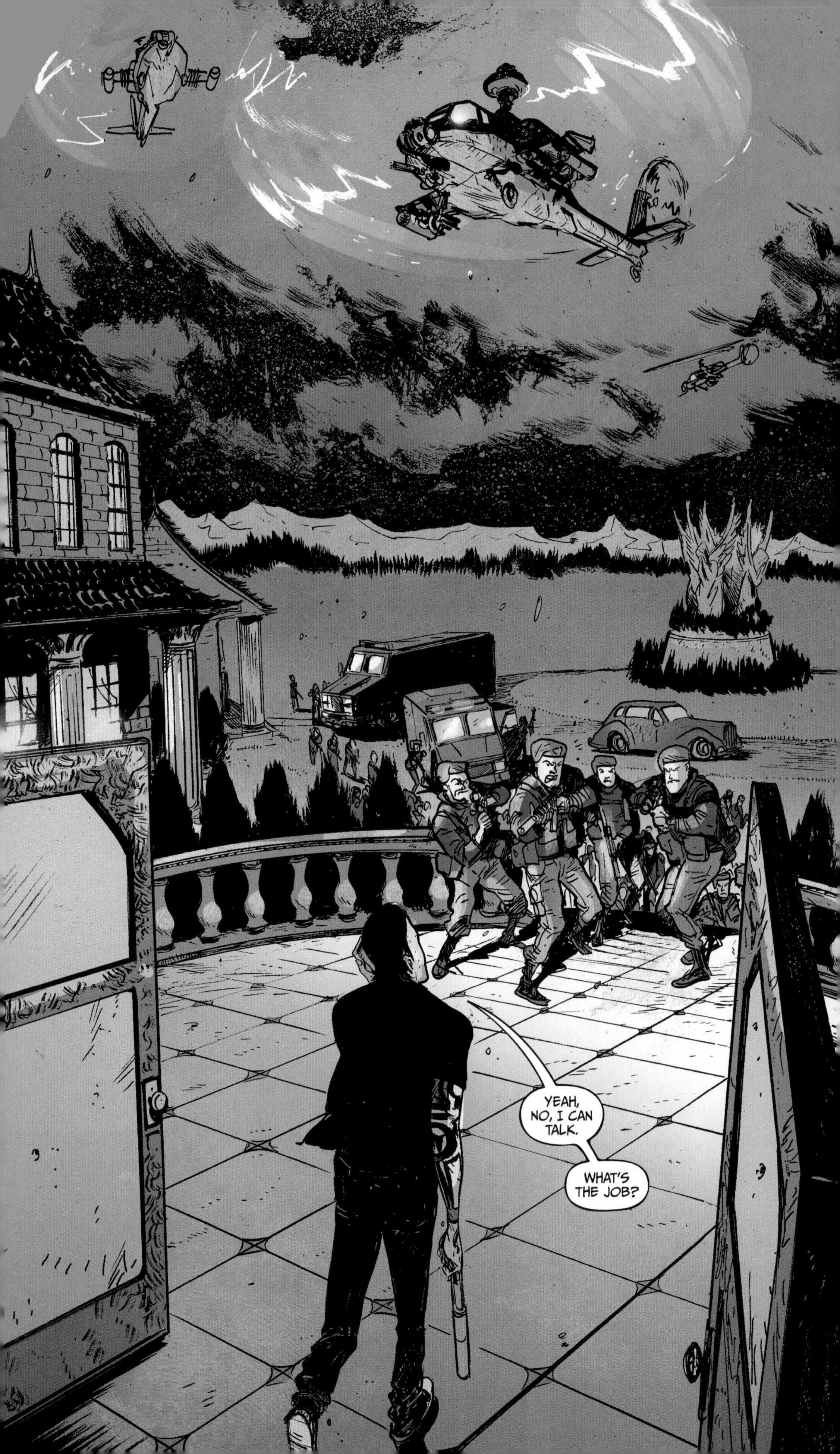
YEAH, NO, I CAN TALK.
WHAT'S THE JOB?

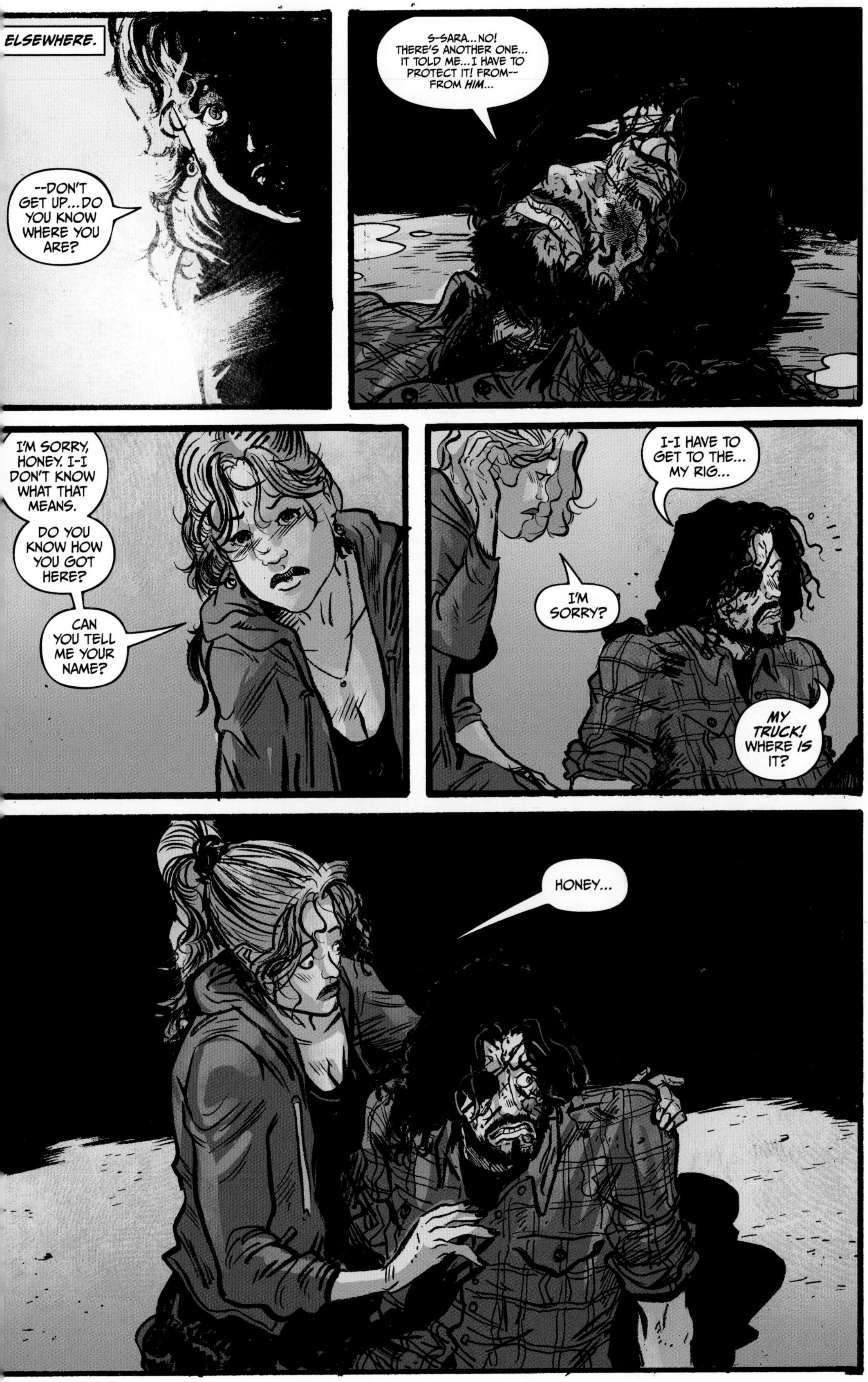
ELSEWHERE.
--DON'T GET UP...DO YOU KNOW WHERE YOU ARE?
S-SARA...NO! THERE'S ANOTHER ONE... IT TOLD ME...I HAVE TO PROTECT IT! FROM-- FROM *HIM*...
I'M SORRY, HONEY. I-I DON'T KNOW WHAT THAT MEANS.
DO YOU KNOW HOW YOU GOT HERE?
CAN YOU TELL ME YOUR NAME?
I-I HAVE TO GET TO THE... MY RIG...
I'M SORRY?
MY TRUCK! WHERE *IS* IT?
HONEY...

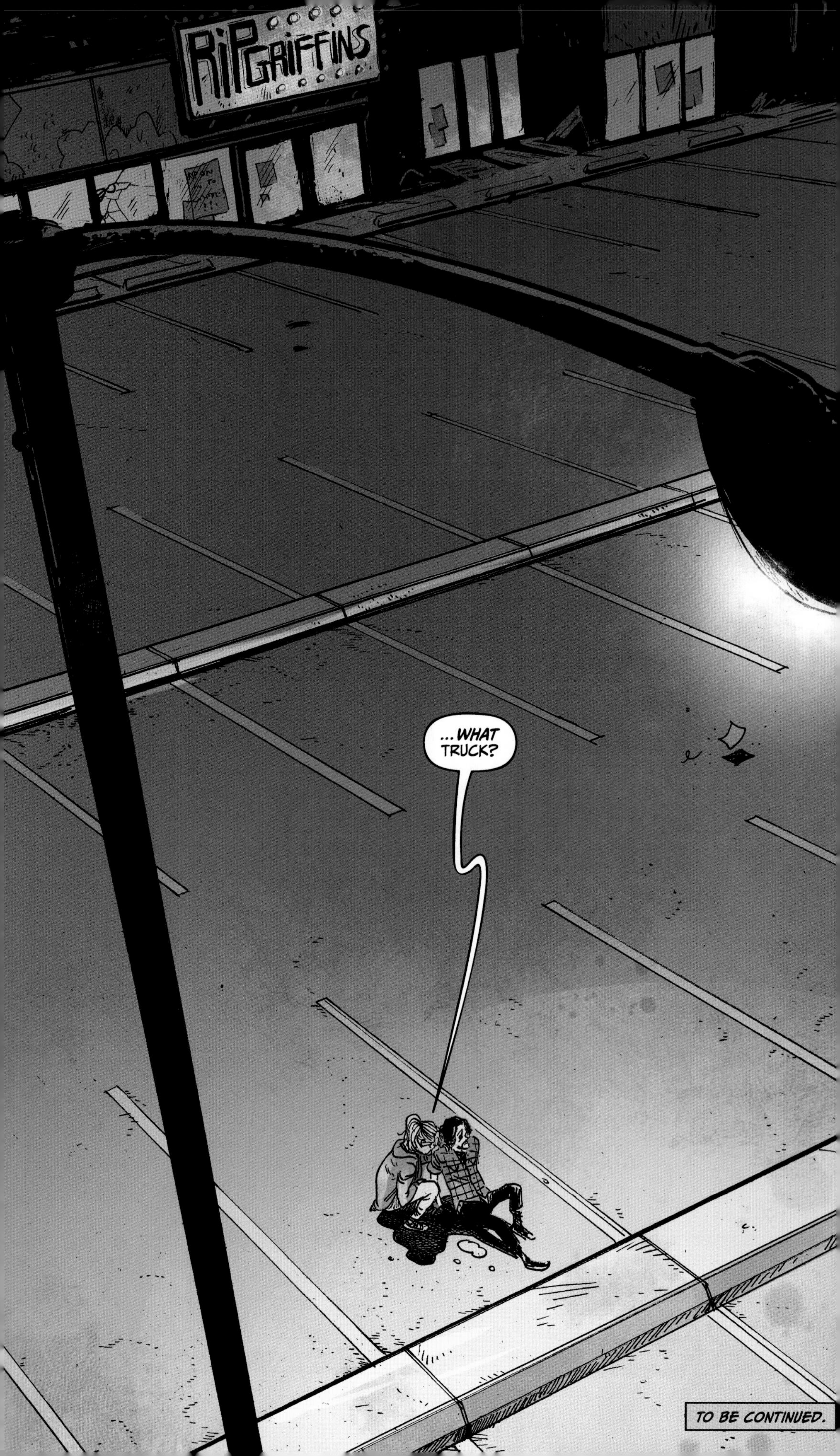
RiP GRIFFINS
...WHAT TRUCK?
TO BE CONTINUED.

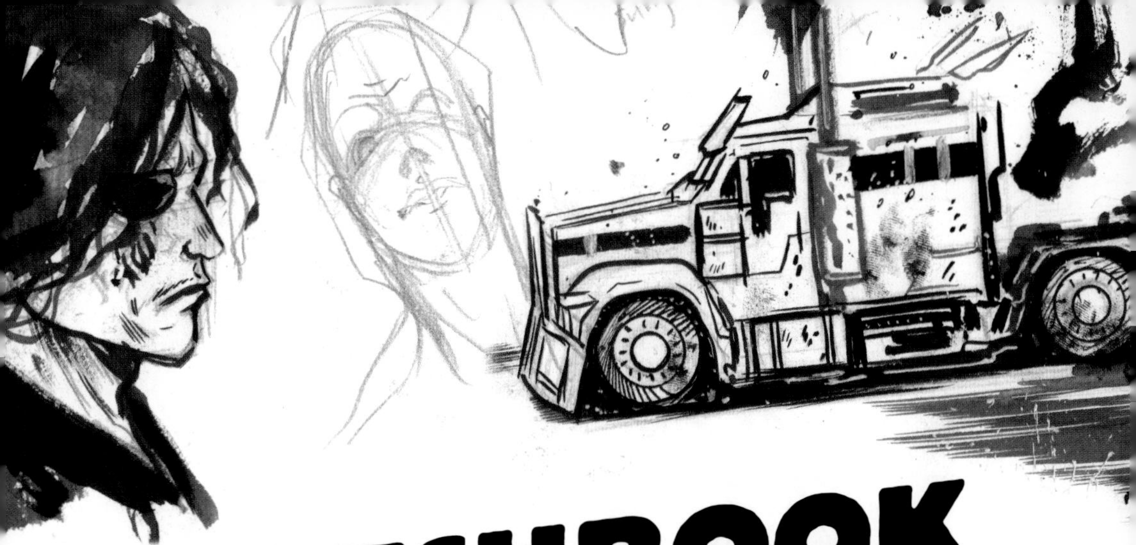

SKETCHBOOK

Preliminary art by

DANIEL WARREN JOHNSON

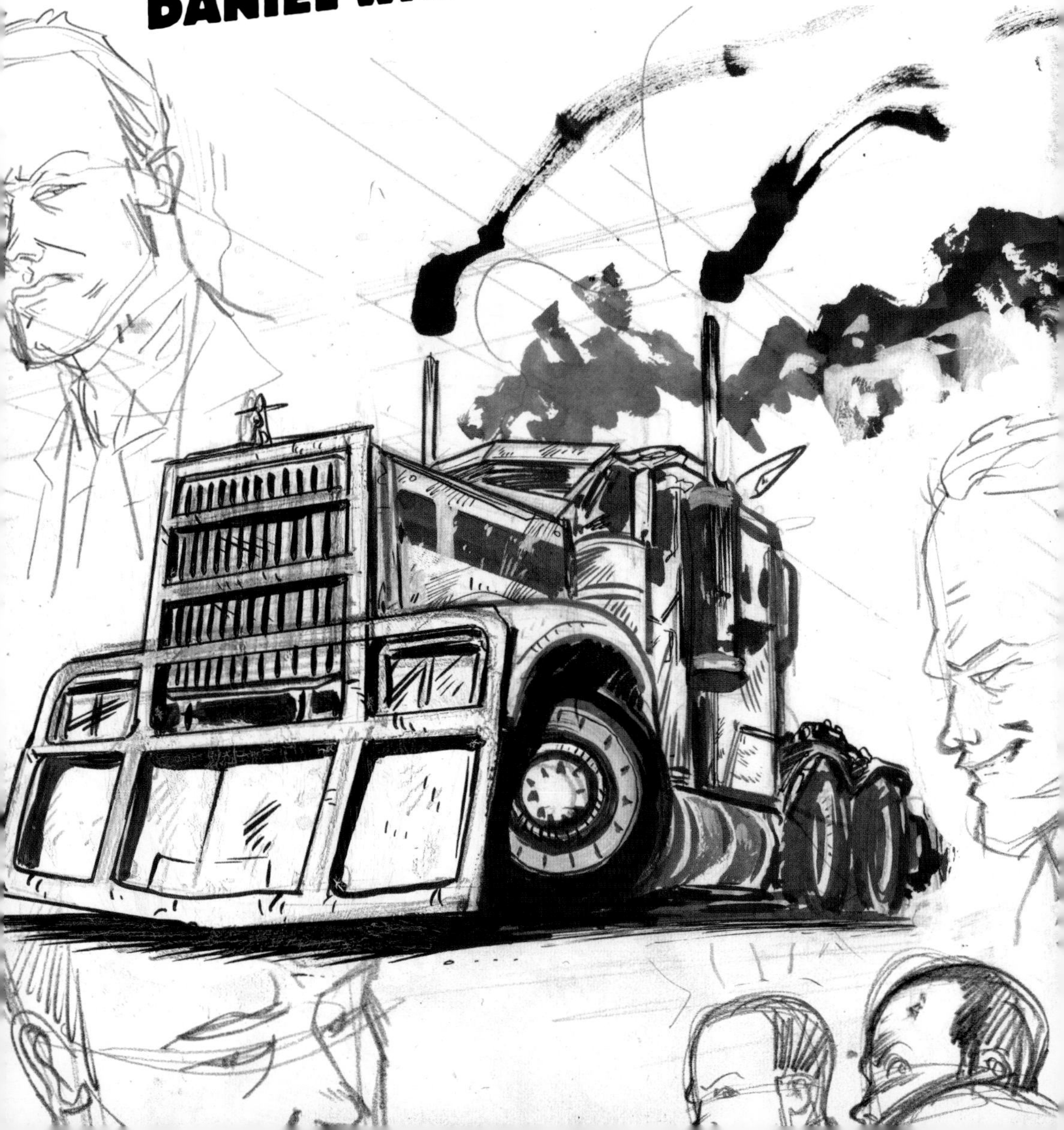

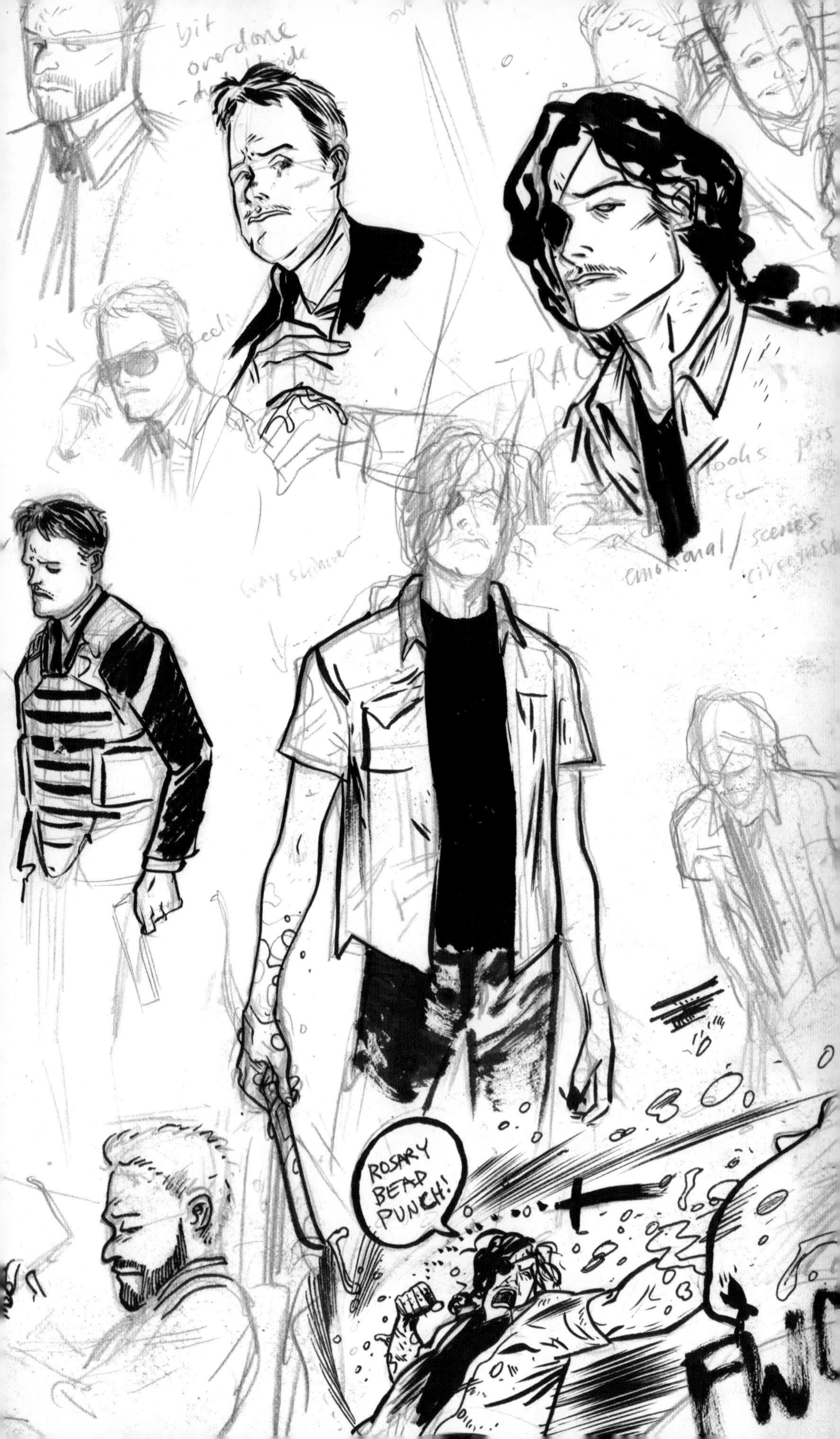
bit overdone
ROSARY BEAD PUNCH!

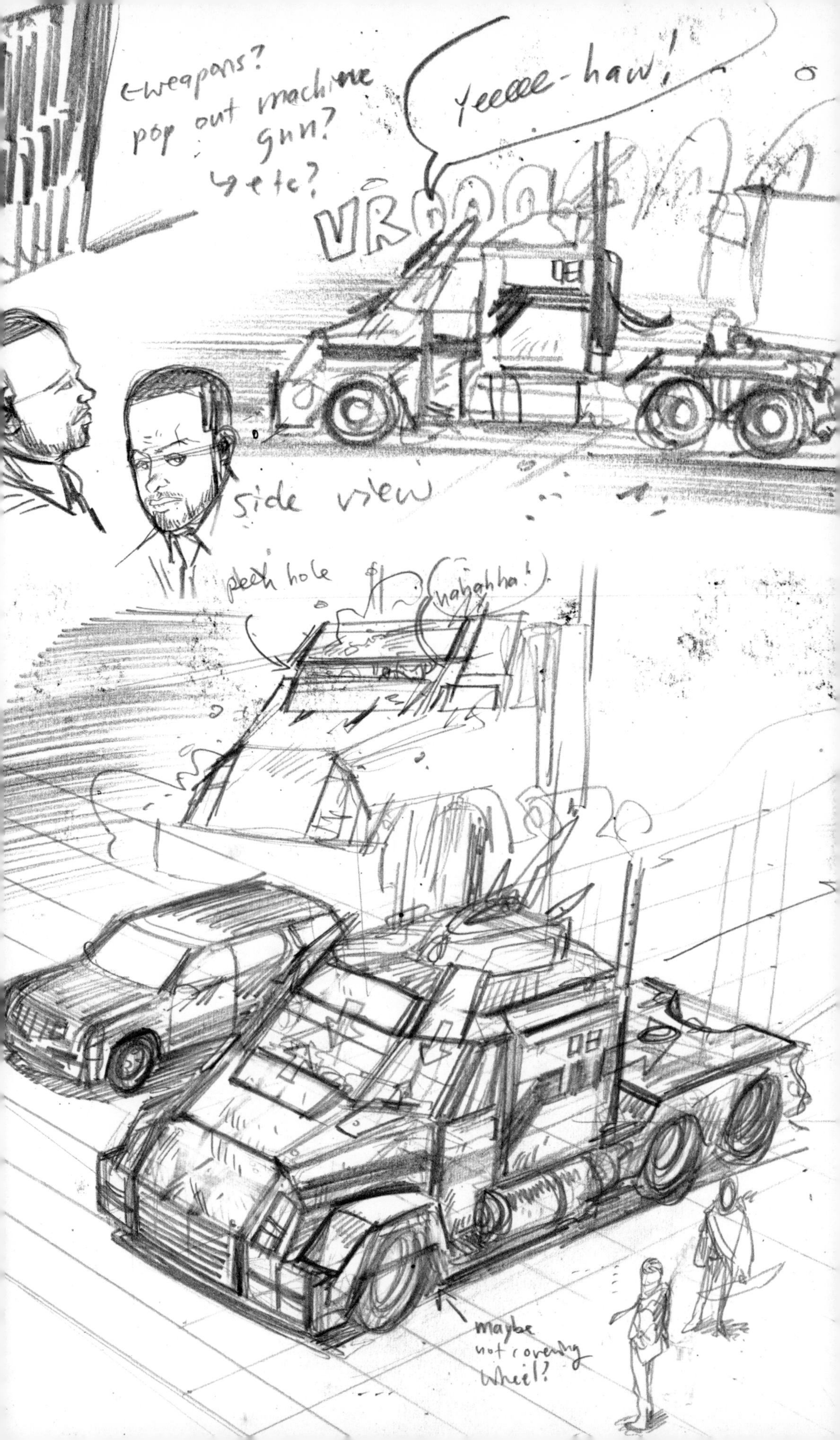

←weapons? pop out machine gun? ↳etc?
yeeeee-haw!
VRooo
side view
peek hole
hahahha!
maybe not covering wheel?

SUPER:POWERED BY CREATORS

"These superheroes ain't no boy scouts in spandex. They're a high-octane blend of the damaged quixotic heroes of pulp and detective fiction and the do-gooders in capes from the Golden and Silver Ages." —Duane Swierczynski

SLEDGEHAMMER 44
Mike Mignola, John Arcudi, and Jason Latour
ISBN 978-1-61655-395-1 | $19.99

DREAM THIEF
Jai Nitz and Greg Smallwood
VOLUME 1
ISBN 978-1-61655-283-1 | $17.99
VOLUME 2: ESCAPE
ISBN 978-1-61655-513-9 | $17.99

BUZZKILL
Mark Reznicek, Donny Cates,
and Geoff Shaw
ISBN 978-1-61655-305-0 | $14.99

THE BLACK BEETLE
Francesco Francavilla
VOLUME 1: NO WAY OUT
ISBN 978-1-61655-202-2 | $19.99

THE ANSWER!
Mike Norton and Dennis Hopeless
ISBN 978-1-61655-197-1 | $12.99

BLOODHOUND
Dan Jolley, Leonard Kirk, and Robin Riggs
VOLUME 1: BRASS KNUCKLE PSYCHOLOGY
ISBN 978-1-61655-125-4 | $19.99
VOLUME 2: CROWBAR MEDICINE
ISBN 978-1-61655-352-4 | $19.99

**MICHAEL AVON OEMING'S
THE VICTORIES**
Michael Avon Oeming
VOLUME 1: TOUCHED
ISBN 978-1-61655-100-1 | $9.99
VOLUME 2: TRANSHUMAN
ISBN 978-1-61655-214-5 | $17.99
VOLUME 3: POSTHUMAN
ISBN 978-1-61655-445-3 | $17.99

ORIGINAL VISIONS—
THRILLING TALES